Advance Praise

"Inspiring! A must-read for anyone interested in contemplative approaches to living in the world. Dr. Chan does a great job articulating connections between classical Daoism, modern psychology, and neuroscience."

—LARSON DIFIORI, Ph.D., Associate Director of Undergraduate Contemplative Studies, Religious Studies, Brown University

"Weaving an intellectual exploration of the ancient wisdom teachings of Daoism and Western philosophical traditions with fascinating hypotheses about the challenges we face in cultivating mental well-being, Aldrich Chan provides us a conceptual journey with practical suggestions for how to create a healthier way to live. This intricate weaving of poetic and contemplative insights with aspects of contemporary science provide much food for thought and invitations to try out new ways of envisioning our mental lives and how to thrive."

—DAN SIEGEL, M.D., executive director of the Mindsight Institute and founding co-director of the Mindful Awareness Research Center at UCLA; author of *Mindsight*, *The Whole-Brain Child*, and *The Mindful-Therapist*

"*7 Principles of Nature* superbly connects classical Daoism to modern psychological insights. Aldrich Chan's valuable book shows us how to align ourselves with the principles of nature and thereby return to our purest selves."

—DENG MING-DAO, author of *365 Tao*, *The Lunar Tao*, *Scholar Warrior*

"A marvelous offering to the world at this very moment when so much pandemonium surrounds us! It is a salve for the stressed and an invitation back to serenity together."

—DARCIA NARVAEZ, Ph.D., Professor Emerita of Psychology, University of Notre Dame and author of *Neurobiology and the Development of Human Morality: Evolution, Culture, and Wisdom*

7

PRINCIPLES
of NATURE

How We Strayed
& How We Return

ALDRICH CHAN, PSY.D.

CNƆ
PRESS

Copyright © 2025 Aldrich Chan

FIRST EDITION

7 PRINCIPLES OF NATURE
How We Strayed and How We Return

ISBN	978-1-5445-4854-8	*Hardcover*
	978-1-5445-4853-1	*Paperback*
	978-1-5445-4852-4	*Ebook*
	978-1-5445-4855-5	*Audiobook*

I dedicate this book to my beloved wife,
Jessica Shraybman.

CONTENTS

AUTHOR'S NOTE

*"Let your mind wander in simplicity, blend your spirit with the
vastness, follow along with things the way they are..."*
—ZHUANGZI

*"Someone who boards a boat and becomes confused,
not knowing west from east, will see the Dipper and a Pole star
and become oriented. Nature is likewise a Dipper
and a Pole star for human beings."*
—from THE HUAINANZI

Before diving into this book, there are a few opening notes that serve
as a necessary prelude for fully appreciating what is to come. First,
I want to state that this book does not promote any particular religion;
I approach Daoist ideas as a philosophy that can be integrated into
many belief systems. Second, a return to natural principles does not
mean abandoning society and inhabiting the world as humans have,
as hunter-gatherers, for 99 percent of human history. While this may
be the answer for some, a true embodiment of nature's principles is a
psychological shift. It means the need to reclaim a way of being that was
our birthright, a way lost amid the rise of technology, political swings,
and cultural changes. There are many benefits to our society, the degree
to which may be controversial, but the fact of which is important to
acknowledge, such as music, art, medicine, communication, and so on.
There are also many ways of hunter-gatherers that I'm sure most of us

would be happy to let go of. These include "infanticide, abandoning or killing elderly people, facing periodic risk of starvation, being at heightened risk from environmental dangers and infectious diseases, often seeing one's children die, and living in constant fear of being attacked."[1] For modern-day hunter-gatherers, I follow Diamond's lead in suggesting there are benefits to adopting specific practices that would likely heighten our well-being. It is also important to note that it would be overly simplistic to assume that all modern-day hunter-gatherer societies are aligned with nature and that their way of life has not changed. There is variability among them. As such, while I use modern-day hunter-gatherer lifestyles as examples throughout, what I endeavored to capture is existential. By that, I mean how overarching principles of nature, which are also universal conditions of life, may translate into a way of life that is congruent with nature's movements. This is where the nature-inspired philosophy of Classical Daoism comes into play. Finally, to support the idea that by harmonizing with the principles of nature, humans may enhance their capacity to flourish, I incorporate neuropsychological science. In short, this book advances a theory of how humanity has become misaligned with nature, and how we may realign with it. Daoism holds that aligning with nature engenders a vital efficacy or *Potency* (*de*, 德). The greater part of this work serves as a guide to cultivating *Potency* through the lived restoration of harmony with the natural order.

Now, why did I choose Classical Daoism? Simple—it complements several facts that have accrued through scientific inquiry. To begin with, however, it is important you know what I mean by Classical Daoism, and what myths continue to live on.

The Chinese civilization is one of the oldest human civilizations (1600 BCE, over 3,000 years ago) to continue flourishing. Daoism emerged around the Warring States Period (475–221 BCE) and has since developed widely, branching off into many schools. This book focuses on Classical Daoism, which encapsulates its earliest texts and contemplative origins. Within the modern parameters of works that highlight Daoist thought,* I will include work from Laozi (老子, pronounced "lao-zuh") and Zhuangzi (莊子, pronounced "zhwaung-zuh") with the Neiye (內業) and The Huainanzi (淮南子) as support.† Later writers added to Laozi and Zhuangzi's writings, and some debate whether these figures actually existed. As such, it's better to view them as symbols rather than actual historical figures.

Sima Qian's *Shiji*, or *Records of the Historian*, provides most of our knowledge of Laozi and Zhuangzi. Laozi or Li Er, also called Lao Dan, was a native of Chu.‡ Scholars speculate he lived in the sixth or fourth century BCE.[4, 5] The Shiji[6] states:

> He lived in [Zhou] for a long time, but seeing its decline, he departed. When he reached the pass, the keeper there was pleased and said to him, "As you are about to leave the world behind, could you write a book for my sake?" As a result, Laozi wrote a work in two books, setting out the meaning of the way and virtue in some 5,000 characters, and then departed. None knew where he went to in the end.

This document came to be known as the Daodejing (道德經).§ According to Daoist scholar Harold Roth,[7(p6)] the earliest excavation of the Daodejing was "no earlier than the beginning of the third century BC... discovered at Kuo-tien in Hupei in a tomb..." Dao (道) is often translated as "the way," or "path"; *de* (德, pronounced duh) as "virtue," "Potency," or "power"; and jing (經) as "classic" or "the book of." As such, the full title may be read as *The Book of the Way and Its Power/Virtue*. It has also been referred to as *The Laozi*. The Dao may be considered a single universal living principle of nature pervading all that is. *De*, or *Potency*, relates to the unique expression of the Dao in each person. According to Chan,[4(p190)] *de* "is [Dao] inherent in each individual thing; that is, [de] is what is obtained from [Dao]. In this sense, [de] is its virtue or characteristic." Kohn's[8(p110)] analysis led her to the conclusion that over virtue it "is inner power, the living vibrancy of Dao activated within."

Image 1: Two of the oldest versions of the DDJ, the first image found in the Kuo-tien/Guodian Chu (300 BCE) on slips of bamboo, and the second excavated from the Mawangdui tomb on silk (168 BCE).

Zhuangzi or Zhuang Zhou (莊周) is estimated to have lived circa 369–286 BCE.[9] According to Sima Qian, as cited by Watson,[10(pvii)] Zhuangzi was a native of Meng (i.e., Henan province) who "once served as an official in the lacquer garden" and "wrote a work in 100,000 words or more that was 'mostly in the nature of fable.'" This work came to be known as The Zhuangzi.[5]

Burton noted that the version of The Zhuangzi that forms the basis of all present works dates back to 312 CE, compiled and edited by a neo-Daoist, Guo Xiang. Roth[7(p6)] building on the work of A.C. Graham, specified there are at least "four different philosophical voices, in addition to [Zhuangzi's]" with its final compilation dating back to around 130 BCE. Continuing, he identified different philosophical strands of thought as individualist, primitivist, and syncretist. The individualist has a primary emphasis on self-cultivation, whereas the primitivist incorporates political and social philosophy, advocating simplicity in societal life. The syncretist incorporates cosmology, philosophy of self-transformation, and techniques for governing, further borrowing relevant ideas from Legalists and Confucian schools. In a later work, Roth[2(p63)] specified that of the three sections in the thirty-three-chapter work—Inner Chapters, Outer Chapters, and Mixed—there are "six basic strata and groups of authors."

Most academics agree that the work of Laozi preceded that of Zhuangzi, and this is evident in the refinement and elaboration of Laozi's work.[4] It is also worth noting that because of the linguistic consistency in the first seven chapters of The Zhuangzi, many believe these "inner chapters" are most authentically Zhuangzi. Not that the outer chapters or mixed/miscellaneous chapters have no value, rather they may be fragments of, and/or elaborations on Zhuangzi's ideas.

There are differences between Laozi and Zhuangzi, but greater similarities.[4] Laozi's writings emphasize harmony, whereas Zhuangzi's emphasize freedom. Whereas Laozi takes a poetic approach to express ideas, Zhuangzi uses parables, parodies, perspectival relativity, and paradox. According to Chan,[4(p163)] Laozi's Dao is one that is "natural, eternal, spontaneous, nameless and indescribable." Zhuangzi additionally emphasizes that nature is a dynamic process in constant flux and transformation. This cosmic process balances everything and unifies all into one. According to Zhuangzi, to connect with the Dao is to experience stillness and a childlike disposition, free and playful, wandering the vast expanse of nature, intoxicated by its immense power. Laozi and Zhuangzi also vary in their symbolic preferences, with Laozi using recurring symbols such as "water, the infant, the female, the valley" and becoming as "uncarved wood,"[4(p13)] whereas Zhuangzi emphasizes, becoming like a "newborn calf,"[4(p20)] blending with the "Great Unity."[10(p82)] In Laozi's work, the message appears as "cultivate the physical and mental qualities of this sage; get involved and help in a non-intrusive way; retire when the work is done,"[12(p25)] whereas Zhuangzi overall advocated involvement only if it may help you align with the Dao.

Both Laozi and Zhuangzi emphasize spontaneity, because acting from a pre-reflective state is considered to harbor the potential of nature. Reflections can bias the extent to which natural processes are mirrored. Yet spontaneous action does not mean simply acting out all your desires. Impulsive actions originate in the egoic system, whereas spontaneity originates within a deeper substratum of nature. Moreover, impulsivity neglects context and complexity.

To find one's home in change, as a constant process, one must let go of any desires for one's life to be anything other than it is in the present. One must trust the process of change while centering oneself in what does not change, which is the still, peaceful field of nothingness. An individual becomes an ally of nature by emptying their mind and living according to their *de* or inner virtue, power, or Potency. This does not mean being a doormat. In fact, Laozi still supported engaging with the world, but emphasized the importance of ensuring thoughts and actions are not contrary to nature.[4]

A common mistranslation of *Wuwei* (無為) is nonaction. The meaning is not so much about not doing anything as it is about not forcing or contriving. Thus, a better translation often used is "effortless action." We will discuss Flow, a more familiar Western term, in a later chapter. This leads many to think if faced with oppression or aggression, it is okay not to act. This is not the case. In fact, Daoism actively opposes oppressive systems. Standing up to injustice may be considered a spontaneous response, as is defending oneself if being attacked.

Another major misconception is the idea of Daoism as being anti-intellectual. The skepticism toward abstraction in Daoism is speaking to *the use* of knowledge for nefarious purposes or "cunning and clever-ness."[4(p16)] Imposing selfish pursuits over reality occludes its true nature, as the intellect believes itself to be the foundation. Classical Daoism is interested in intellectual activity where it relates to fostering creative harmony with natural activity.

A third misconception is that to align oneself with Daoism is to believe in divination, celibacy, and deities. Although this may be true for some schools of Daoism, many of which involve mystical practices and deifi-cation of Laozi, and others such as the Daoist trinity, this is not the case for Classical Daoism. It is my understanding that many religious schools view deities as symbolic. In fact, Laozi and Zhuangzi are both skeptical about whether there is a God overseeing everything:

> "Tao is esteemed and virtue is honored without anyone's order!"[4(p190)]
> "Joy, anger, grief, delight, worry, regret, fickleness, inflexibility, modesty, willfulness, candor, insolence, music from empty holes, mushroom springing up in dampness, day and night replacing each other before us, and no one knows where they sprout from…it would seem as though they have some true master, and yet I find no trace of him."[10(p8)]

The word *Tian* (天) often translates as "heaven," but it more directly means "sky." It is used throughout Daoist texts, and in English it bet-ter relates to "nature" or the process of nature, as it relates to celestial bodies and the patterns that govern them. Most of Zhuangzi's religious expressions can be understood as metaphors. Despite the ambiguity of language use, paradoxes, and fantastical flights of imagination, classical Daoism is actually quite a practical philosophy. Part of the challenge with translations is the lack of linguistic substitutes that capture the full essence of particular words or, in this case, symbols. For example, words like "nonbeing" and "being" carry deep existential connotations in English, but may not necessarily be so in certain contexts throughout Daoist literature. In Chinese, characters that translate to "nonbeing" (無有) and "being" (有) are used in everyday language. The idea that being comes from nonbeing becomes something as evident as you did not exist before you existed. We will revisit Daoist pragmatism throughout this book.

SUPPORTIVE MATERIALS

The Huainanzi contains twenty-one chapters, the culmination of work formed by Liu An, a King of Huainan, and other scholars who attempted to produce a book that synthesized the best ideas from the existing schools of thought.[13(p1)] I consider Liu An to be the eastern parallel to the Stoic Marcus Aurelius and The Huainanzi (however much more comprehensive and with more voices) to his *Meditations*. King An was "an enthusiastic man of letters, whose interests ranged from administrative matters to cosmology, from rhetoric to poetry, from natural philosophy to the occult. He was a great patron of scholarship, and he attracted to his court and lent support to a large number of men of learning. He was known as a quick, adept, and prolific writer…"[13(p7)]

The roots of this text are Daoist, drawing heavily from Laozi and Zhuangzi. Roth[13] specifies that contrary to The Zhuangzi, "the rulers are not reluctant minimalist," but "adept sages engaged in government."[13(p79)] In essence:

…this book was designed to survey the entire body of knowledge required for a contemporary monarch to rule successfully and well. Organized in a "root and branch" structure, the work's early chapters set out the fundamental nature of the world and of human society, while the later chapters deal with the application of that knowledge to various practical concerns. Taken as a whole, the work is in effect a model curriculum for a monarch-in-training.[13(p1)]

Other texts were included as well, such as the famed *Book of Changes*, *The Odes*, which is a collection of poems, and *The Documents*, which relate to Confucian thought. One of the cornerstone additions in The Huainanzi is the discussion of human nature.[2] Throughout this book, I will draw from the foundational elements of Daoism that have been elaborated upon in The Huainanzi.

The Neiye, or "inward training," is currently considered by a scholar of Daoism, Harold Roth,[7] to be the progenitor text of Daoism, and "possibly one of the oldest mystical texts in China." This work was drawn from the Guanzi, a voluminous collection of texts originating in 300 BCE, and Roth speculates it was written around the fourth century BCE. It explicates self-cultivation practices present in the Laozi, Zhuangzi, and Huainanzi. Because it is the oldest known text related to contemplative Daoist practice, Roth considers it the "Original Dao." The text itself consists of 1,622 characters.

I also draw from the Horse Taming Pictures by Gao Daokuan, a twelfth-century Daoist Monk, when elaborating on stages of consciousness as one advances in their inner cultivation. They are based on a quietist model that corresponds well with classical Daoist meditation. This analysis draws much from Louis Komjathy's[14] work *Taming the Wild Horse*. One of Komjathy's major contributions was linking classical Daoism to later periods, viewing apophatic meditations as a constant throughout all time periods (Larson Di Fiori, personal communication, 2024).

Finally, I will integrate some Zen philosophy because of its close connection to Daoism, especially the work of Zhuangzi. Indeed, Zen emerged because of Ch'an Buddhism's migration to Japan; this discipline was a mixture of Daoism and Buddhism. Hinton[14] elaborated that when Buddhism was introduced to China, it was assimilated into Daoism, resulting in a more organic and empirical expression. The resulting founders of Ch'an selected Buddhist texts that were beneficial to deepening their understanding of and relationship to the Dao. The founder of Ch'an, typically identified as the Bodhidarma, even stated that "Tao is Ch'an."[15(p22)] According to Grigg:[16(pxiv)]

> The similarities between original Daoism and pure Zen are far more striking: the simplicity, the directness, the intuitiveness, the paradoxes, the importance of being natural and the prevalence of natural images, the skepticism about words and explanations, about institutions and dogma. Zen is Daoism.

On the Daodejing and Zhuangzi, Grigg[16(pxv)] noted that, like Zen, they "are really descriptive rather than prescriptive, constructive rather than sacred." He further suggested it became labeled Buddhism for political reasons, and as a result evolved into institutional religious-like systems. In fact, the Buddha should be careful if he were to meet any serious Zen practitioner, for he would likely be "killed" (the form of Buddha is also an illusion to overcome).

The goal of this book is not to prove or disprove any argument, rather to share reasons for using certain Zen texts to amplify resources. This book will only include information as it relates to what I am referring to as "Zen Daoism," which includes elements associated with "tactics of attention, simplicity, directness and paradox, together with a skepticism about words, explanations and dogma."[17(p104)] I will not use any Buddhist terms unrelated to Daoism and will mainly focus on Zen philosophers and their insights. Far more research has been conducted on Zen meditation than on Daoism, yet the differences are few. For those familiar with

Buddhism overall, but not Daoism, Table 1 highlights a few differences (adapted from Grigg's *The Zen Tzu*[17]):[**]

Daoism	Buddhism
Primal, elemental connection with rhythms and forces of nature, social and ecological harmony	Detached, abstract, immateriality, spiritual dimensions
Engaged and utilitarian	Austere and psychological
Organic, unstructured, intuitive, spontaneous, practical	Rational, ordered, deliberate, logical, cerebral
Origin in Nature	Quest for liberation
Tradition of Feeling	Tradition of Thinking

Table 1: Contrasting Daoism and Buddhism

Table 1 presents the major principles of nature from classical Daoism that resonated with my readings in neuropsychological science. The multiple themes identified in each chapter share seven convergent principles, which form the acronym "CPR WEST." The acronym implies another purpose of this book: to help revive the importance of nature's wisdom and lessons to help nourish the drought of meaning in which we have found ourselves. Following are the seven principles of nature.

Principles of Nature

► Nature is creative.

► Nature is process.

► Nature is relationship.

► Nature is whole.

► Nature is equilibrium.

► Nature is spontaneous.

► Nature is transformation.

Each principle is an invitation to cultivate a way of being. This sequentially corresponds to becoming adaptive, yet genuine; spontaneous, yet attuned; integrated, yet distinct; simple, yet complex; balanced, yet dynamic; playful, yet wise; and savage, yet virtuous.

My goal in this book is to help you develop an awareness of how we have become separated, alienated, and in discord with nature, and how to cultivate *Potency* by aligning with the seven principles of nature. Each chapter elaborates upon one or more of these principles and dives into how they translate into human experience, besides techniques that may facilitate their embodiment. I examine themes throughout Daoist thought and practice, and how they are expressed in modern-day neuroscience, psychology, and hunter-gatherer culture. Given my profession as a neuropsychologist, I could not help but frame some of these ideas in terms of three neural networks, each corresponding to a specific way of interacting with the world: *Being, Attending,* and *Doing.* A fourth network, reflecting our *original nature,* is also introduced. While this network operates alongside the other three, its relationship with them can be harmonious or conflicted. I will also discuss how violating or detaching from these principles may result in an unhealthy mind.

For therapists, I dedicate the chapter prior to the conclusion, to the potential use of this model in psychotherapy. While it is an advance that allows for substantial integration, at its core I would consider it a contemplative and existential approach, albeit neuropsychologically informed. I am broadly defining existential as having to do with existence, and in this case, an informed therapeutic approach based on universal principles. Following Emmy Van Deurzen, I consider Chinese philosophers during this period to be existentialists. While their ideas may differ from what is traditionally considered existential work, their ideas are most suitable for this category. Finally, because this book focuses on principles that emerged through a conversation between Daoism and neuropsychology, I would call it a *"neurodaonamic"* approach.

The following is an attempt to share in words what would be simply experienced nonverbally by an individual who is harmonized with these principles.

Unfolding Experience in Words

My mind is clear and still; it is serene. In its clarity, I allow the world to disclose itself in all its richness. In its stillness, events are met with the whole of my being. In its serenity, I experience and embody *Potency*.

My being is in constant creation; it is a becoming. I integrate who I was without clinging to it. This enables my process of becoming to be perpetually growing and in alignment with nature's creative advance. I am a natural unfolding of nature's potential through space and time.

Nature expresses itself to me through my intuition. Intuition signals me through feelings that guide my actions. To maintain and cultivate my relationship to nature, I meditate through stillness and movement. The interconnection and oneness I experience in deep meditative states have endowed a natural sense of empathy and compassion toward all living things. It has also led me to a greater appreciation of nonlinearity, and inherent paradoxes in nature. As time transpires, my experiences in waking life gravitate toward my experiences in meditation. Instead of the need for certainty, I have found peace in uncertainty.

I take care of my body through movement and diet, for it is through my body that I engage with the world. It is inseparable from the mind. This lifestyle has afforded me great feelings of vitality. When I encounter an obstacle, I adapt and embrace change. While I feel the same array of emotions that others do, I recognize their nature is to inform me, then be free.

I keep in mind that at times misfortune can become fortune and that which is fortunate can become misfortunate. I view change as a precondition for stability, as new balances emerge in the ever-changing conditions of life. I attune to nature's dynamic equilibrium —a balance of asymmetry and symmetry. I thus completely join nature's spontaneity and proactively embrace its transformations.

I live my life simply, fully engaged in what I am doing in the moment. When I am sitting, I am sitting; when I am working, I am working; when I am socializing, I am socializing. I do what is necessary for my well-being, and I release anything that might result in dependence or excess.

I am in perpetual awe of nature. Intoxicated and humbled by its unending process of adventure, discovery, and transformation, I engage the world with a playful disposition. In alignment, I experience a deep trust and connection, feeling at ease wherever I find myself. Without the weight of the past or the future, it feels as though I am floating, seamlessly flowing with the wind as it effortlessly courses through all terrain.

After chapter two, this book was written in the format of a national park. Each principle serves as a different entrance to the park, with each chapter as the opening to a unique hike. Let go of the need to follow any order, and feel free to roam toward whichever chapter calls out to you in the moment.

Endnotes

* According to Roth,[2(p9)] alongside the Laozi and Zhuangzi are foundational texts, including "the four 'Techniques of the Mind' (Xin Shu心術) texts from the Guanzi compendium, the four 'YellowThearch' texts found at Mawangdui ('Huangdi si jing' [ca. 275 BCE] and the 'Huainanzi.'" Wong[3] also added the writings of Liezi, which elaborate even more on Daoism in simpler form. He will be cited throughout, though he will not be used as extensively as the others.

† Zi simply means "Master." They are not related.

‡ According to the Stanford Encyclopedia of Philosophy, it's been argued by Fung Yu-Lan that Sima Qian mixed up Lao Dan and Li Er, who were actually different people, Lao Dan being the "real founder" of Daoism. The word Dan is supposed to refer to "long ears," which is "a mark of longevity in Chinese physiognomy."

§ The translations of Daodejing came from Wing Sit Chan[4] and D.C. Lau.[5]

¶ The translations of *Zhuangzi* being used come from A.C. Graham,[11] Burton Watson,[10] and Brook Ziporyn.[9]

** For those interested in a synthesis of Zen and Daoism, I highly recommend *The Tao of Zen* and *The Zen Tzu* by Ray Grigg[17] and China Root by David Hinton. *The Zen Tzu* re-interprets the Daodejing by incorporating ideas from Zen. It becomes very evident how easily these two philosophies fit.

INTRODUCTION

"Following nature and putting it into practice is called 'the Way.'"
—The HUAINANZI

"...there can be no living science unless there is a widespread instinctive conviction in the existence of an Order of Things, and, in particular, of an Order of Nature."
—ALFRED NORTH WHITEHEAD

Image 2: Jade

A feature of jade is its signature vein pattern, which shapes how the mineral may fragment when cut. This pattern is the earliest definition of the Chinese character Li (理). These patterns may be seen as valuable and determine whether jade is genuine. In Daoism, the meaning of Li evolved into patterns of nature that course through an individual and the universe. These patterns, largely hidden by human mental activity, may be lived in accordance with or abandoned.[2] An individual who is in complete harmony with these patterns is known as a sage.

It only takes a few seconds to remember that our bodies are vibrant landscapes, worlds shaped by the forces of nature. Within each human are elements forged from ancient stars, rivers of blood reflecting the great waterways of earth, neural pathways branching like sprawling roots of forests, and electromagnetic waves humming in rhythm with invisible forces around us. We are simultaneously mountain, ocean, and sky—a microcosm, home to millions of organisms. It is without surprise that each individual, guided by their unique biology and history, will inevitably have distinct expressions of nature's patterns. These patterns may be understood as dynamic themes that point toward underlying processes. How does modern science understand how grand patterns of nature may be reflected in each human? Fractal geometry. Patterns in nature where the whole is reflected in its parts are known as a fractal pattern. The golden spirals of a Romanesco broccoli, the repeating triangles on a Koch snowflake, or the structure of a fern echoed throughout its leaves, can all be objectively quantified. In the world within us, fractals, within a larger framework of complexity theory, may model our nonlinear subjective life, and its relationships with itself and others.[18]

In this book, we attend to zones of convergence between findings in science and themes in classical Daoism. These zones are defined by seven core principles: creativity, process, relationship, wholeness, equilibrium, spontaneity, and transformation. Each principle is found in nature and conserved through the multiple levels that compose a human being—from biology to our relationships. They are repeated, diversifying their expression through iterations with time. When these principles are cultivated, they will enrich life; when they are deprived, they will impoverish life.

What does it look like to embody these seven principles? Imagine somebody who confronts challenges with an unusual degree of tolerance. Despite the risk of death or social shame, their responses remain genuine, their minds are still, and their emotions balanced. Flexible and adaptive, their actions appear seamless, connected, and in tune with any situation. Their bodies are supple and strong. They may be full of vigor yet patient and present to all things. They simply seem to blend in with the natural world. With clarity of mind and perspicacity, they are spontaneous yet prepared. They do not tremble in the face of uncertainty, entering it with tranquility. Their decisions convey timeless wisdom, yet they simultaneously display a playfulness found in children. Despite these abilities, they remain humble and continually exhibit virtuous behaviors even when they have been slandered. These are all typical descriptions of a sage, and while a sage may be too humble to admit to this, in modern times, we might informally describe this person as *savage yet virtuous, playful yet wise*.

It is not so much about returning to be a "noble savage," whose purity remains unblemished through noncontact from civilization, but to *root in the principles of nature while being authentic to the necessities of society.* This does not mean simply acquiescing to societal pressures, but revolting when it is misaligned. Other than the power associated with the word *savage*, the idea that it comes from the Latin word "silva, silvaticus," meaning "wood, from the woods," is appealing due to the symbolic importance of the uncarved wood in Daoism. Its most recent ancestor is *sauvage*, from old French, meaning "wild." To be savage is to operate from *the wilderness within*, to be a force of nature. In addition, being savage implies the *possibility* of being feral and destructive. Yet it is counterbalanced by virtue.

To be virtuous is to be someone whose principles guide their being and actions. The connection here is the word "de," from the Daodejing, which is often translated as "virtue," yet may encompass "savage," through its alternate meaning, "inner power."*

Thus, to align with nature is to cultivate *Potency,* and one appearance of *Potency* is to be savage, yet virtuous. The becoming of reality, a creative process in perpetuity may be seen as a form of timeless play. In parallel, the sage plays with the expressions of nature that they are attuned to, rousing a childlike disposition of wonder, livelihood, humor, and ease. Yet, it is also because they have tapped into the underlying current of Dao that their actions are wise, with complexity and context seemingly considered every moment. Thus, as *Potency* increases, such qualities shine through, with appearance conforming to inner truth.

The first major premise of this book is that, to our detriment, we have become misaligned with nature. This misalignment may be characterized by varying severities, categorized into separation, alienation, and discord (SAD). Humans have evolved the capacity to suspend the immediacy of space and time. This suspension enables us to reflect, plan, and analyze complex situations. We can mirror the unfolding of natural processes disclosed to us as feelings, sensations, images, and thoughts. We can even think about our thoughts (i.e., metacognition). The added dimension of internal experience is reflected in the development and stabilization of multiple networks in the brain. This sets the foundations for *"the SAD theory,"* which is the subject of focus in chapter two. Separation from the immediacy of time and space also means that being alienated and discordant with nature's flow becomes a possibility, as the ensnarement of narratives, emotions, thoughts, and sensations (NETS) draws one further away. Such NETS have anchored themselves with major cultural and technological shifts throughout human history. One trade-off many of us suffer from today is the experience of ourselves as detached and isolated entities housed in our heads, even though we are deeply interconnected. Our experience has become far removed from the facts. NETS can impede organicity and result in discontent.

The second major premise is we begin cultivating *Potency* by becoming aware of and embodying the seven principles as they express themselves within us. Where do we begin? In humans, nature finds its purest expression in unimpeded organic activity, or *organicity*. Organicity is the natural intelligence and wisdom our bodies are born with, outside of awareness. It is nonverbal, sustains our entire body without "thinking," and signals us toward patterns inherent to its order. Organicity is communicated through our intuition—the old-growth forest of the mind—a nonlinear, dynamic, complex medium through which nature's potential is unveiled. Reason, informed by intuition, considers the context of situations, as it facilitates its creative expression. An individual who is aligned with nature is characterized by readiness and flexibility, navigating within and above the widest range of possibilities.

What is *the way of nature*? The way of nature cannot be defined, only experienced. To define it would be an attempt to limit what is essentially limitless. It would be an exercise in futility. In this book, I use words for what they are, symbols that point to a particular direction. I point to qualities in nature that can be understood as principles to embody. Importantly, the expression of these principles is inherently heterogeneous (e.g., creativity comes in many forms).

We use the word *nature* to refer to the living world and the underlying patterns of activity that give rise to it. Nature is not just matter but the organizing principles that lead to its realization. There is the natural world as it resides within each of us, as well as that which is outside of us. Nature may be seen as a continuity extending from moral intuitions in humans to the trees that populate a forest. Its boundaries are defined by what we know yet are made transparent by what we do not. In the enigma of existence, nature becomes a wordless teacher whose very process serves as a path toward deeper knowledge and insight. Science seeks to understand nature through observation and measurement. Daoism seeks a way of life that is most natural (自然, Ziran), guided by an attunement to nature, the discernment of its patterns, and the expression that follows.[†]

We do not fully understand the workings of this universe, consciousness, or the brain—let alone how thoughts arise, where they come from, or what, indeed, a thought is. This simply means the complexity of the universe surpasses our intelligence. This fact leads Daoists to be reverent and humble when considering the place of humans in nature. Each human is modeled after a fraction of the cosmological process. Humans are composed of a subset of elements in the periodic table, with 99 percent of our composition made up of hydrogen, oxygen, and carbon. We exist in a much grander natural process that encompasses and incorporates our own. There is nature and human nature. They are one, but not the same. This is a fact in science and a foundation of Daoism.

In my previous book, *Reassembling Models of Reality*,[19] I delved into the various ways we filter and shape our experience of the world. This was done so through the lens of psychology, neuroscience, and Western philosophy. My method there was a vertical one, peeling back the layers of experience to touch upon the most elemental of truths. Language, for instance, superimposes a symbolic and conceptual order upon the raw immediacy of perception. Through sustained efforts of definition and reflection, we descend toward the bedrock of experience.

In this present inquiry, I adopt a different path, one that unfolds horizontally. Here, I turn to the interplay of psychology, neuroscience, and Eastern philosophy to illuminate the way we might return to an elemental experience. Rather than framing humankind's condition as a "fall," I consider it a "straying"—a term whose roots can be traced back to the vulgar Latin word *estragare*, which translates to "wander out of bounds." Language, as Daoism observes, deepens this estrangement by carving out distinctions, magnifying the sense of multiplicity and separateness. By systematically dissolving these conceptual edifices, we traverse the horizontal continuum, potentially unveiling a primordial state known as *the uncarved wood* (樸).

Under linguistic and conceptual illusions, it becomes much easier for us to lose ourselves in narrative. We may default toward treating the environment and each other as means to an end, as if negatively affecting others and the environment will have no consequence to us. To live this way is to live farther away from the facts and farther away from well-being. This illusion of separateness, bolstered by the discoveries in science and critiqued profoundly by Daoism, lies at the root of our disconnection from nature and from one another.

Evolution and the Dao are both creative, dynamic, living principles, allied with nature's continual movement, change, and transformation. They can both be described as impersonal, amoral, and spontaneous generative forces that express themselves through the material world. In fact, Zhuangzi, who emphasized these points, has been considered a Chinese forerunner to evolution through his writings on the transmutation of species.[20] Despite these facts of nature, humans continue to live in a way that opposes these conditions. We cling to identities, feelings, and thoughts that constantly change. We suffer from an experiential rigidity that prevents us from embodying the wider spectrum of nature. Learning how to adapt to the transience of life and the uncertainty that follows is important for well-being and is a major theme in Daoist literature.

What exists behind the present moment and at its edge? Nothingness. In Daoism, nothingness is not considered a nihilistic void, but an absence of things, a vacuity, which allows for an inexhaustible opening for the presence of things. Everything is housed inside nothingness, and with no discriminating intellect, everything remains undifferentiated, or one. In nothingness, there is no beginning or end; it is perfect, formless, and tranquil. Nothingness consents to all experiences and becomes everything. Nothingness draws out an experience of absurdity that transitions into freedom and possibility. The essential principles that guide the actualization of life and its transformations operate in this vacuous absence, which permeates all that exists. It is a mystery. This is what Daoists subjectively and objectively refer to as the Dao, and what Western society objectively refers to as the laws of nature. Descriptions of sages refer to the emergent qualities from the embodiment of the Dao. To abide in the Dao is to be wholly open to the process of becoming. It is to be without ties to emotional or historical experiences or entanglements with desires and fixed identities.

There are key differences between Daoism and science. Whereas Daoism is a philosophy of being and nonbeing that emphasizes receiving and spontaneity, science is a method of investigation that emphasizes doing and calculated action. Nature in science is investigated through experimental design and measurement of the observable, whereas nature in Daoism is investigated through self-cultivation, observations of natural processes, and inner experiences. Science attempts to "shed light" over unknowns to improve our understanding of the world, whereas Daoistic practices are aimed at "eclipsing light" to amplify nature's autonomous illumination (明) within. Finally, Western thought attempts to consciously construct a conceptual scheme of reality, which may become an intuitive foundation of experience. In contrast, Daoist practices reverse this process by intuitively grasping the nature of reality and then describing that experience. Daoism and science can walk hand in hand. In my opinion, no other living system that can be adopted by people of all cultures, atheist, or religious alike, has been as fruitful as these practices.

Despite being over 2,500 years old, the Daodejing remains among the most widely translated books (second only to the Bible). Any book with this magnitude of continual impact likely harbors essential truths that remain relevant. At this juncture, we turn our attention to how Classical Daoist ideas converge with a particular scientific framework called complex systems theory.

Endnotes

* Importantly, virtue includes the *appearance* of morality because an alignment with nature naturally leads to virtuous behaviors. There is no trying involved, virtue simply is, and when principles of nature are not followed, virtue simply is not. As will be argued, nature is expressed through moral intuitions in a manner fitting to the context of any given situation. Sometimes, one might be a surging river running a well-defined course, and at other times, a cultivated botanical garden.

† I am using Hanyu Pinyin (Daoism) verses Wade-Giles, which transcribes it as Taoism. Although Taoism is more popular in its usage, it is phonetically inaccurate. The official Romanization in China is Hanyu Pinyin, and I will continue using this approach throughout the book (unless coming from a direct citation).

I

DAO AND SCIENCE

*"Surging forth! It arises with us. We do not see its form,
we do not hear its sound, yet we can perceive an order
to its accomplishments. We call it 'the Way.'"*
—THE NEIYE

*"There is a strong current in contemporary culture advocating
'holistic' views as some sort of cure-all... Reductionism implies
attention to a lower level while holistic implies attention to a higher
level. These are intertwined in any satisfactory description: and
each entails some loss relative to our cognitive preferences, as well as
some gain...there is no whole system without an interconnection of
its parts and there is no whole system without an environment."*
—FRANCISCO VARELA

Nestled within Costa Rica is the Monteverde Cloud Forest Reserve, a 26,000-acre forest hosting exceptional biodiversity. Cloud forests form on higher altitudes, typically on mountains, and as water sources empty into the valleys below, warmer temperatures lead to the conversion of liquid water to vapor. Winds carry vapor back up the mountain, as the cooler temperature condenses it into a thick mist. Blanketing the canopy is now a cloud that decreases light entry and temperature. These clouds provide moisture to many of the plants. In addition to rain, the crown of trees accumulates moisture from clouds, forming a fog drip, nourishing the ground, and contributing to the water cycle. Due to these unique conditions, many endemic species and a diverse range of flora, fauna, and fungi interact to maintain the ecosystem.

Image 3: Monteverde Cloud Forest Reserve

Imagine walking through a cloud forest. Looming over you are exotic trees, and from their leaves you can see droplets of water gently dripping over plants and the earth. Fragments of sunlight scatter as they enter through the canopy and become increasingly diffuse as they merge into the fog. In the distance, you hear the songs of birds communicating with each other, and below you encounter worker ants carrying leaves while soldier ants protect their passage. It doesn't take a scientist to intuit that many elements of the forest work together to sustain something greater than the sum of its parts. These interdependent elements interact at many levels forming a complex system.

A complex system is characterized by hierarchy, heterogeneity, self-organization, openness, adaptation, memory, nonlinearity, and uncertainty.[21] Complex systems are both stable and flexible. The cloud forest system can accommodate changes, such as variation in the amount of rainfall, because its requirements are not overly rigid. The behavior of the cloud forest system is not so wildly chaotic or unpredictable that birds and other animals can't survive. Not too rigid, not too chaotic, but stable and flexible—like a Daoist sage.

The mind, too, is a complex system. The brain is *hierarchically* organized, and within the brain each level has varying degrees of influence upon others. From the perspective of the brain, we might consider multiple levels of analysis, beginning at the genetic and cellular level, proceeding to neural networks, electromagnetic activity, and even the environment. Individual differences among these levels (heterogeneity) lead to a variety of creative interactions. These interactions form *emergent* patterns, incorporating feedback loops from the crown of the hierarchy back down to the roots. This is spontaneous *self-organization*. Another connected term is *recursion*, where a system can change that from which it emerged. The mind can influence the brain, just as the brain can influence the mind. It is also *open*, meaning boundaries are not solid but porous, resulting in an exchange of information and energy between the world and our inner lives. The brain is also an *adaptive* organ, changing in response to external stimuli. Change is not blind or restricted to the present moment; rather, it stores information so future developments are based on *memory*. Memories help us predict the future. Interactions may be linear or nonlinear, meaning that responses may have a disproportionate output-to-input ratio. In addition, there is always a degree of chance, due to randomly determined probability distributions that occur naturally within the components of a complex system, rendering predictions *uncertain*.[21]

One of the greatest neuropsychological advancements in the last few decades was the integration of complex systems theory,[1] providing a framework for a better understanding of how our bodies, brains, and relationships interact to shape an intricate inner system of experiences.[22] Our minds are no longer imprisoned in our brains, and there are myriad findings to support this assertion. For example,

- Our gut health may affect our thinking ability, emotion, and even personality.[23, 24]
- Our diets affect mitochondrial functioning, which has been correlated to several mental illnesses.[25]
- Our physical health may significantly influence our mental health.[26]
- Positive social relationships are necessary for the development of healthy neural systems.[27, 28]
- Enriched environments optimize neural circuitry for resilience and learning.[29]
- Our brains and bodies operate through cycles synchronized with our environment.[30]

Interestingly, from the perspective of Daoism, these findings are not so much advancements as they are a return to what humanity has long known to be true. First, the Chinese language has no symbol designated for mind in isolation. Mind as we typically understand it is known as Xin (心), which refers to the "heart-mind"—firmly locating the mind within the body. In Classical Daoism, taking care of the body so it is healthy, supple, and strong facilitates the process of harmonizing with nature. The main centers of influence in Daoism include three regions of body (called the three cinnabar fields) that correspond to three systems of intelligence that have been investigated in science: the brain, the heart, and the gut. The bidirectionality of physical and mental health was noted long ago in Daoism (this also extends to eating habits and the environment). Even in basic Daoist-seated meditation, the focus of awareness is on the abdomen, which is referred to as the lower dantian (下丹田), usually translated as "elixir field."

Fractal systems are a part of complex systems. In nature, we find many types of patterns. Throughout grade school, we learn about geometric figures and how to quantify them mathematically. When we look at a branching tree or a mountain range, we are looking at fractals, in contrast to traditional Euclidean geometry.[31] Fractals are complex and may be symmetrical or asymmetrical, and linear or nonlinear;[32] self-similarity is when the whole is reflected in the parts.[31] It is an encompassing form of geometry not restricted to any point in time or space, embraces paradox, and even penetrates symbolic dimensions. Fractals may be scale invariant, meaning the structure remains the same regardless of the scale of observation. The visual Image 4 (on the left) is the Mandelbrot set, an indefinite pattern that repeatedly presents itself as one continues to zoom in from larger scales to smaller scales. It is defined by the simple mathematical formula $Zn + 1 = Zn2 + C$. These patterns may be seen over time and through space.[32] The image on the right is a fern from the French Alps. Notice how the whole is reflected in its parts.

Image 4: Mandelbrot Set and Fern

Terry Marks-Tarlow asserts that fractal mathematics is ideal for modeling the relational and inner lives of humans. As an example, she elaborates that fractals play a large role in boundaries. Boundaries are not uniform, but "rough, bumpy, paradoxical and interpenetrating."[33(10:40)] They are not clear-cut in humans, perspectives are limited, and often people present with contradictory thoughts and feelings. Boundaries in humans may be open and closed simultaneously, which makes them paradoxical. When a person is resistant to change, they are a "closed" system. Yet humans are constantly affected by outer conditions, and changes in an individual's surroundings may be sufficient to prompt change in what was previously resistant. This would be an example of interpenetration and how boundaries may also be open. She further notes that in the nonlinear world of human life, fractals are found through dreams that map onto our external life, repetition compulsion (i.e., unconscious repetition of relational patterns we learned from history), as well as the therapeutic phenomena of transference or countertransference.

More recently, neuropsychologists have described cognition through the 4Es[34]—cognition as *embodied, embedded, extended,* and *enacted.* We know the mind is influenced by the body's internal environment and that bodily states can affect cognition and emotion. Heart problems can impact one's attention, speed of processing information, memory, and executive functioning. The mind is embedded because the brain is embedded in a body that is embedded in a world; this embedding imposes constraints on what the individual might do. Where you are, what you are doing, and how you are feeling will highly impact the activities of your mind. Have you ever practiced and mastered a speech at home, and when the time came for a public presentation, your execution was completely different? Cognition is extended, meaning it extends into objects in the environment. When you use a calculator to estimate the tip for a bill or when you use a GPS to navigate, you are coming together with tools in your environment to solve problems. In this sense, cognition becomes distributed. Finally, the mind is enacted because it results from the interplay among the body, environment, and feedback processes from those interactions. Social interactions depend on what's on your mind, what's on the other person's mind, what's happening, facial expressions, body language, and other factors that inform where the conversation may lead. The mind never works in isolation; it is always in relationship to something.

What does all this have to do with *the Way*? From a macroscopic scale, Daoism views nature as a whole and attempts to embody its overall movements through an individual's life. Complex systems begin with guiding principles. Biologically, guiding principles constitute and reconstitute our bodily forms with every passing moment. Despite millions of cells continually dying and replenishing, we remain recognizable as ourselves. We understand this today through biological mechanisms, such as the parameters our genes dictate. These guiding principles ensue in interactions among elements in your body, psychology, and social surroundings, leading to a diversity of emergent properties. Emergent properties are *unique* properties that arise from an interaction. These properties go beyond what each part interacting initially contained or expressed. For example, two hydrogen molecules and one oxygen molecule look quite different when separated than when they bond (forming H_2O, the molecular composition of water). Psychopharmacology embraces the concept of synergy (i.e., 1 + 1 = 3), whereby, when combined, two medications with particular effects generate novel ones beyond their individual profiles.

In Daoism, the narrative self or the incessantly chattering mind may be considered an emergent property of nature. One facet that makes humans special is that we can decouple or separate from the immediacy of time and space. Our minds need not be tethered to the present. We can be angry in a completely peaceful environment, and completely calm in a stressful situation. This decoupling is a facet of our emergence from nature—an advantage because we can analyze and plan with far more scope, and a disadvantage because we no longer need to flow with nature and can act in many ways contrary to it. This separation is the prelude to the possibility of not being in tune with our original nature in Daoism.

If you peel away the narrative mind, you'll find organicity or organic activity. This includes automatic processes like seeing, hearing, smelling, and balancing. Most of us take these for granted, but they require a stunning amount of ingenuity! Our heart pumps blood, our breath brings oxygen to cells, our digestive system breaks down food—all on autopilot. You could call this a kind of intelligence.

Intelligence does not require meta-cognition, or the ability to think about thinking. Consider geniuses who can calculate very complex mathematical equations without being aware of the process, or people with photographic memories who have no idea how they stored what they can remember. Even slime molds are known to solve mazes! These pre-reflective forms of intelligence do not require "you" to be there. In fact, the inclusion of "you" might lead to an adverse effect.

You may be impressed by a visual scene reproduced to near perfection by a painter after a few months, yet have you ever wondered how your mind perceives the world with such vividness in a matter of a few milliseconds on a continual basis? This activity is ordered, necessary for these coordinated processes to function. At another level are "aha! moments," such as solutions or ideas that arise without a linear process. Many of the best ideas have emerged from the cessation of continuous thought and reflection. These are all examples of organicity, how multiple hidden processes may combine to inform or signal an individual.

After years of practice, processes that used to require conscious effort become effortless. This is what Daoists "strive" for. Wisdom occurs when intelligence and experience combine into an effective and coherent spontaneous expression. The wisdom in organicity may very well come from millions of years of evolution and may appear at different levels of psychological experience, such as the feeling of inner movement, images, sounds, and/or ideas. Organic activity exists outside of our awareness and forms the foundations for it. The following quotations from celebrated artists, scientists, and thinkers offer powerful examples of organic activity and wisdom at work.

MC Escher (Visual Artist): "But then there came a moment when it seemed as though scales fell from my eyes. I discovered that technical mastery was no longer my sole aim, for I became gripped by another desire, the existence of which I had never suspected. Ideas came into my mind quite unrelated to graphic art, notions which so fascinated me that I longed to communicate them to other people. This could not be achieved through words, for these thoughts were not literary ones, but mental images of a kind that can only be made comprehensible to others by presenting them as visual images."

Mozart (Composer): "...thoughts crowd into my mind as easily as you could wish. Whence and how do they come? I do not know and I have nothing to do with it. Those which please me, I keep in my head and hum them; at least others have told me that I do so. Once

I have my theme, another melody comes, linking itself to the first one, in accordance with the needs of the composition as a whole: the counterpoint, the part of each instrument, and all these melodic fragments at last produce the entire work."

Simone Weil (Philosopher): "Man only escapes from the laws of this world in lightning flashes. Instants when everything stands still, instants of contemplation, of pure intuition, of mental void, of acceptance of the moral void."

Nikola Tesla (Inventor): "But instinct is something which transcends knowledge. We have, undoubtedly, certain finer fibers that enable us to perceive truths when logical deduction, or any other willful effort of the brain, is futile."

Georgia O'Keeffe (Painter): "I have things in my head that are not like what anyone has taught me—shapes and ideas near to me—so natural to my way of being and thinking that it hasn't occurred to me to put them down."

Tchaikovsky (Composer): "It is a purely lyrical process. A kind of musical shriving of the soul, in which there is an encrustation of material which flows forth again in notes... Generally speaking, the germ of a future composition comes suddenly and unexpectedly. If the soil is ready—that is to say, if the disposition for work is there— it takes root with extraordinary force and rapidity, shoots up through the earth, puts forth branches, leaves, and, finally, blossoms. I cannot define the creative process in any other way than by this simile. The great difficulty is that the germ must appear at a favorable moment, the rest goes of itself. It would be vain to try to put into words that immeasurable sense of bliss which comes over me directly [when] a new idea awakens in me and begins to assume a definite form. I forget everything and behave like a madman. Everything within me starts pulsing and quivering; hardly have I begun the sketch, before one thought follows another."

Anaïs Nin (Diarist and Essayist): "I thought of my difficulties with writing, my struggles to articulate feelings not easily expressed. Of my struggles to find a language for intuition, feelings, instincts which are, in themselves, elusive, subtle, and wordless."

Frank Lloyd Wright (Architect): "In nature there is a continuous, ceaseless becoming. There is the great in-between of which [Laozi] speaks, which is alive, which never ceases to be. When you become the pencil in the hand of the infinite, when you are truly creative in your attempt to design, the thing that we call good design begins and never has an end. Once you are aware of the importance of this spirit living in nature, you will never have to copy nature."

Socrates (Philosopher): "The favor of the gods has given me a marvelous gift, which has never left me since my childhood. It is a voice which, when it makes itself heard, deters me from what I am about to do and never urges me on."

Carl Jung (Psychiatrist/Analytical Psychologist): "Philemon and other figures of my fantasies brought home to me the crucial insight that there are things in the psyche which I do not produce, but which produce themselves and have their own life... He said I treated thoughts as if I generated them myself, but in his view thoughts were like animals in the forest, or people in a room, or birds in the air... He confronted me in an objective manner, and I understood that there is something in me which can say things that I do not know and do not intend, things which may even be directed against me."

This list includes several well-known individuals who were intimately in touch with organic activity. There are organizing principles directing the expression of organic potential relevant to each person. The resulting uniqueness of each person may be understood as part of an individual's *de*. Daoism asserts that hidden within the clutter of human mental activity resides guiding principles, a natural Way that can be experienced. *The way* is a return to the foundational terrain of experience, an opening up to the organic wisdom operating below incessant mental activity.

Many dedicated meditators across the world have described experiences of this primordial stratum of nature as pure non-differentiated oneness, a genuine simplicity without any discrimination. This is referred to as guarding, realizing, or maintaining the one,[7, 35] by Laozi as "return to the state of [uncarved wood],"[36 (verse 28)] or Zhuangzi as the "oneness"[9(p46)] or when one may "join in great unity with the deep and boundless… dark and undifferentiated chaos."[10(p81)] To dispel any misconceptions, experiencing oneness does not lead to the perception of the world as an amorphous mass of impressions. While certain meditations may lead to temporary perceptual alterations, the long-term effect is that illusions of duality are still seen so long as one continues to exist in a body with senses, but how one experiences, interprets, and thinks of what is perceived remains altered. In deeper states of meditation, the experience of oneness pervades even when perception insists on separation. Finally, an experience of oneness with the world does not suddenly mean you can read people's minds or that your social skills become optimal. Core empathy and an increased insight into your intentions may increase your patience and understanding for others and yourself, thus reducing conflicts, but does not equate to technical social skills that allow you to accurately infer what people might be feeling and thinking.

Attuning to nature refers to a way of being that emerges when an individual recovers and embeds herself in organicity. For many, it can take several years of self-cultivation practices before experiencing this recovery. Western culture emphasizes self-consciousness and its development, which is secondary to organicity. From the perspective of the brain, as we will discuss later, this relates to frontal, left hemisphere-biased functions focused on differences, discrimination, and details. So long as one inhabits the narrative self, organicity can only be understood intellectually. In contrast, right hemisphere-biased functions correspond quite closely to the characteristics of a sage.

II

HOW WE STRAYED

"The more taboos and prohibitions there are in the world,
the poorer people will be. The more sharp weapons the people have,
the more troubled the state will be. The more cunning and
skill man possesses, the more vicious things will appear."
—THE DAODEJING

"Coming down to the era of decline, [it transpired that]
people were abundant, but wealth was scarce; people labored to
the utmost, but their nourishment was insufficient.
Thus competition and strife were born, and Humaneness was
valued. The Humane and the petty minded were, [however,]
not treated equitably. Neighbors formed groups, and
friends formed cabals. They promoted falsehood and deceit,
cherished a spirit of contrivance and artifice,
and lost [their] natural tendencies."
—THE HUAINANZI

Most individuals would readily concede that humans are part and parcel of nature, yet how few among us truly feel this connection in the depth that one might expect? This lack of connection leads to a contradictory experience, an intellectual acknowledgment that we are an expression of nature without any emotional resonance. Thrown further into the complexities of a culture that dominates us—one rife with conflicting social norms, competitive pressures, and relentless technological advances—the severing of our bond with nature appears almost a foregone conclusion. But how did this unraveling come to be, and by what forces was it driven?

I propose that a threefold process is responsible for this misalignment: separation, alienation, and discord (SAD). Separation began with the evolution of brain functions that enabled us to disengage from the immediacy of experience and drift amid an inner world of ideas. Separation encourages individuality, which may be in harmony or discord with that from which it has separated. Thus, separation is not necessarily negative. In fact, it is quite important for nature's creative advance. Alienation relates to historical events and modern-day practices that have empowered divisive narratives. And discord refers to our belief systems, technologies, and practices that actively promote conflict.

Two important developments in human brain functioning are the capacity for inhibitory control and working memory. Inhibition enabled humans to transition from reflexive to intentional responses. The ability to suppress competing responses passively or actively, in favor of an alternative response marks a major step in our cognitive evolution. Two important regions related to inhibition are the orbital frontal cortex (OFC), and the dorsolateral prefrontal cortex (DLPFC).* Of note, the DLPFC is also of great importance for working memory, which allows us to think, after we disengage with the world. It relates to an "inner space and time" where thoughts can linger, examine, and shape itself. It is commonly thought that children are more attuned to the purity of nature, and it is interesting that many executive functions mature around age twelve, which coincides with the maturity of the neural networks.[19]

In any given moment, a distributed set of regions in the brain are connected and synchronized in their activity. The collection of active regions is called a neural network. Humans have many neural networks that work together, but we will just focus on four. What the SAD theory ultimately leads to is an imbalance within and between these networks, or in short, a *neurodynamic imbalance*. Let me first clarify what these networks relate to, and how they might relate to our misalignment with nature.

The four networks are: the Default Mode Network (DMN), the Salience Network (SN), the Central Executive Network (CEN), and the Subcortical Midline Structures (SCMS). We could say the DMN supports being, the CEN assists doing, the SN facilitates attending, and the SCMS aids in the expression of our "original nature" and is the only system that functions in tandem with the three. I am using these networks only as *representatives* for these concepts; while they are not causal, they are related. While I highlight these four networks, it is the DMN, SN, and CEN or this triple network model that forms the basis of the separation from our original nature (SCMS). A metaphor that may be of assistance is to envision the SCMS as a stage with a melodic soundscape, the DMN as the storytellers, the SN as the director, and the CEN as the actors. They are all necessary for a good play, but a lack of synchrony can lead to complete chaos. Alone they are neutral, similar to how stress or neuroplasticity can be good (e.g., beneficial change) or bad (e.g., addictions) depending on the context. Following are images of these three networks and how they interact.

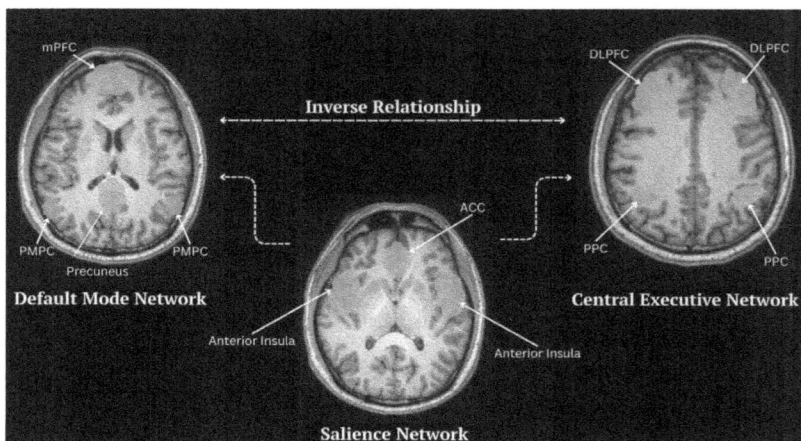

Image 5: Rendition of the image from Marks-Tarlow, M. Solomon, and D. J. Siegel (Eds.), Play and creativity in psychotherapy (pp. 39–63). W. W. Norton & Company. Brain image from Chan, 2024.

The DMN correlates to functions related to mental time travel, others and the self (MOATS). It is defined by the ability to project oneself into the future to simulate a scenario, into the past to retrieve a memory, to an imagined social interaction, or outside of oneself to reflect upon the self. These are all necessary for character development and good story-telling. In contrast, if left unchecked, it may lead to mind wandering.[38] Thus, it enables us an added spatial dimension to our psychological landscape, yet this may also be experienced as a boundary, like an actual moat. Consider that when your mind wanders, you are no longer present with reality around you but instead absorbed by fantasies, stories, or thoughts. Up to half of the time when we are in our minds, they are not present but wandering, and the more our minds wander, the more likely they will wander to a negative place.[39] A storyteller may get lost in the details, losing the interest of the audience. Importantly, *intentional* mind wandering usually leads to more positive places, and some degree of mind wandering is beneficial, for example for creativity, memory encoding, memory consolidation, or for rest and recovery.[40] This would provide spontaneous ad libs appropriate to the context. One study[41] sampled 226 participants and found that 64 percent of our mind-wandering content was future oriented, and the topic of highest frequency was work. The modern DMN has become too noisy, and this is partly reflected as work stress, and additionally (as will be argued) self-absorption, loss of ability to be present, and increased levels of problematic stress.

The CEN enables us to engage in goal-directed tasks requiring executive functions, such as problem solving, working memory, and cognitive flexibility.[19] When the CEN is active, it deactivates the DMN. Continuing our metaphor, when the acting begins, the storyteller must stop, otherwise there would be too much noise. Part of this network is the DLPFC as discussed earlier. One can actively "work" on items held in short-term memory for a specific problem through reverberating neural circuits. Importantly, the DLPFC is a central hub for most executive functions. The CEN, however, is also linked to the posterior parietal cortex, which relates to visual-spatial reasoning and attention. Together, they play a role in regulating emotions, coordinating behavior, controlling attention, and decision-making. The CEN maximizes our ability to focus and work through external tasks. It is about performance.

The CEN has become overly emphasized in the modern day. What you can do is more valued than who you are. Our cultural emphasis on productivity has exalted "doing" over "being," sidelining the DMN's reflective potentials. This does not mean that the CEN is disproportionately more active, rather that people have become more focused on finessing this system, which also results in the DMN being more preoccupied with work (as indicated in the study). In this process, the potential for DMN development is lost. As an example, emotion regulation, coping skills, interpersonal abilities, introspection, and mindfulness are generally not part of the core curriculum in schools. Remember, these networks also inhibit or turn off each other when they are active. For this reason, you may have heard of many CEOs who are extremely productive, but terrible with social relationships. Part of the challenge is our culture forgives those who are extremely skilled at what they do, even if their character has major flaws (as if their productivity justifies harmful actions).

Third, the SN helps determine what the individual should pay attention to, acting as a switchboard for the DMN or the CEN. It is the director, and one of her jobs is to provide direction. The SN's two main areas include the anterior insula and anterior cingulate cortex (ACC).[38] The anterior insula is a central hub that integrates information and signals the brain for higher-order action. Importantly, it also plays a role in sensing physiological signals within the body, or what we call interoception. The ACC is known as the "oops center" for its relationship to emotional awareness and error correction. It has also been linked to an affective component of pain and empathy. Overall, the salience network determines what is most relevant and significant to the person at any given time, and will either attempt to optimize resources toward focusing on a goal-directed activity (the CEN) or to engage in self-reflective processes (DMN). Without surprise, it is also related to many tasks that measure cognitive flexibility. It serves to maintain the overall homeostasis in this way.[42] It spotlights what you pay attention to.

Given our evolutionary history and its mismatch with modern-day civilization, it is plausible our salience network may not be sufficient to account for our modern ways. The SN may be deceived into triggering one network over the other without consideration of the context. Artificial drugs or technological temptations hijack our natural reinforcement systems into believing we are meeting a goal that is important for survival. This deception increases their value and presence while reducing the importance of more beneficial interests. We can be like moths swarming around an artificial light, believing it is the moon.

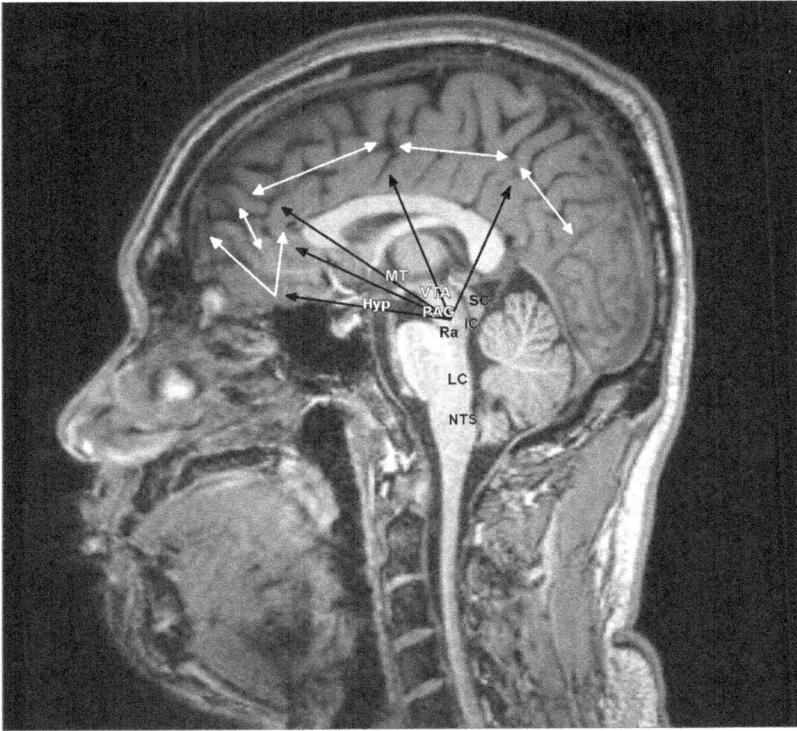

Image 6: Subcortical and Cortical Midline Structures with influences from Georg Northoff, from chapter entitled "The Neuroscience of Ethics" (2023) in *Neuroethics and Cultural Diversity* and secondly Antonio Alcaro, Stefano Carta, and Jaak Panksepp from "The Affective Core of the Self" (2017) in *Frontiers of Psychology*. Brain image from Chan, 2024.

Finally, the subcortical midline structures (SCMS) include fundamental areas related to basic physiological functions like breathing, vitality, movement, primary emotions, homeostasis, and autonomic regulation. Thus, even if dominance among the three networks shifts due to cognitive demands, the influence of the SCMS remains present. For this reason, it aptly represents our unconditional ground of being. It is always active and necessary for the functioning of the others. Like an empty stage, it is ever present, and provides the foundations for which storyteller, actor, and director must work upon. It also holds the potential for what types of sets are available for use. The music, on the other hand, refers to the primordial rhythms inherent in our nature, our breathing, core emotions, and possibilities for sensory-motor experiences and expressions.

The SCMS includes major areas within the brain stem, thalamus, and hypothalamus. Damage to this area may leave you in a vegetative state. It additionally supports our capacity to synchronize our bodily movements with higher cognitive functions, which may lead to actions that are spontaneous, effortless, and in alignment with the natural world—hallmarks of the Daoist ideal of ziran. As the deepest layer of our self, it is primarily emotional and sensory motor. When we quiet the mind (especially parts of the DMN) and allow these subcortical systems to function in their natural, balanced state, we may rediscover our original nature.

Interactions among the DMN, SN, and CEN confer humans the ability to override the immediacy of space-time, enabling conceptual thinking, which may promote survival and flourishing. According to Northoff, this conceptual world is enveloped by three inner dimensions of "space-time," which may be measured by neural structure and activity (i.e., space) and electromagnetism (i.e., time).[43] Furthermore, measurable disruptions in spatiotemporal synchrony have positively correlated to verbal reports and objective data providing a new lens for understanding clinical conditions. In collaboration, my research group devised a model clarifying how distinct levels of space and time in the mind may be expressed and utilized to assist in psychotherapeutic practice.[44]

In summary, the phase of separation relates to recent functional developments in the brain. There is an expansion of "inner space-time" which has given rise to the capacity to inhibit/override the demands of the present. The benefit provides an open range of responses that may be intentionally chosen to outcompete reflexive behaviors. Clearly, these provide us with a survival advantage, but unintentionally have also made us more *susceptible* to being alienated from and in discord with nature. Importantly, although advancements in brain development may have separated us from nature, they also provide us with access to greater potentials that nature has to offer. Here lies a profound irony, the very faculties that distance us from nature also afford us the potential to rediscover it in new and meaningful ways. If human experience is folded into nature's order, then so too must we regard our moral intuitions, our sense of beauty, and our quest for meaning as natural unfoldings. Might it be that through understanding and harmonizing these faculties, we may not only reconcile with nature but unlock deeper potentials?

ALIENATION

The bridge between separation and alienation is language. For most people, communication is its primary function. Language, however, represents the natural world through symbols. This means that the inner world is now populated by words, phrases, and narratives, which may provide humans with advantages in analysis and planning.[45] Trial and error through direct experience is no longer necessary, as we can strategize symbolically (i.e., words). The problem, though, is that we may now be one step further away from nature, as we anchor ourselves in our inner narratives in contrast to the actual experience around us. Coating the perceptual world is now a symbolic world. Like the other functions, language is neutral, but the possibility for narratives to be biased and inaccurate arises through communication and dissemination of false information. Furthermore, we harbor a left-hemisphere known to be confident,[†] yet frequently inaccurate and ever attached to the need to be certain.[45]

Another important consideration is the invention of currency. Currency has the same effect, as it is a widescale-shared belief that confers coin and paper the power to "make or break" someone. In other words, a symbol overrides reality. It is believed that metal objects were already being exchanged at 5000 BCE, with formal systems beginning around 600–700 BCE. The ability for symbols and concepts to outweigh experience clears a path into alienation. To be alienated is a step further from mere separation; it is an estrangement. The potential in the be-ing of humans has increased, yet artificial narratives may now supersede preexisting natural patterns. In alienation, there is an overgrowth of artificial narratives.

During the first agricultural revolution dating back to circa 10,000 BCE, hunters and gatherers were transitioning from a nomadic lifestyle to a sedentary one. At that time, selection pressures to conserve energy were dominant. Societies expanded based on the stability that was afforded through farming, deforestation, new tools, and other methods. This was a necessity for the flourishing of civilization, as the hunter-gatherer lifestyle was not conducive to stationary living. This epoch also marked the beginning of the intentional manipulation of nature, a surplus of available resources, and the eventual establishment of more formalized governments and regulated roles. Ten million hunter-gatherers are all that could be sustained due to their lifestyle,[46] which translates into an estimate of 100–200 million people by 500 BCE. The mobile restrictions consequent of dense spaces and the speed of movement that typically follows have been in fact linked to increased stress.[47] Humans may now jockey for roles and compete for resources and social standing in a way that was quite different from hunter-gatherer society. The amplification of stress may consequently lead to a cascade of problematic alterations in brain structure, plasticity, neurogenesis, memory, learning, cardiovascular health, metabolism, and increases in anxiety, depression, and a host of other psychological conditions.[48]

In fact, Jared Diamond[49] believed agriculture was "the worst mistake in human history." His argument was derived from modern-day hunter-gatherer communities, many of which challenge common conceptions about them. First, leisure time is not sacrificed in hunter-gatherer communities; in fact, the opposite is true. This is strange, considering the purpose of technology was to provide us with more leisure time and to engage in more complex and meaningful tasks. Second, diets are a healthier balance. Agriculture restricts the diets of many previous foragers due to selecting crops that would grow in their regions. This led to malnutrition. It was further exemplified in lifespan decreases in post-agricultural communities and a height decrease from the end of the ice age to 3000 BC (in Greece and Turkey). Third, sedentary settlements brought higher levels of infections and diseases due to crowding. Finally, industrialized societies have higher levels of socioeconomic differences and inequality among sexes. Hunter-gatherer communities tend to have higher rates of well-being and lower incidences of psychological conditions when compared to industrial civilizations. While there are many theories as to why this is, Chaudhary and Salali[50] highlight equality, present orientation, social support, explorative learning, and alloparenting as major differences from industrial society that have led to this beneficial outcome.

In agreement, Narvaez[51] elaborates that cultures of small-band hunter-gatherers are characterized by high levels of social support and embeddedness, considerable physical contact, cooperation over competition, high levels of autonomy for adults and children, egalitarian relationships, mutual sharing, and communal joy. These are all in contrast to what is normative for Western society, which, as an example, has expectations of competition over cooperation, low levels of social support, physical contact, hierarchical relationships, and expectations for others to be selfish in contrast to generous and cooperative. Rather than dominating nature and extracting it for resources, hunter-gatherers partner with the natural world, whose gifts they request and rely upon and whom they respect with reciprocal gifts. If the hunter-gatherer lifestyle sets the conditions for species-typical development, we have strayed.

She further asserts that many of these changes are related to modern-day child-rearing practices. These include but are not limited to the lack of alloparenting, unfounded fears of "spoiling the baby" by giving it too much attention and care, over emphasis on independence, ignoring biological rhythms, undermining play, sleep training, over prioritization of cognitive development, use of technology as a substitute, and mechanized routines. In her words, we have been "parenting baby-as-machine." They become "good candidates for authoritarianism" (Darcia Narvaez, personal communication, 2025). When babies are reared in a species atypical way, they are primed to grow up conflicted, as human nature is twisted to fit human convention.

The notion we have strayed can be found in all four seminal Daoist texts listed in the author's note. The clearest examples come from The Huainanzi (i.e., monarch's guide to ruling well), especially in a chapter translated as "The Basic Warp," where modern-day living is criticized for losing *The Way*. As an example,

> So things reached the stage when [people] built great mansions, houses, and palaces... Yet [even] this did not suffice to fill the desires of the rulers of men. Thus the pine, the cypress, and the flowering bamboo drooped and rotted in the summertime; the Yangzi, the Yellow River, and the Three Streams became exhausted and ceased flowing...marauding wild animals became [even] fiercer. The common people had only small reed huts for houses, with nowhere [for travelers] to find lodging; those who died of cold and hunger lay as close together as pillows to mats. Thus it came to pass that they divided mountains and streams...to make territories and boundaries. They counted the population to divide the masses of people by numbers...they created insignia for those who managed affairs, made regulations of clothing and rank, differentiated between noble and base...weapons and armor flourished, and contention and conflicts broke out; that the common people suffered extermination, repression, and disasters...was all due to this.[13(pp269–270)]

As such, writings on misalignment date back to circa 2,500 years ago, with the birth of Daoism, which coincides with what Karl Jaspers[52] termed the Axial Age (around 500–300 BCE). The significance of this period relates to the emergence of thinkers such as Laozi, Zhuangzi, Liezi, Buddha, Confucius, Homer, Heraclitus, Plato, etc. This period may have marked an expansion of consciousness or a major updating of our "software," likely due to the necessity for it. Daoist literature often criticizes abstractions that may provoke unnecessary strife. Social hierarchies, for example, may be a catalyst for an insatiable cycle of desire and wealth accumulation. These social drivers engrained the importance of being useful in the minds of many. This is partly why Daoist writings attempt to shed light on the usefulness of the "useless." It has now become a primary mode of perceiving the world, and even oneself, as a commodity. People become objects to possess, and our self-worth becomes conditioned upon our success as opposed to our character. What ensues is a disproportionate focus of energy on maintaining an empty façade and, ultimately, a life wasted on a delusion. This is only accentuated by the psychological impact of technological advances. Human "mastery" over elements all the way to the domestication of animals entrenches the idea that the natural world is something humans use for their advantage. Instead of viewing animals as companions, they became pets or livestock. Slowly but surely, an echo chamber is created between individuals, and these deeply embedded societal narratives passed down through the generations. People are birthed into a society, inculcated into the notion of being greater than nature.

A related theory comes from Mcgilchrist,[45] who argued that historical, societal, and artistic developments paralleled brain development, ultimately leading to the dominance of the left hemisphere over the right hemisphere. Many of us now view the world predominantly through a narrow lens, a perspective that is fixed, mechanistic, decontextualized, and overly assured. In a public conversation we had[53] touching on the misalignment with nature, he noted the Industrial Revolution as being particularly relevant. The Industrial Revolution was a historical epoch beginning circa 1760 that clearly amplified the relationship between "man and machine," supplanting the idea of "man and nature" and further escalating the dynamic of "man over nature." The image of a train spewing out pollution as it traverses many miles of natural splendor is a perfect expression of this era. The introduction of trains also initiated the standard time zones still used today. We live our days according to an artificial construct that is useful for coordination across large distances. Instead of living in direct contact with nature, we are several steps removed: from the food on our plates (e.g., on average, food travels 1,500 miles before arriving on your plate), to the clothes we wear (e.g., production, distribution, retailer, delivery), to the spaces we inhabit (e.g., average human is 9.7 km away from natural spaces; in Germany, it's 22 km[54]). As the distance between humanity and nature grows, our inner life reflects it. The natural world has become a place for people to "disconnect" rather than "reconnect." Estranged from nature, there is no feeling of returning home, and the experience of "belonging" in nature disappears, as home becomes the artificial structures and rules developed in society. Nature appears more and more foreign, as separation turns over to alienation.

DISCORD

The roots of discord incorporate all the previous levels and can be found budding on multiple levels of analysis, from the individual to the societal, historical, and spiritual. Discord occurs when separation becomes wrought with alienating artificial narratives *and* opposition. Several religions align with the philosophical idea of dualism, which pervades the minds of many today. We are born into this world with a body, a direct connection to nature, yet many are indoctrinated into the prevailing notion that the mind (or soul) and body are separate, with the mind being greater than the body. From this perspective, the value of our bodies depreciates, as we think of our bodies as a ball and chain in contrast to who we are. The body becomes a scapegoat for anything society deems distasteful. Inappropriate outbursts of aggression, lust, or gluttony are all blamed on the body; all that is base is related to the body while all that is pure, sacred, and of value resides in the soul or mind. This is a recipe for a human being that is perpetually in conflict with itself.

Furthermore, the use of social media to drive dopaminergic excess, and exploit our attentional resources has led to a greater susceptibility of consuming false and polarizing information. At a biological level, our natural reinforcement systems, which have evolved for hundreds of thousands of years, are now being targeted and repurposed for reinforcing ideologies and products. The continual presence of instant gratification changes the way our brains organize information. People now develop the preference of feeling excited over meaningless content, over long-term rewards, which leads to the erosion of meaningful activity. The strong desire to conform to social pressures drives a greater wedge of discord between being and nature. As the virtual world grows in significance, the value of nature is quietly relegated to the annals of history. When humanity loses touch with the natural world they evolved in, so does their understanding and perceptions of its value, followed by their motivations to protect it. Without awareness of consequence or experience of connection, humans become myopic, and the world is abused for self-gain.

If we trace neurodevelopmental functions throughout the lifespan, we will find the gradual increase in inner space and time. From age two we begin with an explicit sense of self, to age three with explicit memory and theory of mind, to age five with representational theory of mind, to moral reasoning, inhibitory control, and DMN maturation by age twelve.[55] This age also aligns with puberty, where independence becomes typically a key goal. The expansion of psychological terrain finds its foundations in the experiences we encounter, alongside its impact on brain development. If children are exposed early on to social media (without reservation), narratives that overstimulate may become prioritized, potentially setting a rigid structural baseline for their thinking.

The functioning of the three networks reflects this incongruence, with excessive DMN activity related to conflicted narratives surrounding who we believe we are, who we actually are, and who we are trying to become; the SN confounding on what we pay attention to, and how we pay attention to it, and the CEN unsure of what to do, yet with increasing pressures on how to do it (well). What remains is the isolated human—self-absorbed, living through virtual avatars, chasing the next rush through extremes, competing for influence, seeking controversy through polarizing posts—detached from the present, disconnected from their own body, unhealthy, lacking real friendships, poor social skills, driven by a consumer mindset, ecologically irresponsible, and operating on a foundation of incomplete or inaccurate facts.

What are other major problems related to humankind's misalignment with nature?

	Problems	Why?
Biological	• Higher risk of unhealthy lifestyle	• Care for body becomes secondary
Psychological	• Fragmented inner world • Self-absorption and pride • Feeling isolated, disconnected • Feeling inauthentic	• Aspects of nature are rejected, loss of wholeness • No experience of interconnection with natural world • Belonging related to an artificial world promoting conformity
Social	• Lack of empathy • Objectification of others • Jealousy	• Other people are not viewed as ends, but as a means to an end. • Competitive drive heightened
Ecological	• Ecologically irresponsible • Lack of long-term foresight leads to unsustainable practices.	• Belief that nature is here to serve humans • Lack of interconnection with natural world, views nature as "other"
Spiritual	• Feeling incomplete • Feeling empty • Reduced sense of awe • Accentuated fear of death	• Lack of unity leads to loss of belonging, appreciation, and meaning. • Death is not viewed as a natural transformation but as a forced choice. Experience is subject to the imagination of the individual.

Table 2: Problems Related to Humanity's Misalignment with Nature

Narvaez[56] identifies our disconnection as covering several directions: horizontally, or from our evolutionary heritage; developmentally, or from optimal ways of child rearing; and vertically, which relates to the natural world itself. We subsequently have lost all the advantages associated with them. To further the mistake we are making, she makes the simple case that our baselines should be reflective of the 99 percent of human history as small-band hunter-gatherers, not on 12 percent of the global population (and 1 percent of human history) that most of our studies use as baselines. In fact, evolutionary psychologists and anthropologists refer to us as a WEIRD society, an acronym that stands for Western, Educated, Industrialized, Rich, and Democratic—punctuating how strange our culture is in comparison to many others.

We must find a way to integrate our inner wilderness with the demands of modern-day living and reclaim the *Potency* that naturally emerges with this alignment! With an understanding of how we strayed, we now turn our focus on our return.

Endnotes

* Each region has been correlated to different aspects of inhibition, for example, the DLPFC with holding rules and goals in working memory, and OFC with the actual motor suppression.[37]

† This alludes to the very famous split-brain studies that found out that when our hemispheres are split (for intractable epilepsy), our left hemisphere will make up responses to answer choices that the right hemisphere makes, because the right hemisphere's relation to language is for most, non-verbal (it is related to pragmatics, prosody and context).

PRINCIPLE I

CREATIVITY

Nature is a ceaseless process of creativity. It is continuously forming through the activity of creating itself. This means nature dances at the edge of existence and nothingness. Every experience is a realization of its endeavor, its self-generating activity brimming with variety. We are just one expression of nature. In humans, diversity exists on many levels: from the biological to the psychological and sociocultural. Technically speaking, we are a different person with every moment that passes; some cells have died, a thought has passed, an emotion has settled. Every mind is different, and every person is unique all the way down to the beginning of humanity. Broadening your perspective, you might peer into a history book and note the progression of ideas that have captured the minds of many in their respective times; these similarly change with new advances in science and the humanities. New movements surge into the sociocultural fabric in reaction to previous ones, initially causing disruption and polarization as they slowly stabilize into the foundation of the next epoch.

Each of us provides nature with a unique path for experimenting and experiencing a different angle of its potential. We can find meaning in creativity. Our unique character, upon encountering a shared existential condition, may lead to an experience that has never been felt in the history of humanity. The emergence of distinct-feeling tones accompanied by thoughts may birth novelty into the world. Can you rest in the bosom of creativity and find solace in this? There is no need to create a masterful artwork; your experience is nature's oeuvre.

Creative *being* is a means to ensure nature's creativity advances unimpeded, and to do so, we must develop the ability to be present, with an attitude of openness and acceptance. We move with the flow of potentials that are seeking to unfold within us, and learn how to integrate those, which at first glance, may appear to threaten our being. Openness provides us with the largest dynamic range of actions to select from, enabling us to adapt to any context. Openness arises when we are uncertain. It is a flexibility that allows us to move through the most challenging times with serenity.

Creative *attending* refers to the flexibility of attention. Changing how you pay attention to others, yourself, and the world may birth novel pathways and experiences. This flexibility in attention holds the potential to transform not only our ways of relating but also the very fabric of our experience, fostering a deeper sense of harmony with ourselves and the world that sustains us.

Creative *doing* refers to the variety of artistic ways we may express ourselves and our relationship with the world. This can appear through music, dance, and painting, as well as inventions, fiction writing, and other forms of divergent-thought expressions. Being and doing need not go hand in hand. An amazing visual artist may have a very rigid and closed personality; and a very open and accepting individual may have no particular skill toward traditional acts of creativity.

Many hunter-gatherer societies are present-oriented. The BaYaka hunt for their food on a day-to-day basis and favor the present over the future.[50]

When goals go unmet, they accept it and move on. This is unlike the obsession with goal completion, to the extent where persistence becomes burnout and depression in our WEIRD society. Creativity comes in many forms, from accepting the difficulties of life to creativity in problem solving and adapting to uncertain conditions. This society further engages in communal singing, dancing, swaying, and clapping, for which all members are present.

Under the principle of creativity, we find the Daoist notions of nothingness, the uncarved wood, and change. Nothingness is not mere emptiness but the fertile expanse from which all possibilities arise. The uncarved wood, a metaphor for untouched potential, reminds us that creativity flourishes when we honor the raw essence of things, unshaped by the demands of artifice. Change, the eternal flux of existence, is creativity in motion—the ceaseless renewal through which life reveals its boundless capacity for transformation.

III

"NO-THING" MATTERS

"You cannot do better than to place yourself in darkness and in unknowing."
—MEISTER ECKHART

"When conducting an analysis, one must cast the beam of intense darkness so that something which has hitherto been obscured by the glare of the illumination can glitter all the more in the darkness."
—WILFRED BION

Creativity finds its genesis in nothingness. In Daoism, nothingness is conceived with a depth and vitality that sets it apart from a traditional Western conception—a formless "living presence"[57(p9)] over a void, a fertile expanse rather than nonexistence. It is the cosmological background for Dao's expression. The emergence of things results in a universe forming through relationships between the absence of things and the presence of things, like objects requiring space to inhabit.[*57]

It is the space between things that allows objects and people to maintain individuality. Nothingness is vacuous of things, yet it harbors an inexhaustible playground of dynamic potential. In this way of thinking, pure nonexistence finds its place in the world of words, but not reality.

The Dao acts as the underlying creative principle that brings all things into being. Hinton[58(p25)] spoke of the Dao as a "generative source-tissue" or "existence-tissue" that encompasses both the *ten thousand things* (a term in Chinese literature to convey the empirical world of variety) as well as nothingness. Possibilities always exceed achievements, thus the frontier of human potential seems to recede after every accomplishment.

Nothingness has a practical use. For example, in D.C. Lau's[5(p15, Ch.11)] interpretation of the Daodejing, we find:

> Thirty spokes share one hub. Adapt the nothing therein to the purpose in hand, and you will have the use of the cart. Knead clay in order to make the vessel. Adapt the nothing therein to the purpose in hand, and you will have the use of the vessel. Cut out doors and windows in order to make a room. Adapt the nothing therein to the purpose in hand, and you will have the use of the room. Thus what we gain is something, yet it is by virtue of nothing that this can be put to use.

This passage shows that empty spaces can be advantageous. Nothingness need not be mired in philosophical thought and can enrich your approach to the world. One typically notices objects in a room; however, understanding spatial occupation is equally, if not more, crucial. Comedians may strategically use periods of silence before the punchline of a joke, or a skilled luthier might pay special attention to the space within a guitar they are crafting. When talking, it is hard to listen. When the mind is producing, it is hard to receive.

With nothingness as the center, being becomes peripheral.[57] Nothingness implies things have yet to come into being, meaning it lies in the realm of possibility. When we strive for an ideal self, but have yet to embody them, where are they? The horizon of nothingness. It is our engagement with possibilities therein that grant us access to more encompassing ways of living. Therefore, in the Daodejing we find the phrase "know the white, but keep to the role of the black."[5](Ch. 28) Even more clearly stated in The Huainanzi, "For this reason sages based in nothing respond to something and invariably fathom the underlying patterns; based in the empty accept the full…"[13](Ch. 7) Lodge yourself in nothingness, while also appreciating the world of things.

Nothingness may be a reference point that enlarges our capacity to think. Contemplating nothingness can bring about overwhelming feelings of absurdity, yet it is this absurdity that may give us the power to dissolve the old and usher in the new. Nothingness is at once creative and destructive, twin aspects of transformation.

We can also think of nothingness metaphysically. According to Zhuangzi,[10](p88)

> In the great beginning there was nonbeing; There was no being, no name. Out of it arose one; There was one, but it had no form… Out of the flow and flux, things were born, and as they grew, they developed distinctive shapes; These were called forms.

The idea that formlessness precedes form has been speculated by many physicists and philosophies that challenge materialism. A discussion of these may be found in my previous book.[19] Daoism is a nondualistic philosophy, meaning it does not separate the physical and mental. Yet it is clear that formlessness is more fundamental in this philosophy.

In our direct experience, what is formless: mind or matter? Mind. It is quite interesting that this assumption (i.e., the universe can be reduced to matter), which many medical professionals hold to be true, is not so widely agreed upon by physicists. Many physicists, such as Nobel Prize-winning physicists Wolfgang Pauli, Niels Bohr, Schrodinger, Max Planck, and Werner Heisenberg, believe the fundamental substrate to be more of a mental quality than material.[60] There are three viable options that I can think of for the metaphysics of Daoism. Mind and matter may be understood as processes on a single dipole, as in Whitehead's[59] work. Matter may also be described as a phase of a consciousness,[60] or simply what consciousness looks like as it is expressing itself,[61] such as in objective or analytical idealism. This idea, which has existed in ancient wisdom traditions, is no longer just an idea, but is currently being explored scientifically (i.e., "conscious realism") and mathematically.[62, 63] Third, mind-matter relations may be collapsed into a category that encompasses and transcends them both, such as in neutral monism.

It is an error to assume that the mind comes from matter. It is actually impossible for us to conceive of anything outside of our mind, for everything is experienced in the mental arena. This includes all that is observed and all that we quantify. How is it possible that dead lumps of matter give rise to an entirely new dimension of deep rich inner experience? And where does everything come from? What birthed our existence? As Jung noted long ago, if there is anything that would extend beyond the confines of space and time, it would more likely be mind. A far more rigorous discussion can be found in the following references.[19, 60, 61, 62, 63]

Nothingness in Daoism is the foundation of nature. To harmonize with nothingness, we engage in practices that assist in developing a mind that is clear. First, we recognize thoughts are options, not orders. Our heart pumps blood throughout the body, like how thoughts arise in relation to our brain activity. It is easy to be swayed by the illusion you are just the content of your thoughts, but you are *also* the process that can transcend and guide them. They are options, just information to be considered, not who you are.

We then continually dissipate the being and becoming of thoughts. A clear mind gives way to stillness. A stilled mind allows a more objective perspective on phenomena being observed. A healthy distance from their presence allows us to experience the quiescence between our thoughts. Where does this information and energy pass to once our attention is no longer focused on them? Nothingness. To identify with nothingness is to allow organicity to naturally unfold with the process of becoming.

> I do my utmost to attain emptiness
> I hold firmly to stillness
> The myriad creatures all rise together
> And I watch their return
> The teeming creatures all return to their separate roots
> Returning to one's roots is known as stillness
> This is what is meant by returning to one's destiny
> Returning to one's destiny is known as the constant.[5(p20, Ch.16)]

To experience the silence between thoughts is to merge with a form of nothingness. From this point, "be-ing" is experienced as a non-differentiated process, or what Zhuangzi calls "oneness." Oneness presents as a united wholeness emerging from pure potential.[57] By keeping the dominant foot in the Dao's abode and the other in the phenomenal world, one establishes a process of continual harmonic resonance with Nature's way. Importantly, the Dao is both root and branch, meaning the primordial nature is its creative potential and its subsequent nature, the phenomenal world. The individual aligns with nature's own principles that pervade. One embodies the openness, tranquility, and stillness of nothingness; emotional and intellectual empathy from the deep sense of oneness; and the complete entering into the spontaneous becoming of things. Instead of being trapped by probabilities, we free ourselves by entering the vast terrain of possibility. Nothingness becomes primary, with being secondary. Interactions are then always balanced by this deeper domain of nature, as opposed to the tyrannical imposition of belief systems and logic that emerge from the self.

Existentially, the idea of nothingness brings fear to many individuals, especially in relation to death. But does it need to be seen this way? The following passage illustrates how differently it may be viewed with a Daoist mentality. Note that I am substituting nonexistence with nothingness (which is how Ziporyn[9] translated it) given how I refer to these two words throughout this chapter:

> Bright Dazzlement asked [nothingness], "Sir, do you exist, or do you not exist?" Unable to obtain any answer, Bright Dazzlement stared intently at the other's face and form—all was vacuity and blankness. He stared all day but could see nothing, listened but could hear no sound, stretched out his hand but grasped nothing. "Perfect!" exclaimed Bright Dazzlement. "Who can reach such perfection? I can conceive of the existence of [nothingness], but not of the [nothingness], of [nothingness]. Yet this man has reached the stage of the [nothingness], of [nothingness]. How could I ever reach such perfection!"[10(p185)]

Nothingness and being are not opposites in this line of thought. Instead, they are viewed as complementary. That which exists is praising that which does not. In fact, existence personified views it as a paragon of perfection, something worth striving for and learning from. Meditative techniques, such as "sitting in oblivion," as discussed in the subsequent chapter, may be considered a form of practicing death.

Reflection and Practice

Several distinguishing attributes of nothingness can be captured in the acronym SPACE: silence, potential, absence, creativity, and emptiness.

How might adopting the Daoist conception of nothingness enrich your life?

1. Might it make you feel less fearful of death?
2. Might you design your home space differently?
3. Might it make you appreciate the aesthetics of the space around objects more?
4. Might you become more comfortable with silence and its potential use in conversation?
5. If you are a painter, might it affect your work by strategically including space?
6. If you are a musician, might it impact your music by strategically including silence?
7. If you are struggling to regulate an emotion, might emptying your mind be beneficial?
8. In relationships, how does absence play a role? Does physical absence change the emotional presence?
9. Immerse yourself in silence or other forms of sensory deprivation. Experiment with the experiences that emerge.
10. Try minimalism, see how less can bring more.
11. Try operating throughout the day without expectations. See how that might change your psychological responses.
12. Consider a world where every person could clear their thoughts and still their emotions. With every mind being in a state of serenity, where is there room for violence? At minimum, we concede that the world would be more at peace, should every mind be at peace.

Think about your daily activities. How does nothingness or emptiness play a role?

From my professional perspective, we have many uses for nothingness in its various presentations. Silence is often used as an intervention, especially in dynamic approaches. A therapist can learn a lot about their patients based on how they interact with silence. We also diagnose based on the presence or absence of symptoms. The absence of emotional continuity from a previous session may indicate a change or reversion. The play of presence and absence can be analyzed at many levels.

In Daoism, emptiness refers to a state of mind that is empty of thoughts and clear of disruptive emotions. While this chapter focused on the beneficial outlook of nothingness, and nonbeing, the common Western outlook is emptiness as negative. In psychotherapy, many forms of emptiness can emerge that differ from what is being discussed in this chapter. Emptiness can also be understood as a form of suffering, linked to a loss, and it is usually followed by a restlessness that attempts to fill the gap. People describe themselves as feeling "empty," for many reasons. Importantly, a negative experience of emptiness may still lead to a positive outcome. As an example, emptiness can arise when an individual realizes the emptiness in their maladaptive habits. This may guide one toward adaptive behaviors.

The following are a few that lead to negative experiences (notice it spells out ROGUE).

1. Relationships: when someone feels as if their relationship has lost momentum or feelings of excitement.
2. Others: neglecting the self as one focuses too much on others may lead to feelings of emptiness.
3. Grief: emptiness felt when somebody passes away, or one endures a break-up.

4. Unmet Need: emptiness felt when the object desired is not available.
5. Existential: when someone feels like their life lacks meaning, or if a meaningful pursuit has been disrupted (e.g., creative roadblock).

The mind is empty when the heart is full, and when the heart is empty, the mind is full.

Endnotes

* Chai distinguishes between nonbeing and no-thingness. No-thingness cradles this dyadic operation, and is the Dao's playground. He categorizes nonbeing as ontic, meaning it relates to the empirical reality of humans, and nothingness as ontological, which encompasses the universe as a whole or "'absentia' forms of existence (trace, shadow, void, hollow, etc.)" p. xiii. To keep things simple, I will use nothingness to encompass both.

IV

UNCARVED WOOD

*"My thesis is that…there is only one primal stuff
or material in the world, a stuff of which everything
is composed…pure experience…"*
—WILLIAM JAMES

*"In this regard, pure experience is identical
with direct experience. When one directly experiences
one's own state of consciousness, there is not yet
a subject or an object, and knowing and
its object are completely unified.
This is the most refined type of experience."*
—KITARO NISHIDA

Image 7: Redwoods

One might venture to say that the first stirring of being, as it arises from the abyss of nothingness, reflects the symbol of the uncarved wood. The uncarved wood is a term Laozi used to refer to a state of simplicity and wholeness brimming with possibility; for the wood has yet to be carved. In this state, creative ideas swell and only one becomes realized from moment to moment. It is synonymous with our "original nature," a pure process of becoming with a direct line to nothingness. This process effortlessly flows in most of nature, but in humans, it is obscured. Categories and concepts are imposed upon nature, and in doing so, the inherent potential of the natural world becomes hidden. The mind reshapes the world into artificial constructs, in contrast to a presence that reveals and nurtures its potential.

From the perspective of time, the uncarved wood is found in the imme- diate present, before memories of the past or anticipations of the future can stamp their expectations onto the present. In space, it precedes our experience of material diversity, or what Daoists refer to as "the ten thousand things." If we think of it as lying on a horizontal axis, it would be the moment just after the world was sensed, but before it was realized through perceptual groupings, concepts, and labels. It is thus a pre-reflective state. Thought of, from an evolutionary perspective, it was a time before our cognitive faculties allowed us to suspend the immediacy of our engagement with the world. For this reason, it has been called our "original nature," for this way of being was the template upon which we have developed.

One of the greatest imports from Daoism and extended upon in Zen[15, 16] is the discovery that this primary way of experiencing the world can be recovered, and its recovery brings with it a host of benefits. For those with a Christian background, an interpretive angle identifies Eve eating the apple as a symbol of gaining egoic consciousness. Although ego consciousness was gained, suffering came with it, and she was cast out of paradise. From the Daoist perspective, one could say we never left paradise; we have strayed into a maze of NETS (i.e., narratives, emotions, thoughts, sensations) and simply forgotten that paradise is still with us.

In Costa Rica, we say *Pura Vida*, an expression often used as a greeting, farewell, or synonymous with "all good." It translates to "Pure Life." It is a perfect term to describe the way of the uncarved wood. Other terms have been used, such as "pure experience," but this implies an "experiencer" and the experienced, which contradicts the notion of nonduality.* For this reason, I use the term "pure life" to describe consciousness without conceptual divisions, life as a pre-reflective happening in the immediate moment, and as pure oneness.

What is it that creates division? The thinking mind, which houses narratives empowered by emotions and impulses. When one is no longer attached to those, their power is lost. The mind, clear of thoughts and any emotional agitation, becomes serene. There is but the expression of pure life. The thinking mind dissipates from the foreground to the background, and with ample time in this utter stillness, the movement of nature becomes present. The individual is now joined with "the great unity,"[10] has returned to the state of the uncarved wood, and "holds fast to the one."[†7]

When a new sensory experience is presented to us, it is so rapidly grouped and discriminated against that we lose touch with the present. Pure life is always present, but in our inability to extend and prolong it without judgment, we lose our way. As you look around you, your mind will automatically view specific objects. Your mind is primed to focus on a figure placed on a background. Although this perceptual ability is important for survival, it now functions as a limitation. (Because there will always be the chance that you may be focusing on something maladaptive. It may also not be entirely conducive to well-being, even if it may be beneficial for survival.) It is also possible for you to disengage with this selective function and distribute attention equally to all you see. Open monitoring meditations may facilitate this capacity. Essentially, the figure dissolves into the background, and the entire field of experience becomes the foreground. Perceiving the world this way requires the cessation of cognitive systems involved with identifying and discriminating objects. When thinking is completely silenced, awareness merges with the flow of becoming.

Roth[67(p7)] introduced the term "cognitive attunement" as the ability to "live free of attachment to rigid, egocentric third-person objectifications of self and other, free from excessive self-consciousness, able to act effortlessly, without intentionality, in a mode of no-person orientations to first-person, second-person, and third-person experience." In other words, clear, fluid, spontaneous cognition emerges based on pure experience. The "no person perspective" is another term he pioneered, speaking to perspectives that arise from selfless conscious states whereby the subject-object divide has been transcended. An experience of pure life is the occupancy of a no-person perspective.

Roth believes Zhuangzi's central theme and goal in his writings include this idea of cognitive attunement that involves a trait change, rather than a state change that may heighten or become altered during meditation practice. Individuals may thus become "free of attachment to a fixed identity."[67(p8)] To bolster his view, he points out a discussion in Chapter 22 between Laozi and Confucius, noting, "…the Sage neither misses the occasion when it is present, nor clings to it when it is past. He responds to it by attuning himself, that's the Power; he responds to it by matching with it, that's the Way."[67(p715–16)]

Zen practitioner Sekida[68(p108)] divided moments into what he called a "nen," which he approximates to a "thought impulse."

> Let us call the outward-looking action the first nen, and the reflecting action of consciousness the second nen…another reflecting action of consciousness that immediately follows in turn. This action is a further step in self-consciousness. It consolidated the earlier levels. We shall call it the third nen. This third nen will think, for example, "I know I noticed I had been thinking, "It's fine today."[68(p109–110)]

He went on to note,

> Descartes' "cogito ergo sum" seems to be commonly accepted without question. But "I think" is the action of the first nen. If it is not recognized by the reflecting action of the second and third nen, no cognition of it occurs. One must say, "I recognize my thinking, therefore I know I am."[68(p182)]

Thus, the goal is quite similar in the recovery of what he terms "intuitive cognition,"[68(p184)] which equates to the first nen. His view of the human ego also resonates with it being an emergent property, because he views it as arising from the third nen: "the sequence of three nen actions—I live, I notice my living, I know I am."[68(p183)] From a scientific perspective, these ideas match well with Vanderkerckhove and Panksepp's[69] anoetic consciousness, noetic consciousness, and autonoetic consciousness, as well as Damasio's[70] protoself, core self, and autobiographical self.

Today, a similar experience has been popularized through the use of psychedelics, such as LSD and psilocybin. These experiences are usually followed by "ego dissolution," or what I inadvertently called "disillusion." Pure experience may be conceived of as a primordial state of consciousness prior to the intellectually discriminatory faculties that arose in response to survival needs. One of the main differences between psychedelic and meditative experiences of oneness is that in heightened states of meditation, there is a simultaneous retention of individuality in things.[68] Daoist practices promote the recovery and primacy of this primordial state of consciousness, with divergence leading to suffering.

Pure life can be defined as the moment experience is conceived. It is the surging of all life in the immediate moment. There is no concept of time; in fact, no concepts at all. Just a happening. All comes together as ONE: *Original Nature Emerging.*

THEORY AND SCIENCE OF MEDITATION

Are there practices that may help one attain the way of the uncarved wood and embody the value of wholeness? And returning to the SAD theory, how do we silence an overly noisy Default Mode Network (DMN)? The storyteller is of no use if he continues rambling on, focusing on irrelevant details. One response is meditation. One line of connection between all classical Daoist texts is the mention of *Jing* (精, essence), Qi (氣, breath/energy), and Shen (神, numen/mind). Daoist practices are often centered on becoming aware of, regulating, and cultivating these *Three Treasures.* Jing is what we inherited: the bestowal of spontaneous energy from our family lineage—energy involved with the development of our bodies, as well as that which dissipates as we age. It is energy involved with the expression of our genes and our resultant biological disposition. Qi relates to our vitality experienced daily. Biological properties like blood flow, metabolism, and sweat are all connected to it. Finally, Shen is highly cultivated energy connected to consciousness, creativity, and spirituality. A wonderful old metaphor, a source unknown, describes Jing as a candle's wax and wick, Qi as the flame, and Shen as the resulting light.

One of the most important methods for self-cultivation impacting all three treasures is meditation. The science of meditation has been surging in the past few years, partly due to its associations with cognitive, psychological, and physiological benefits. James Austin[71, 72, 73] identified two orientations toward the world—an egocentric and allocentric (i.e., other-oriented) cognitive orientation. He stipulated that meditation may elicit a shift in attentional dominance to an allocentric orientation. Indeed, there is little to no debate that meditation can change neural structure and functioning. For example, one area of the brain (i.e., the posterior cingulate cortex) related to self-referential processing was found to be diminished in long-term meditators.[74] He also[72, 73] noted bottom-up influences (i.e., inferior occipito-temporal pathway to inferior frontal) relate to receptive meditative practices that focus on global awareness and allocentric attention, in opposition to top-down influences that relate to concentrative approaches, which are focused narrowly and include egocentric attention (i.e., occipito-parietal processing pathways overlapping with somatic and motor cortices).

Overall, meditation consists of two categories: focused attention (FA) and open monitoring (OM).[75] Focused attention, as it sounds, is the focusing of attention on particular internal or external stimuli. It is worth noting that meditations typically begin with breathing, which is a function directly related to the subcortical midline structures (i.e., representative of original nature) in the brain. The most common form of focused attention meditation is breath awareness practice, whereby the individual focuses on the sensations of their breath every time their mind wanders.‡ From the perspective of the brain, cortical systems (evolutionarily, more recently developed systems) silence subcortical areas (more primitive systems).

Open monitoring is a form of receptive attention whereby an individual observes all experiences without particular focus or attachment. The field of awareness is thus in a ready state, completely open to anything that arises.[§]

Neuroanatomically, open awareness activates bottom-up systems of attention (i.e., alerting system), as the individual suspends interpretative processes (e.g., reduced thalamic activity) and elicits a small percentage of the executive system involved with monitoring. The result is an overall reduction of limbic activity and overall executive systems. Both inhibit, but they do so through different mechanisms. Both types of meditation lowered the connection between the striatum (areas involved with motor functions, emotion, reward, and habits) and DMN regions (a network in your brain that is active when you are resting and not engaged in any task) linked to mind-wandering.[77]

From research on the minimum time to meditate, duration matters, but frequency may be more important.[78] A study by Norris and colleagues[79] used a "minimum dose" of meditation of thirteen minutes for eight weeks. It was found that individuals who finished eight weeks of brief mindfulness meditation may improve attention, working memory, and recognition memory while reducing negative emotional states. A simple meditation, such as breath awareness practice for ten minutes a day for sixteen weeks, can drastically improve brain functioning.[80] Jha[81] suggests that people generally see benefits when they practice for about fifteen minutes a day, five days a week, for around four weeks. Long-term meditation practice may also decrease responses from the autonomic nervous system, which houses your sympathetic system (fight/flight) and parasympathetic (rest/digest), and reduce reactions to emotions.[82]

Meditation is a process, some would say a lifestyle, and to reap its benefits requires continual dedicated practice. A study by Tanaka and colleagues[83] investigated changes in attentional function with brief one-time FA and OM in a single thirty-minute session. It was shown that one-time meditation did not improve attention functions universally. A limitation of this study was that the brief one-time meditation might have some effect, but it may be very small.

Overall, meditation has been found to correlate to improved allocation of brain resources, executive functioning, sustained attention, memory, impulse control, emotional regulation, conflict monitoring, and the immune system. Meditation can also influence the efficiency of brain activity alongside structural changes.[19, 82]

While meditation can be a powerful tool, it is also important to consider its *dark side*. First, it is not a cure for all psychological distress, and second, in a conversation with Dr. Steven Hayes (founder of ACT) on my podcast, the CNC Dialogues (2024),[284] he revealed evidence to support that it may lead to higher levels of self-absorption. More specifically, they become "nicer to themselves, but nastier to others." Why isn't it a cure for all psychological problems? Because the foundations of your psychological functioning are based on interactions between genetic guidance and early experiences. While you may have the ability to quiet the mind of chatter, difficulties impacting that foundational level may still exist and arise in moments of interaction. The process and content of thoughts that populate the mind are intimately connected with these foundations. As an example, while you may achieve the capacity to distance yourself from thoughts, and strategically select one over another, you may not be presented with many good options with a tenuous foundation. The world of feeling is also much greater than thought, and regulating yourself when you are alone is not the same as with others. For these reasons, meditation cannot supplant psychotherapy, though it may help. In time, many experiences in meditation generalize, but this takes time, patience, and humility. With this more balanced view, let's now dive into the practical components of meditation.

BREATHING FROM THE HEELS: DAOIST-SEATED MEDITATION

"Tranquility and calmness are that by which the nature is nourished. Harmony and vacuity are that by which potency is nurtured."
—THE HUAINANZI

"On inner cultivation 'concentrate your breathing and attention and relinquish thoughts, feelings, and desires,' 'cast aside wisdom and precedent.' eventually, you will reach a condition of complete equanimity and pure emptiness, a state in which your inborn nature is merged with the way. Then when returning to the world of dualities, you will have many valuable qualities. Your sense perceptions are always clear and accurate; your emotions are always calmed; and you rest in harmony amid the turmoil of the world."
—THE HUAINANZI

Classical Daoist texts refer to various types of meditation; however, they do not offer specific instructions because these texts were not designed to do so. As such, any meditation derived from them is to be considered an approximation based on the information provided. That said, classical Daoist meditation involves cultivating a serene mind, meaning one that is clear (qing, 清) and still (jing, 靜).[84] The mind is cleared of thoughts, and emotions are stilled. As the mind is released of all conceptual human activity, the new clearing allows natural activity to unfold without hindrances. Although many modern Daoist meditations may involve a proactive approach that includes visualizations, breathwork, self-massage, and other active practices, the most ancient Daoist texts demonstrate a preference for more passive approaches.

We are limited by our identities, preferences, and viewpoints. Meditation provides us with a way to free ourselves *from* ourselves. As we begin our meditation practice, we continue a process of emptying and filling. Achieving a state free from constraints begins as temporary during meditation, as one eventually returns back to them. However, with practice and time, the constraints loosen, and one achieves a deeper connection with nature.

Daoist meditation begins with awareness of the alignment among the body, breath, and the mind. The earliest seated posture known in Daoist meditation is thought to be "upright sitting" (正坐, zhengzuo, jing co), which "involves kneeling, with the sit-bones resting on the heels."[85(p157)] In texts like the Neiye and Zhuangzi, it may be referred to as "aligning the four limbs."[7] If there is too much stress on the heels, one may use meditation pillows and/or rest the ankles slightly off the edge of the meditation mat. This is similar to the position used in Zen practice. Other seated positions popularly known as Lotus or Half Lotus are believed to have been integrated after exposure to Buddhist and Indian practices.

One of the current hand positions commonly used in Daoist meditation is that of *ziwu* (子午), whereby the hands are interlocked like a yin-yang. Typically, for males, the left hand is wrapped over the right with the tip of the middle finger of the left hand touching the outer base of the right ring finger and the tip of the thumb on the left hand touching the inner base of the right ring finger. The remaining fingers rest beside them. For females, the formula is inverted, with the right hand over the left. The purpose of the hand positioning is symbolic, but also serves to keep you minimally active to maintain wakefulness.

The eyes may be open or closed, depending on the meditation. When eyes are open, they are still half closed, with the gaze gently rested on the tip of the nose or on a point on the floor. This may help with generalizing benefits gained from meditation into everyday life, combat sleepiness, and reduce the occurrence of visual hallucinations that may arise during extended practice. Breathing is through the nose, as that is what our nose was designed for. The mouth is closed with the tip of the tongue touching the roof of the mouth.

Daoist meditations are referred to as apophatic, meaning that negation becomes a path for experiencing more. It is also interesting to note that in the Daodejing, the Dao is not often described directly. Instead, it is described indirectly through descriptions of what it is *not*. In meditation, individuals practice "movement in stillness," one attunes to stillness, even in the presence of mental contents in ceaseless flow. Excessive movement in our minds results in a disconnection with nature. *Breathing from the heels* is a Daoist saying from The Zhuangzi, which informs technique and implies that the sage's breath penetrates the entire body, not just from the throat and lungs. For this reason, deep breathing is of particular importance in Daoism, and coincidentally corresponds to interventions commonly used to assist with emotion regulation. For all the following meditations, you can follow the general rule of thumb that begins by *aligning* the body, breath, and mind. As breathing continues, you reach a point of *clarity*, which leads to *emptiness*, and the mind becomes *still* (ACES). Importantly, if your mind wanders at any point, simply redirect yourself to the exercise without any judgment or criticism. This is actually not a mistake, or "bad," but natural, and each time you redirect, it strengthens your attentional circuitry.

Meditation 1

We begin with the most ancient text and practices noted in the Neiye.[7(p78)] This first practice comes from verse 17.

> "For all [to practice] this Way: / You must coil, you must contract, / You must uncoil, you must expand, / You must be firm, you must be regular [in this practice]. / Hold fast to this excellent [practice], do not let go of it. / Chase away the excessive; abandon the trivial. / And when you reach its ultimate limit[,] / You will return to the Way (*Tao*) and its inner power (*te*)."

Coiling and uncoiling refer to breathing, as one coils with every inhalation and uncoils with every exhalation. Many Daoist practices begin by focusing on what is called the *lower dantian*, which resides three inches below the navel and on the inside. This area is seen as the roots of a system of energy or, more practically, the center of gravity and balance. In science, this corresponds to "gut-brain." With every inhale and exhale, the individual is continually allowing mental contents to dissipate as they concentrate on the upper abdomen, lower abdomen, and then the whole field as they breathe and empty out mental contents.[7]

Meditation 2

The second meditation from the Neiye[7(p72)] is a mantra-based meditation focusing on the word "Dao." This was reconstructed by Roth, inspired by verse 14.

> The way (Dao) fills the entire world; it is everywhere that people are, but people are unable to understand this. When you are released by this one word: you reach up to the heavens above; you stretch down to the earth below; you pervade the nine inhabited regions. What does it mean to be released by it? The answer resides in the calmness of the mind. When your mind is well ordered, your senses are well ordered. When your mind is calm, your senses are calmed. What makes them well ordered is the mind; what makes them calm is the mind. By means of the mind you store the mind: within the mind there is yet another mind. That mind within the mind: it is an awareness that precedes words. Only after there is awareness does it take shape; only after it takes shape is there a word. Only after there is a word is it implemented; only after it is implemented as their order.

To be released by the one word means to repeat the word Dao in your mind so that you may free yourself from all other internal activity until you become completely identified with it. What is "it"? Here, it is described as an awareness that precedes words, the mind within the mind. Once you have inhabited the state, you gain a deeper connection with it and may develop an increased frequency of contact with it.

Another practice may be to engage in prolonged vocalizations of the word *Dao*. This may be especially helpful for early phases of meditation, by more actively engaging your breath and assisting with the maintenance of attention.

In the Daodejing, verses 10 and 16 are most relevant for references toward meditation. Verse 10 states:

When carrying on your head your perplexed bodily soul can you embrace in your arms the one and not let go? And concentrating your breath can you become as supple as a babe? Can you polish your mysterious mirror and leave no blemish?[5](p14)

We can also combine this with one of my favorite verses from the Daodejing, verse 16.

I do my utmost to attain emptiness, I hold firmly to stillness, The myriad creatures all rise together, And I watch their return, The teeming creatures all return to their separate roots, Returning to one's roots is known as stillness.[5](p20)

Moving into the dialogues in Zhuangzi, we find more details regarding meditation techniques that can be reconstructed. For example:

You have only to rest in inaction, and things will transform themselves. Smash your form and body, spit out hearing and eyesight, forget you are a thing among other things, and you may join in great unity with the deep and boundless. Undo the mind, slough off spirit, be blank and soulless, and the 10,000 things one by one will return to the root—return to the root and not know why. Dark and undifferentiated chaos—to the end of life, none will depart from it. But if you try to know it, you have already departed from it. Do not ask what its name is; Do not try to observe its form. Things will live naturally and of themselves.[10](p81)

Returning to the roots is a shared theme. Meditations related to this theme are found in more detail in The Zhuangzi. The two most well-known include Zuowang or sitting and forgetting (or Sitting in Oblivion[66]), and xinzhai or fasting of the mind.

Meditation 3

Sitting and forgetting or sitting in oblivion (坐忘, Zuowang) refers to the process of emptying one's mind until one is no longer identified with their preferences, identities, body, and internal activity. Interestingly, "forgetting" carries a negative connotation, often used when something has been unintentionally lost. If we look at the word itself, however, it's composed of forgetting. To intentionally forget is to gain something. What do we gain? The gift we call the present, an invitation to become and experience something new. One is temporarily suspended in "forgetting," or oblivion and, as a result, the individual merges into nonbeing, allowing oneself to flow with the current of the Dao. This is found in Chapter 6 in the Inner Chapters.[9](p62) In this first meditation, Yan Hui shares his progress with Confucius. He begins by noting how he has "forgotten human kindness and responsible conduct." This then transitions to forgetting "ritual and music." Finally, he arrives at the assertion: "I just sit and forget." When Confucius asks him what he means, he responds: "It's a dropping away of my limbs and torso, a chasing away of my sensory acuity, dispersing my physical form and ousting my understanding until I am the same as the transforming openness. This is what I call just *sitting and forgetting*." Confucius replies, "The same as it? But then you are free of any preference! Transforming? But then you are free of any constancy! You truly are a worthy man! I beg to be accepted as your disciple."

There is a version of this that is comprehensive, lasting a much longer time than a single day from Sima Chengzhen. If we stick to the classics, however, according to Roth,[86](p14) the practitioner "gradually lose[s] visceral awareness of the emotions and desires...cut[s] off awareness of sense perception...[and] lose[s] bodily awareness and banish[es] all thoughts from consciousness." This apophatic practice is about completely emptying the mind until it merges with emptiness, and in emptiness it also becomes everything. Chan, quoting Lu Ch'ang-Keng, said that "to forget means to have one's mind in all things but not to have any mind about oneself, and to have one's feelings in accord with all things but not to have any feelings of oneself." [(p201)]

The following is a personalized rendition of this meditation that follows the dialogue straight from the text.

> Begin with your eyes closed and simply focus on your breath. When you've reached a state of calm and centeredness, imagine three rings orbiting around you—an outer, center, and inner ring. Beginning with the outer ring, allow your thoughts to revolve around social rules and expectations of what it means to be a good person. And when a feeling of satisfaction and knowing arises in relationship to this theme, empty your mind with every exhalation. Notice the outer ring disappearing with every breath until that ring has disappeared entirely. For the center ring, allow your thoughts to revolve around your name, who you are, how you identify yourself, your habits and preferences, likes and dislikes. Allow this ring to form until you have a feeling of satisfaction and knowing. When you've reached this state, similarly, begin dissolving this ring with every exhalation until the second ring has completely disappeared. For the inner ring, bring into awareness your body, scanning yourself from your feet to your head. Now gently begin releasing body awareness alongside any other thoughts that may accompany it. Allow the image of this ring and yourself to disappear and evaporate entirely. Continue collecting any lingering thoughts or images in your mind with every inhalation and expelling them out with every exhalation. Completely open up to the silent process of becoming and transformation.
>
> When you feel ready to conclude, gently return awareness to your breath and the expansion and contraction of your body with every inhale and exhale. Slowly begin opening your eyes as you return to the world around you.

Meditation 4

Fasting of the mind (san zaai, Xīn zhài, 新寨) can be found in Chapter 7 in the Inner Chapters. The passage is as follows:

> "May I ask what fasting of the mind is?"
>
> Confucius said, "Make your will one! Don't listen with your ears, listen with your mind. No, don't listen with your mind, but listen with your [breath]." Listening stops with the ears, the mind stops with recognition, but [breath] is empty and waits for all things. The Way gathers in emptiness alone. Emptiness is the fasting of the mind.[10(p25)]

Three stages, as indicated in this practice, include sensory focusing, mental awareness, and merging. The method of "fasting" continues into the Zen tradition with Zen Master Bassui indicating:

> Fasting does not mean refraining from the formal eating of food. It means refraining from feeding on the roots of delusion. Fasting means looking into your own nature and illuminating your consciousness, cutting off diluted feelings arising from analytical thinking, remaining apart from external phenomena and unattached to the internal void, completely purifying yourself so that things with no more than a threat of meaning become nonexistent in your life[10(p48)]

Script: "Begin by listening to inhalations and exhalations of the breath. Notice any other sounds, detaching meaning from them, noticing them as simply bits of information. Follow through by noticing anything else engaging your senses, such as taste, touch, smell, and sight (if your eyes are open). With time, transition to the awareness of thoughts. Observing the breath, and any other thoughts that arise. Who is it that is noticing the breath? Who is it that is noticing thoughts? Finally, merge consciousness with the breath, becoming the breath itself."

Meditation 5

Komjathy and Townsen[85] categorized quiet sitting as a meditation related to guarding the one (*shouyi*, 守一), fasting of the heart-mind quiet sitting (*jingzuo*, 靜坐), and sitting and forgetting. This practice includes simply sitting while focused on the abdomen and letting thoughts free themselves in complete nonattachment to whatever content arises. Guarding the one is derived from the Neiye[7 (p92)] verse 24:

> When you enlarge your mind and let go of it, When you relax your vital breath and expand it, When your body is calm and unmoving: And you can *maintain the One* and discard the myriad disturbances. You will see profit and not be enticed by it, You will see harm and not be frightened by it. Relaxed and unwound, yet acutely sensitive, In solitude you delight in your own person. This is called "revolving the vital breath": Your thoughts and deeds seem heavenly.

Meditation 6

For this last meditation, I use some creative license and integrate a meditation called Tugu Naxin (吐故納新), as well as insight from Eva Wong. It is inspired by the passage "to spit out the old breath and draw in the new"[10(p119)] and also makes its way into The Huainanzi:

> Now Wang Qiao and Chi Songzi exhaled and inhaled, spitting out the old and internalizing the new. They cast off form and abandoned wisdom; they embraced simplicity and returned to genuineness; in roaming with the mysterious and subtle above, they penetrated to the clouds and Heaven.[59(p414)]

According to Wong,[87 (p8)]

> Meditation is about becoming aware of consciousness, not watching or gazing at it. When we tune our awareness to thoughts and experience them directly, we are totally involved. When we are merged with thought and non-thought, the duality of subject and object disappears. In contrast, if we observe or look at our thoughts, we become bystanders. Worse, we often become critics and analysts, and the duality of watcher (subject) and thought (object) is never dissolved. If we understand we are not watchers, and fundamentally there is no watcher and watched, we can relax and flow with the activity and non-activity of consciousness.

Keep in mind, the mind in Daoism includes the body, specifically the three cinnabar fields that correspond to three brain systems that have been investigated in science: the brain, the heart-brain, and the gut-brain. Image 8 illustrates this concept through the most widely known Daoist diagram of the human body.

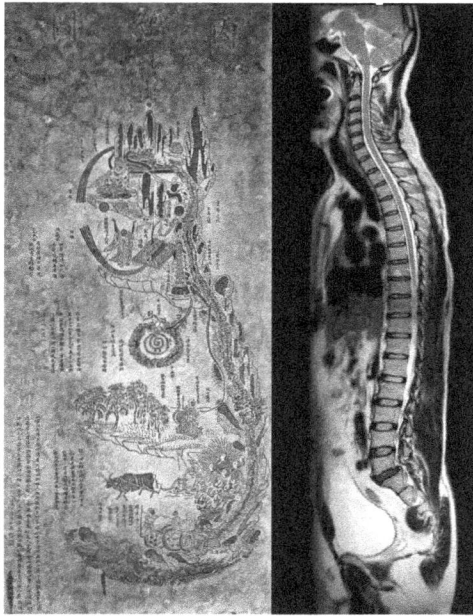

Image 8: The Neijing Tu (內經圖, Inner Landscape, late nineteenth century) is an engraving on a stele in the White Cloud Monastery in Beijing. While this may not fall into the domain of Classical Daoism, rather Daoist alchemy, it is a beautiful example of how the body is a cosmos and inseparable from the mind. From the bottom up, you find the lower torso, connecting to the spinal cord, rising to the head. The three elixir fields (gut, heart, brain) are represented as the ox and farmer, the cowherd, and the old sage (Laozi) sitting below the mountains. In general, the ox (abdomen) represents unrefined energy (i.e., Qi) that becomes refined through practices (farmer working hard). The cowherd is seen holding the big dipper (center of the cosmos), representing our conscious effort to guide the ox. The sage represents our complete integration with the Dao. They represent stages of Daoist cultivation, like climbing up the spine as a mountain (personal communication, Sam Wuest, 2025). There is far

too much symbolism to review all elements, so I would suggest you view papers from Louis Komjathy for more information. This image is licensed under Creative Commons Attribution-Share Alike 2.0 Generic license; no changes were made. On the right is an MRI scan of the spinal cord. ("Mapping the Daoist Body: Part I: The Nèijīng tú in History," *Journal of Daoist Studies 1* (2008), 67–92 and "Mapping the Daoist Body: Part II: The Text of the Nèijīng tú," *Journal of Daoist Studies 2* (2009), 64–108.)

Instructions:

Begin by focusing on your breath. Allow the stillness of your body to be reflected in the rhythm and tranquility of your breath. Then merge your mental activity with your breathing. Observe how each inhalation collects thoughts in your mind and each exhalation releases them. Continue this for a few moments in silence. This process will permeate the entire exercise.

Now focus awareness on the lower abdomen. Notice its expansion and contraction, and any other sensations. Breathe in, gather any thoughts or emotions, and breathe out, releasing everything. Shift awareness to the center of your abdomen, continuing the gathering and release of all thought content or emotions. Notice the still point: periods of non-thought, commonly right in between the inhale and exhale. Let the mind and body open to the process of becoming; let the still point expand its presence. "Enter with the inflow and emerge with the outflow.[11 (p136)]

Then gently shift focus to your heart, allowing your awareness to engage this area. Notice any sensations, gradually exploring all experiences your heart offers. Allow the breath to facilitate the transition of any thoughts, emotions, or impulses. Remain non-reactive to any of them, releasing them from any hold they may have on you. Notice them and let them free themselves.

Now turn awareness to your mind's eye. Notice any narratives, emotions, thoughts, or sensations and simply allow them to drift in and out of awareness. If, at any point, your mind wanders, that is okay. Bring it back to the activity with judgment or criticism. Continue filling and emptying.

If your eyes are closed, you may notice darkness, but even that is visual, so be aware that you are observing the darkness. Then be aware of your consciousness observing the darkness. Become aware of both the observer and the observed, dissolving their boundaries. Continue this exercise until all that remains is the pure process of life itself.

When you feel ready to conclude, shift your awareness to any sensations you have in your body. This may be the weight of your body resting on the cushioned surface below you, or the fabric of your clothing lightly wrapped around your body. Continue for ten more breaths. If your eyes were closed, begin fluttering them open as you return from your journey.

Endnotes

* "Pure experience" comes from William James and was adopted by Japanese philosopher/Zen practitioner Kitaro Nishida to refer to primary experience with no conceptual additions. Whereas James describes the metaphysical notion of the universe made of pure experience, Nishida approached Western philosophy through the lens of pure experience as a phenomenological experience from Zen practice. He describes pure experience as a meaningless non-differentiated presentation of facts, as well as a "unifying activity,"[61(p8)] or "an animated state with maximum freedom in which there is no gap between the demands of the will and their fulfillment."[ibid] James[62(p50)] went on to note that "attention carves out objects, which conception then names and identifies forever—in the sky "constellations," on the earth "beach," "sea," "cliff," "bushes," "grass." Out of time we cut "days" and "nights," "summers," and "winters." We say what each part of the sensible continuum is, and all these abstracted whats are concepts."

† Kohn[66(p154)] shared that "oneness" in the context of certain meditative techniques may refer to "the recovery of a primordial oneness lost in the course of life on earth or to the realization of an original unity that has always existed and will exist in eternity." Throughout the text, she notes that oneness can be understood in four different ways: (a) as the primordial state of the universe in its non-differentiated form; (b) as a formless principle that guides and unifies; (c) as a force or material energy; and (d) as characteristic, which means that everything stems from the same source, the Dao.

‡ Neuroanatomically, Corbetta and Shulman[76] identified the bilateral dorsal frontal-parietal system as playing a major role in top-down systems of attention (cortical-subcortical). This system relates to voluntary focusing on particular figures upon a background and has been found to be recruited during this practice.

§ Corbetta and Shulman[76] identified the right-lateralized ventral frontoparietal system as being involved with the alerting system, an attentional system developed to detect anomalous and salient activity outside of the focus of attention. In meditation, this system may become less active, demonstrating increased readiness and lower consumption of neural resources. Another study found that OM decreases the ventral striatum's functional connection with the visual cortex and the retrosplenial cortex. This means deliberate, focused attention has decreased connections to memory functions related to DMN. Findings imply that OM enhances detachment from autobiographical memory while decreasing consciously focused attention. This distance may be crucial for maintaining an impartial and unreactive mindset throughout OM.[76]

¶ In a meta-analysis of 21 neuroimaging studies examining 123 brain regions in 300 meditation practitioners, Fox and colleagues[82] determined eight core areas consistently altered in meditators: the frontal polar cortex, sensory cortices and insula, hippocampus, anterior and mid-cingulate, orbital frontal cortex, superior longitudinal fasciculus, and corpus callosum. Overall, these correspond to potential functions such as meta-awareness, exteroceptive and interoceptive body awareness, memory consolidation and reconsolidation, self and emotion regulation, and intra- and interhemispheric communication.

** The word translated literally to "breath" is Qi. Watson translated it as *spirit* and Ziporyn as *vital energy*. Ziporyn also notes its literal meaning is breath. For the sake of clarity in practice, I have incorporated the meaning of breath.

V

CHANGE

*"You once happen on the shape of a human being and are
especially pleased. But humanity has a thousand alterations and
ten thousand transformations, never reaching its limit, wearing
out and then renewing; should not your joy be incalculable?"*
—THE HUAINANZI

*"If today a master swordsmith were smelting metal,
and the metal should jump up and say 'I insist on being
made into an Excalibur,' the swordsmith would surely think it
metal with a curse on it. If now having once happened on the shape
of a man, I were to say 'I'll be a man, nothing but a man,'
he that fashions and transforms us would surely think Me a baleful
sort of man. Now if once and for all I think of heaven and earth as
a vast foundry, and the fashioner and transformer as the
master Smith? Wherever I'm going why should I object?
I'll fall into a sound sleep and wake up fresh."*
—THE ZHUANGZI

In line with modern science, Zhuangzi viewed the universe as constantly changing and transforming. The sage lodges their mind in
nothingness, attunes to the uncarved wood, and pivots to an uncertain

attitude as they embrace the changes that nature intends. In his typical humorous fashion, Zhuangzi noted: "Wonderful, the process which fashions and transforms us! What is it going to turn you into, in what direction will it use you to go? Will it make you into a rat's liver? Or a fly's leg?"[11(p88)]

Most of us do not choose to be uncertain, yet to be intentionally uncertain is to be engaged with the present, to be alert, flexible in our responses, and open to creative possibilities. Above all, it prevents us from the premature closure that certainty[18] so often brings. In life, uncertainty is a certainty. As Zhuangzi notes:

> Things have their life and death—you cannot rely upon their fulfillment. One moment empty, the next moment full—you cannot depend upon their form...the life of things is a gallop, a headlong dash—with every movement they alter, with every moment they shift.[10(p182)]

To embrace a stance of certainty is to be static, narrow, and rigid. Certainty is the death of a question, whereas uncertainty allows both question and answer to remain alive. A question like "what meaning to life do I wish to aspire toward?" can bring up responses that develop with the individual, making it a question worthy of continual inquiry. Uncertainty births adventure, the quest of which brings about curiosity, insight, excitement, development, and the overall "joie de vivre" that we feel as we navigate the mysteries of life. All of this would simply collapse into predictability and boredom, if all were certain. Thus, uncertainty is a creative stance, allowing thoughts and feelings to pulsate with the rhythms of creativity, rather than stagnating with fixed beliefs.

It is a curious tendency of the human mind to treat the world, others, and us as if they were static, unchanging entities—permanent fixtures in the flux of experience. This commonplace presupposition hides in plain sight, lurking within the familiar phrase, "People don't change." How often have we heard this assertion, even made it ourselves, as though it was an immutable truth? Yet, if we pause to consider the matter, it is evident this view is both fundamentally mistaken and dangerously limiting. The individual identifies their being as a noun, negating its true essence as a verb.

People wield this outlook as a kind of rationalization, an excuse for behavior that undeniably harms others. "This is just who I am," the person says, as though their character were a stone, worn smooth by the passage of time. "What can I do?" The phrase may be uttered quietly, even with a shrug of humor, but it betrays a deeper, more primitive resistance to change. It may be a defense provoked by the terror of the unfamiliar territory. Or perhaps it is a misguided and superficial understanding of what it means to be "authentic"—a mistaken belief that oneself must remain fixed and unalterable. Even ignorance may be a candidate, a failure to understand how transformation takes place, or worse, sloth, an aversion to the effort and discipline required for change. Human beings, after all, have an extraordinary capacity for inertia, and for clinging to the past, even when that past is less than ideal.

The notion that we can remain unaltered, that we can avoid growth, will lead to increasing disorder and dissonance in our lives. Change, however difficult, is not merely desirable—it is essential. If we are to navigate the world in a way that is at all coherent, it requires us to be open to change, to accept that who we are is not fixed but subject to the ceaseless flow of life itself. It is not change we should fear, but the refusal to change. The refusal to embrace the ongoing, creative impulse that strives to bring us closer to something greater than we were before.

In Zhuangzi's Dao, there is an inherent trust in the process of change. Change may be labeled positive or negative in our analytical minds, but in Daoist thought, *change maintains balance, it is a precondition, a necessary counterpart.* When someone works against the process, they become imbalanced. To align with the process of becoming is, as Alan Watts comically states, to "groove with the Dao." As an example, when a person experiences prolonged stress, the body's stress response system, particularly the autonomic nervous system, becomes dysregulated. This dysregulation leads to an imbalance in the body's homeostasis—manifesting as elevated cortisol levels, impaired immune function, and disrupted sleep patterns. These physiological changes contribute to a broader imbalance, influencing not only the individual's health but also their relationship with the environment. It is harder for an anxious individual to be empathic, because their systems involved with such behaviors (e.g., the default mode network) disengage in favor of the fight/flight systems. The human organism, in this case, may move out of harmony with its surroundings, leading to disharmony. In both the positive and negative cases, the process is a dynamic interaction between the human organism and the surrounding world.

The human body, with its complex systems, does not exist in isolation; it is part of a greater whole, deeply intertwined with the forces of nature. Just as the Daoist sage seeks to live in rhythm with the Dao, the individual who adapts their internal processes to the natural world can restore equilibrium—both to themselves and to the environment they inhabit. Thus, human change is never merely a personal phenomenon; it is a ripple within the larger ocean of nature, affecting the balance of the whole.

Some might argue that individuals who cling to unhealthy habits are greedy, trapped in narrow self-interest. But perhaps, as Zhuangzi might suggest, the true folly is not that they are greedy, rather they are not greedy enough. For why limit oneself to a single, fixed identity when one could, instead, embrace the boundless potential of becoming anything? As Zhuangzi puts it: "Without praises, without curses, now a dragon, now a snake, you transform together with the times, and never consent to be one thing alone."[11(p121)] The idea here is not one of greediness in the conventional sense, but a radical freedom—a refusal to be confined to any one form, any one state, or any one condition. It is in this capacity to change, to move with the tides of time and circumstance, that true liberation lies—not in the rigid definition of self, but in the expansive freedom to flow with the currents of life.

"Primordial chaos" plays a role in Daoist metaphysics. Chaos involves chance, and chance is involved in change. Peirce's[88] scientific metaphysics defines existence as an argument that will eventually lead to some form of perfection. While this is not a Daoist thought, there is a resonance with his three descriptors that may enrich Daoist metaphysics. These include nature as mechanistic (i.e., ananchism), chance based (i.e., tychism), and further defined by Agape (i.e., agapism), meaning there is a form of familial love enabling our existence. Agape, Laozi might further suggest, can be noted beyond our mere existence in experiences of harmony and peace, when one is attuned to nature itself. Change naturally occurs when mechanistic processes encounter novel circumstances, requiring a new form of adaptation. It may also occur in the reverse form, such as when a mechanistic process like aging necessitates new adaptations to circumstance.

As we reflect on the dynamics of change, we can turn to the example of chronic pain, a condition I often encounter in my clinic. The experience of pain serves as a microcosm for the larger processes of adaptation and transformation within nature. Pain, in its essence, acts as a signal—an indicator that something has gone awry within the organism. Yet, as with the continual flux of nature, a multitude of factors can shape it beyond the physical sensation. We distinguish between "clean" and "dirty" pain: the former being the raw, unavoidable sensation that arises from injury or illness, while mental scripts, emotional overlays, and cognitive interpretations that intensify and prolong the experience compound the latter. "Dirty pain," when it accumulates, amplifies the suffering, creating a cycle that, much like the chaotic interplay of mechanistic and chance forces in the universe, becomes self-perpetuating.

Drawing from Peirce's notion of "tychism," or the role of chance in bringing about change, we find a parallel in the way emotional and cognitive responses can transform the experience of pain. When a person is unaware of or cannot address the psychological aspects of their pain, they are caught in a loop, resisting and avoiding the very experience that could lead to growth. The paradox of pain, then, is by consenting to it, by allowing it to unfold without resistance, one opens the door to adaptation. The very act of accepting pain—whether it is "clean" or "dirty"—can diminish its grip, not by denying its reality but by shifting one's relationship to it. This mirrors the process of change itself: adaptation comes not from fighting against the inevitable, but from embracing the fluidity of circumstance, much like Laozi's harmony with the Dao. When we cease to demand that pain serve a fixed purpose or meaning, we make space for new possibilities—the development of resilience, the refinement of psychological skills, even the deepening of one's spiritual life. Just as in nature, where mechanistic processes encounter novel circumstances and adapt, so too does the individual, when they reframe their relationship with pain, adapt and evolve. By divesting pain of its undue significance, we allow the mind to focus on other aspects of life, thus reducing both clean and dirty pain and enabling us to move more freely in the world.

When working with clients, psychologists often consider the stages of change model, pioneered by the work of Prochaska and DiClemente.[89] Other health models have arisen to be more specific toward particular problems, but the general stages are still quite applicable overall. It is important to note that this model is more like a spiral, especially with substance addictions, where relapse is always a possibility and it takes time for stability to concretize. This transtheoretical model includes five stages:

1. precontemplation, when there is no desire to alter behavior;
2. contemplation, when there is now an intention to change, but delay in behaviors;

3. preparation, when change behaviors are soon (e.g., one month) to be implemented;
4. action, when change has occurred for a period </= six months;
5. maintenance, when change has been maintained for six months or more.

Depending on the stage identified, psychologists facilitate the process with techniques to assist in change. In the precontemplation phase, we may help increase awareness; in contemplation, we may help resolve ambivalence; in preparation, we may help develop a plan; in action, we may assist with the anticipation of vulnerable states and experiment with the best courses of action; and in maintenance, we may assist with teaching new coping skills, reviewing old ones, and continuing to help others develop insight.

The flow of mental life unfolds as an ongoing stream, marked by phases of development shaped by our interactions with the world. Picture when a quote strikes you not just intellectually, but experientially—when an idea sinks into your being and transforms your understanding. What shifts within to allow this deeper realization? My group[44] proposed a model to track these shifts, showing how mental content matures over time in dynamic cycles, much like a spiral of change. With each turn, raw experience transforms into insight, and, eventually, into integrated wisdom.

Our minds move through phases, each tied to the interplay of time and space. Our awareness begins when the external world meets the body and brain—a dance between the inner and outer. Over time, these impressions evolve: bodily sensations and emotions contribute to images, images inform associative thoughts, and so on—until abstract ideas emerge and, finally, align into an integrated understanding. Crucially, this process is not linear. A truth understood in abstraction might still need the grounding of experience to fully mature into wisdom. As T. S.

Eliot put it, "We shall not cease from exploration, and the end of all our exploring will be to arrive where we started and know the place for the first time." A visual representation can be found below:[44]

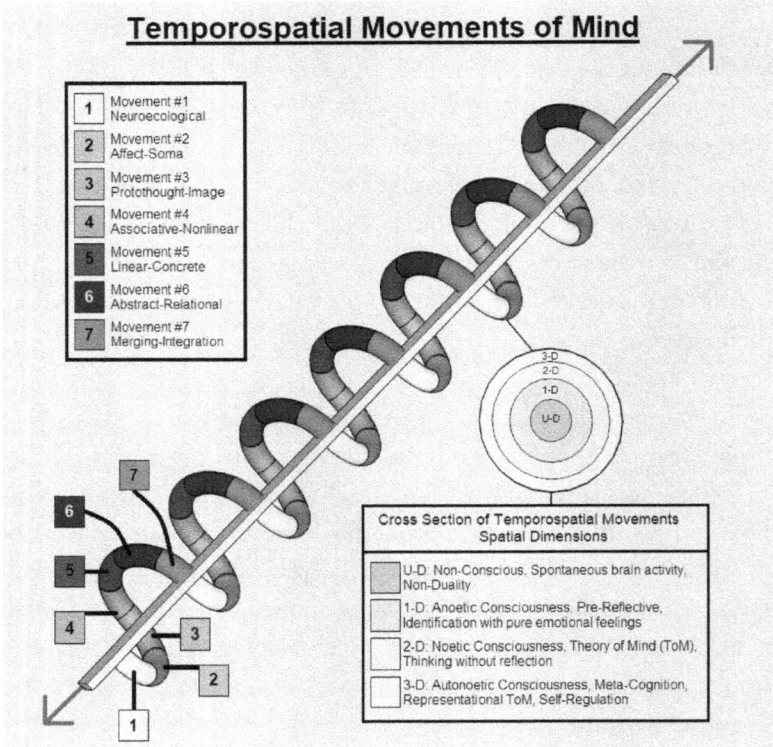

Temporospatial Movements of Mind

1	Movement #1 Neuroecological
2	Movement #2 Affect-Soma
3	Movement #3 Protothought-Image
4	Movement #4 Associative-Nonlinear
5	Movement #5 Linear-Concrete
6	Movement #6 Abstract-Relational
7	Movement #7 Merging-Integration

Cross Section of Temporospatial Movements Spatial Dimensions

U-D: Non-Conscious, Spontaneous brain activity, Non-Duality

1-D: Anoetic Consciousness, Pre-Reflective, Identification with pure emotional feelings

2-D: Noetic Consciousness, Theory of Mind (ToM), Thinking without reflection

3-D: Autonoetic Consciousness, Meta-Cognition, Representational ToM, Self-Regulation

Image 9: This is a visual representation of the temporospatial model. Each ring comprises a full temporospatial cycle. The end (Merger-Integration) is reconsolidated into the beginning (Neuroecological), as the beginning builds upon the end. They are iterative in nature and can move in either direction (i.e., regression, progression). Temporal cycles are coded to corresponding numbers, a cross section of which reveals their volumetric composition as spatial dimensions. Spatial dimensions are illustrated as rings to a tree trunk, colored in light gray. Note that spatial volume and temporal movements form a single stream, and each phase within respective cycles is nested within one another. Artwork by Daniel Icaza.

From the spatial perspective, we begin in a state of pure potential—a reactive, reflexive existence without self-awareness. As our understanding grows, we move from simply reacting to the world to recognizing ourselves and others as separate minds. This second dimension brings awareness of relationships and linear thought. Eventually, we reach a third dimension, where we think about our own thinking and consider others' perspectives in depth. Here, we gain the ability to step back, reflect, and hold space for ambiguity, transforming reactive emotions into thoughtful responses. This broadening of mental space allows us to reframe challenges, fostering inner peace even amid uncertainty.

By recognizing where our mental content resides within this tempo-rospatial framework, we may find ways to nurture its growth, helping knowledge evolve into wisdom. Below is a table from our paper that may assist with the localizing of where problematic mental content may be found in the spectrum (see Chan and colleagues, 2022,[44] for more information about theory and application).

Temporospatial Grid	Undifferentiated Dimensions (U-D) Nonconscious - Non-duality - Attachment - Implicit, Body, Autonomic System - Secondary Emot. - Passive	1-D Anoetic Consciousness - Primary Emot. - Preconscious - Acting out, projection, transference - Passive-Active	2-D Noetic Consciousness - ToM, self-rep - Thinking - Semantic - Insight w/o application - Active-Passive	3-D Autonoetic Consciousness - Meta cog. - Mentalizing - Self-regulation - Explicit mem. - Active
Temporal Movement 1 (TM1) Neuroecological				
Temporal Movement 2 (TM2) Affect-Soma				
Temporal Movement 3 (TM3) Protothought-Image				
Temporal Movement 4 (TM4) Associative-Nonlinear				
Temporal Movement 5 (TM5) Linear-Concrete				
Temporal Movement 6 (TM6) Abstract-Relational				
Temporal Movement 7 (TM7) Merging-Integration				

Table 3: Temporospatial Grid

The Daoist attitude of change even extends into death itself, with death viewed as an invitation to transform into something else. Daoism remains agnostic about what happens after death; it accepts the mystery and trusts the unfolding of nature.

Man's life between heaven and earth is like a white colt passing a chink in a wall, in a moment it is gone. In a gush, a rush, everything issues from there; melting, merging, everything enters there. By a transformation you are born, by another you die.[11(p133)]

The men of old, their knowledge had arrived at something: at what had it arrived? There were some who thought there had not yet begun to be any things—the utmost, the exhaustive, there is no more to add. The next thought that there were things, but they preferred to think of life as the loss of something, of death as its recovery, by which dividing comes to an end. The next said: "at first there is not anything, afterwards there is life, living we soon die. Deem "being without anything" to be the head, "life" the torso, "death" the rump. Who knows that something and nothing, death and life, have a single ancestor? He shall be my friend.[11(p104)]

The Daoist model of change emphasizes its acceptance, trust in the process, and staying in the present. This is fundamental to achieving a nature-aligned lifestyle. While an intentional stance of uncertainty may be beneficial, not everyone may tolerate it, as their minds are populated with imaginary monsters. In psychology, we work with the intolerance of uncertainty (IU).* In science, the intolerance of uncertainty is governed by the need for certainty. This need must be reduced, as fears of uncertainty paradoxically decline with its acceptance and consideration of other possibilities.

We must first be aware of why uncertainty in the present is fueling worry. We then must normalize it, as every day we face it. In fact, encountering triggers of uncertainty is inevitable.[91] Change is inevitable in the Dao, and to work against it creates an imbalance that results in human suffering. Those who find uncertainty intolerable are susceptible to excessive worrying that may hinder their well-being. When our fight/flight systems are triggered, our perspective narrows, and our inner "demons" appear. Yet, the certainty is uncertainty![18] This means it's also possible for there to be "angels." To discount that is to be further away from the facts. Is it possible to view "threat" and "opportunity" as opposite ends on a spectrum rather than perceiving them as separate? Doing so on a spectrum helps cultivate a more realistic and balanced perspective.[91]

It is true, that in the immediate future, the odds are stacked against you. Change can bring unfortunate consequences, but who is to say in a more distant future, what you deem an unfortunate consequence may not result in positive effects? This type of "faith" is a part of Daoist mentality. Paraphrasing a parable from The Huainanzi:[13(p729)]

> A family of skilled diviners had a beautiful horse that ran away. Fellow villagers gathered, sharing their sympathies for him. The father said, "this will bring good fortune."† Several months later, the same horse came back and brought three more horses, and when the news arrived, the villagers celebrated. The father replied, "this will be a disaster!" After a week, the farmer's son attempted to ride one of the horses but was thrown off and broke his leg. The villagers shared their sympathies. The father said, "this will turn to good fortune." The next year, the army arrived looking to draft his son but because of his broken leg they rejected and left him. Later it was known that his 9/10 people died at the battle he was being recruited for.

This story emphasizes a view of the world from a broader perspective. One that is not attached to the immediacy of how events unfold because the future is always unknown. Adopting a vantage point much greater and expansive than your own narrative may confer benefits:

> If you know the immensity of the cosmos, you will not be concerned about life and death. If you know the harmony of nourishing vitality, you will not be attached to the world. If you know the happiness of not yet being born, you will not be afraid of dying.[13(p256)]

This advice very much corresponds to embodying the theme of nature as limitless.

Introspective Exercises

The acronym for this section is BUOY.

1. To optimize change, take on the perspective that change is a precondition for *balance*. What needs to be balanced in this moment?
2. Take a stance of intentional *uncertainty*. Embrace the possibilities within, and the alertness, adventure, and presence it brings.
3. Be open to how change may lead to short and/or long-term *opportunities* yet unknown.
4. Finally, embody "*yes*" toward all events that have happened or are out of your control. To embody "no" is nonsensical, as you are resisting something that has already happened.

Question to use pleasurable in vulnerable moments of clinging or craving (pleasurable can be substituted with comfortable, safe, familiar, etc.).

It's pleasurable, but is it costing your potential?

Facilitating Change

At the center of creativity, is the question: what potentials within you are seeking to express themselves?

Other questions to consider:

▶ What might you be clinging to that is holding you from evolving as a person?
▶ Is there something you are struggling to change about yourself?
▶ If so, where might you be on the stages of the change model?
▶ Where might you locate your challenge in the temporospatial model?

▶ What might be most beneficial for you in this moment?

▶ Who would you be, and what might your life be like without that clinging?

Improving Coping Skills

Perspective taking: When change is inevitable, but you find yourself resistant to it. Ask yourself, *Who is to say that things won't get even better? How could things get better?*

Another simple exercise you can do to cope with resistance to change is to expand your horizons. View yourself from the perspective of friends, family, and community. What might they say? What would you tell a friend if they were in your situation? You may even try on the perspective of our 13.8-billion-year-old universe. How might that influence your feelings?

Working with Uncertainty

To counter fears of uncertainty, one exercise is to place the thought of the future being a "threat" as being on a spectrum with "opportunity." This will at least provide a more balanced perspective on what might come to be.

When uncertainty is paired with fear, try reframing it. View uncertainty as a stance rather than a confrontation. It is only a confrontation if you inhabit a stance of certainty. Remember, uncertainty is a creative stance that anchors you to the present, enlivens you, offers the greatest possible number of responses, and births adventure and excitement. Certainty, however, brings relief, but also lacks many qualities of uncertainty.

It is the nature of all expectations about the future to be uncertain, so either learn how to act without expectations, or choose to interpret events that encourage tranquility. There is always a fictional side to our view of the world and relationships, and you have the option to be practical about it. According to The Huainanzi, "Human

nature is nourished by tranquility; *Potency* is attained through emptiness; when external things do not disturb our internal realization of
spirit, our nature attains suitable and harmonious expression in the
world." [13, p81]

Endnotes

* The Cognitive Behavioral Therapy (CBT) model of intolerance of uncertainty (IU) was devised to understand and treat generalized anxiety disorder (GAD). Individuals affected by GAD are fixed in a cycle of excessive worrying due to IU. The model addresses how the cycle of worrying in GAD begins with an internal or external trigger that drives individuals to ask the question of "what if…?" and sets their worries and anxieties into motion.[91]

† A more popular version of this parable introduces a reply from the farmer: "maybe."

PROCESS

Nature is alive and always on the move. It is not a static noun, but a dynamic verb. It is like jazz improvisation, because where there is a preserved order, there is spontaneity. Nature progresses from moment to moment, developing and evolving through continuous interactions: successions of interrelated processes endlessly forming, integrating, and disbanding. The universe is in perpetual flux, as its becoming shifts into a transformation, then informs the next phase of its becoming. As soon as a snapshot is made at any point in space-time, it loses its direct correspondence to reality. Nature is a horizon that forever recedes from our grasp. There is no end goal in nature, though from a human perspective, there appears to be a direction—chaos to complexity.

As an inner principle of being, the process begins with a serene receptivity to your intuitive signals. It is crucial to acknowledge that the inner life is constantly evolving, and we must recognize and interpret those signals, whether we perceive them as positive or negative. It is to flow with the natural unfolding of these signals and facilitate their expression through our self. If the context is not yet suitable for intuition, it is to be flexible and engage your analytical abilities.

Most simply, attending is about being present with the process at hand. If you are thinking about the future, be present with those thoughts; if you are reminiscing about the past, be present with them; and of course, if you are engaged in an activity, be present with that activity.

As a process of doing, it is to be oriented toward the world in a particular way—to be explorative over analytical, discovery driven over solution focused, attuned to movement over stasis, and to engaged with experience over abstraction. Complete engagement with the process means equality for all experiences. A central question to ask yourself is: what is preventing me from full engagement with the present?

Process is thus about multiple components, moving in harmony. It begins with intuition, which is itself a nonlinear process that discloses potentials of nature, and with these potentials, our original self is continuously revealed. As nature ceaselessly flows from one moment to the next, so have we inherited the ability to tap into the universal experience of *Wuwei* encompasses the concept of Flow.

BaYaka hunter-gatherers allow their children to learn through discovery.[50] They play, practice, and are given free rein to simply explore their environments. Autonomy and presence are valued by adults and children alike. This is, of course, in contrast to the overcontrolled parent who micromanages all the child's affairs, as their minds career toward the future. Hunter-gatherer parents create learning opportunities for their children, but don't interfere with the process. Learning feeds into intuition, and the ground of nature connects and births every member of the tribe.

The chapters here are: intuition, original nature, and *wuwei* and flow. These concepts are but different facets of the same great principle: the unfolding process of life. Intuition arises when the mind, unencumbered by deliberate effort, taps into the living currents of reality, revealing truths that seem to emerge as if by grace. Original nature, as conceived in Daoism, calls us back to a primordial harmony, a state where life's rhythms guide us effortlessly, unspoiled by over-calculation or artifice. *Wuwei* and flow, too, exemplify this principle—a state where action and awareness merge, and the self moves perfectly with the moment, free of hesitation or resistance. These ideas converge in showing us that life is not a series of static points to be reached but a continuous, fluid stream of becoming, where our deepest potentials unfold naturally in concert with the world.

VI

INTUITION

"...A stream that falls from the mountain to the sea.
A man would know the end he goes to, but he cannot know it
if he does not turn, and return to his beginning, and hold
that beginning in his being. If he would not be a stick whirled
and whelmed in the stream, he must be the stream itself,
all of it, from its spring to its sinking in the sea..."
—URSULA LE GUIN

"I have learned that my total organismic sensing of a
situation is more trustworthy than my intellect."
—CARL ROGERS

Organicity brings us to life and keeps us alive, so we do not have to think about breathing to breathe or think about digesting to digest food. These natural propensities also manifest in our minds at even more complex levels. It does so through a nonlinear, subconscious process that operates with far greater capacity than our conscious linear thinking—intuition.

Zhuangzi distrusted conceptual ideas and language, though he believed intuition to be a form of higher truth. He also believed it was rare but possible for people to embody these truths. Zhuangzi did not believe that "small knowledge" from the intellect could ever reach a whole truth. Rather, for him, "greater knowledge" comes in the form of pure intuitive responses. As mentioned in the introduction, Daoist practice is about intuiting the nature of reality through practices, rather than trusting conceptions that only represent parts of the whole. What truly separates us as a species is an increased access to the mental fabric of nature that paralleled the development of our brains. As an example, it is in the conceptual realm where values take root, shaping the course of our human experience.

It is important to reiterate here that Daoism is not anti-intellectual. It is a matter of how to relate to knowledge that is being acquired through means outside of intuition. Instead of memorizing and regurgitating facts, it is about deeply understanding and allowing them to rest within you, as your intuition integrates and guides you with a spontaneous response. As Chai [57] clarifies and elaborates, "Resting in knowledge rather than allowing it to dictate courses of pursuance provides one with the opportunity to reflect upon the state of affairs in the world and adjust one's participation accordingly... It is through this resting that all things return to a state of quiet equilibrium, one in which they mutually cultivate one another, ensuring their continued freedom and longevity." [57 (p156)] Thus, in contrast to a purely active approach, it favors one that is passive-active. The balance of "opposites" is reiterated here.

For Laozi and Zhuangzi, living under the Dao leads to peace of mind, which promotes virtuous behaviors. This means that values and morality form part of the ground of nature. When morality is seen as something to strive for, like in Confucianism, Daoists believe people will inevitably fail. Whereas some existentialists focus on the construction of meaning in one's life, Daoism views values as an inherent part of nature. Values are discovered and attuned to. During this process of attunement, precepts that Daoists from different lineages follow (for a list, see Kohn,

1993[66(p97–106)]). Importantly, however, a Daoist would not use the words "morality" and "good" or "bad;" rather, they would assert simply that *things just are.*

What support might there be for such ideas? To answer such a question, we peer into the science of morality.

RATS

Many of us assume that reasoning births morality; therefore, it is a social construction. Yet many studies have challenged this assumption, several of which have been conducted with other animals. Beginning with rats, one study by Bartal, Decety, and Mason[92] found that if you place a rat in a trap, it will vocalize fearful expressions as it struggles to escape. Experimenters were curious to see if another rat released to roam the cage freely would help. The rat would have to run into an open space that is typically perceived as dangerous (which is why many rats scurry behind walls), as well as overcome the fearful cries of the trapped rat. Despite this danger, twenty-three out of thirty free rats saved the trapped one. To introduce a more complicated situation, experimenters added another lever to open a door filled with chocolate chips. In the same situation, rats will typically save the trapped rat, open the door with chips, and share the food.

While studying the primary emotional system devoted to play, Panksepp[93, 94] found that play activity in rats helped establish dominance hierarchies. This parallels human dynamics. During play, the dominant rat would pin the other rat 70 percent of the time. But here's the twist—if the dominant rat exceeded the 70/30 ratio, the losing rat would then refuse to play, thereby injecting the notion of *fairness* into the equation. For humans, by the way, the ratio is 60/40.

MONKEYS

Although animals may fight when jostling for social status, they more commonly expend energy maintaining peace and protecting each other. For example, many males will provide "anti-predation services" to protect the group. These services are costly signals because they also alert predators. This behavior is an expression of care, especially for their families.[95] Masserman, Wechkin, and Terris[96] identified that some rhesus monkeys refuse to deliver an electric shock to other monkeys even if they are given food. One of the monkeys in their experiment starved itself for five days; another monkey starved itself up to twelve days. This likelihood increased when they experienced electric shocks.

When uncooperative brown capuchin monkeys are given the option to reward themselves or reward themselves and another, they more often reward both themselves and another.[97] Presumably, prosocial choices may have increased rewarding experiences versus selfish ones. Warneken and colleagues[98] found that regardless of rewards or costs of helping, semi-free-ranging chimpanzees will spontaneously assist humans and members of the same species. They included eighteen-month-old human infants as well. More specifically, in their first experiment, an object was placed out of the experimenter's reach. Twelve out of eighteen chimpanzees and sixteen out of eighteen infants helped. Rewarding the helping did not change the rate of help, and infants were faster at helping. In the second experiment, they replicated the same situation but with much more effort required to help. We found no significant difference; the majority still helped. In the third experiment, genetically unrelated chimpanzees could release a chain barring off a recipient from another room with food. The chimpanzees were already skilled at opening the door mechanism. As the recipient tried to open the door, eight out of nine chimps helped over several trials. In the control condition, there was a distractor door with no food on the other side, and although helping occurred in the earlier trials, later trials showed reduced help because there was no food on the other end. Increased help was shown whenever chimpanzees were in front of the target door.

HUMANS

Humans are quick to react when their sense of fairness has been violated. What most people are unaware of is that this can be traced back to fifteen-month-old infants. In one study by Schmidt and Sommerville,[99] infants were presented with two conditions: one of equality and the other of inequality. The condition of inequality generated a behavior indicative of the violation of the sense of fairness. In part two of this study, the infants were presented with two toys. They chose one and the other was given to them. This is followed by a request phase, whereby 26/38 infants shared a toy, and twelve actually shared the preferred toy. This study suggests that fairness wins out over greed in babies and infants.

What about the question of good versus bad? In a study by Hamlin and Wynn,[100] babies were presented with a puppet show. In this show, there is a "good" puppet who is helpful and a "bad" puppet who interferes. They found that approximately 75 percent of babies, clearly not yet capable of moral reasoning, will demonstrate a preference for the good puppet to the bad puppet by showing preference by reaching or staring. This study has been replicated. There are a host of clever studies examining morality in babies, demonstrating that, for example, witnessing unequal distribution of resources leads to consistent reactions from infants. The idea that we are born with a moral template is called *social intuitionism*. This construct refutes the idea that morality is superficially constructed; it seems to run much deeper than we understood previously.

In another study, Jin and colleagues[101] found that twelve-month-olds and four-month-olds demonstrate reactions to events that violate their expectations. In two experiments, the infants were presented with a comforting event, where they would view, via monitor, a mother performing a household chore; the mother notices a baby crying and will either comfort or ignore the baby. Infants spent significantly more time looking at the ignoring event. In their third experiment, infants watched two computer monitors and were shown that touching them would trigger the events. One showed the comfort event, and the other one showed the ignoring event. The babies gave significantly more touches on the monitor, demonstrating the ignoring event. All effects were eliminated when the baby on the monitor chuckled instead of cried. One could interpret the preference for watching the ignoring event as indicating that an expectation was violated, namely the expectation of maternal warmth.

These studies suggest that we, and many other animals, are born with the seeds of morality. Morality is not just a human creation, rather a fundamental tide shaping the flow of psychological existence. As has been found, however, in an extensive review[102] from Narvaez, human moral development often relies on attachment-based experiences to reach its full potential. These conditions can be found in small-band hunter-gatherer (SBHG) cultures. In their developmental studies,[103] moral potential is followed by moral understanding and subsequently, practical wisdom or its application. Of interest, she notes that morality in SBHG tribes is most closely related to virtue ethics (a branch proposed formally by Aristotle). In parallel, Kohn,[8] notes that the ethical orientation Zhuangzi's writings appear to align with most are also virtue ethics. This is the idea that true virtue is embedded in the individual's character and the moral traits they cultivate and live under (in contrast to the emphasis on duty, or optimizing consequences in decision-making).

INTUITIVE DECISION-MAKING

*"There is more wisdom in your body than
in your deepest philosophy."*
—FRIEDRICH NIETZSCHE

Intuition is not blind. It is a hidden, rapid, automatic, and nonlinear process that integrates somatic, emotional, and cognitive information to produce a signal that may facilitate decision-making. All theories examining the neuroscience of intuition involve the recruitment of multiple regions, suggesting that intuition is highly informed. Intuition will not provide you with conceptual facts, though it may offer us markers for character growth, and responses under uncertain situations. Moreover, at least some intuitive responses are coming from "datasets" that have been inherited via evolution. Intuition automatically generates inferences for incomplete sets of data presented to us, in contrast to our analytical abilities, which involve an active cognitive exploration, which includes the gathering of more data and the weighting of each. Analytical thinking also depends on crystallized intelligence, or information we already know, whereas intuition quickly generates a response, likely through interacting implicit patterns. When individuals face a high cognitive load, intuition is more likely to play a role in decision making, and the opposite is also true, where a low cognitive load becomes more amenable to analysis.[104] Errors in intuitive reasoning often stem from biases formed by experiences or momentary influences, such as the salience of specific information or emotional states, whereas errors in analytic thought occur because of issues with data entry or the inappropriate use of formulas.[105] Intuition allows us to address the problem, considering its intricate nature. Analytical thinking, with its tendency to focus on specific aspects and overlook other important parts, and may introduce biases and become challenging because of logical inconsistencies in such cases.[106] Due to the differences between our civilization and our biological inheritance, it is likely that some of our intuitive responses are no longer as valid as they were.

One line of investigation comes from the *somatic marker hypothesis*.[107, 108] From this standpoint, the body's physical reactions to a situation are ultimately registered in the ventromedial prefrontal cortex during decision-making. This area signals the brain about an individual's emotional response to an experience. These bodily cues, known as somatic markers, contribute to cognitive processing by providing feedback. The ventromedial prefrontal cortex is a convergence zone, with highways of information flowing from places such as the amygdala (e.g., fear processing), anterior cingulate cortex (e.g., conflict resolution, emotional processing), hippocampus (e.g., memory formation, autobiographical memory recall), insular cortex (e.g., interoception or sensing internal bodily states), and orbitofrontal cortex (e.g., inhibition, value-based decision making).

Another theory, *dual-process theory*, comes from Kahneman,[109] who divided our brain systems into two types: one that is conscious, deliberate, and effortful (system 2) and another that is rapid, effortless, and intuitive, relying on heuristics and pattern recognition (system 1). These systems are reflected in neuroimaging studies, with system 1 tasks recruiting areas corresponding to reflexive responses in the brain—such as the amygdala, insula, and ventral striatum—and with more logical/analytic-based tasks activating more conscious and executive systems, such as the dorsal lateral prefrontal cortex and the anterior cingulate cortex. Lesion studies also show corresponding functional disruption to these systems.

The third theory comes from Clark,[110] who incorporates *predictive processing theory* into the mix. This theory posits that intuition relates to predictions based on prior knowledge and expectations. Intuition emerges when there is a match between non-conscious prediction systems and expectations.

Several studies have demonstrated how intuition can outperform rational decision-making, besides the disadvantages of relying on intuition. These include:

	Citation	Description
Advantages	Belloc and colleagues (2019)	Relying on intuition can lead to more cooperative behavior than relying on deliberation.
	Nalliah (2016)	Intuition allows experts to subconsciously store information in frameworks and quickly extract it with no need for conscious effort.
		Intuition may be suitable for time-sensitive situations, complex, or unclear, or those lacking scientific evidence.
	Hogarth (2010) Pétervári and colleagues (2016)	In situations where the number of solutions is close to limitless, intuition is a fundamental component in specific stages of the creative process. Specifically, creative intuition is linked to the idea-generation phase, whereas problem-solving intuition is linked to the idea-evaluation phase.
	Brown and colleagues (2020) Hogarth (2010)	Intuition may help people in moral decision-making. Damage to the VMPFC, an area believed to play a role in representing emotional state and homeostatic information when assessing ethical violations, has been linked to reduced guilt and empathy, decreased physiological responses to moral decisions, and a higher tolerance of immoral behavior.
Disadvantages	Brown and colleagues (2020) Dunn and colleagues (2010) Hogarth (2010)	Intuition may unhelpfully guide people toward high-risk decisions because it is based on limited and subjective information.
	Brown and colleagues (2020) Dunn and colleagues (2010) Hogarth (2010)	Personal experiences, beliefs, and emotions can influence intuition and lead to biased decisions.
	Kump (2022)	Intuition-based decisions can be difficult to defend, because they are often not based on a clear and well-defined process, making it challenging to communicate the rationale behind a decision.
	Balas and colleagues (2012) Kump (2022)	Our emotional states may affect intuitive judgment, because a positive mood increases the accuracy of intuitive choices, whereas a negative mood limits it. Therefore, intuition may be unreliable.

Table 4: Advantages and Disadvantages of Intuition

As shown in this table, some disadvantages of intuition involve the influence of an individual's personal beliefs, emotions, and experiences. Daoism would advocate for the idea of "pure intuition," which expresses natural activity without influences from the egoic and emotional systems. Future studies on long-term meditators and their intuitive systems would be quite fascinating to explore. Extant literature does not draw any serious conclusions about their relationship at this point. Theoretically, mindfulness would likely benefit the reception of untrammeled intuitive responses.

Intuition and analysis are both needed in our everyday lives, and the following table describes a few helpful circumstances whereby intuition may be useful for decision-making:

	Intuitive	Analytical
Task complexity (Hogarth, 2010)	When dealing with increasingly complex analytical tasks, intuition becomes more advantageous.	When dealing with simple analytical tasks, analysis becomes more advantageous.
Morality (Julmi, 2023)	In situations with high moral complexity and conflicts, where problems cannot be easily broken down into smaller parts, intuition appears to be more advantageous.	When a moral problem is clear cut and straightforward, allowing it to be broken down into individual parts that be combined and arranged sequentially, an analytically derived moral judgment appears to be more advantageous.
Interaction between students' level of experience and use of different cognitive styles on problem-solving (Pretz, 2008)	In the intuitive condition, first-year high school students scored significantly better than juniors. Juniors in the intuitive condition performed significantly worse than juniors in the analytical condition. Intuition reliance among experienced participants may cause them to overlook relevant information.	In the analytical condition, first-year school students scored worse than juniors.

Table 5: Intuitive and Analytical Decision-Making

From the perspective of Zen, Nishida[64(p30)] introduces the term "intellectual intuition," which can be defined as "an intuition of ideal, usually trans-experiential things. It intuits that which can be known dialectically." He distinguished between ideas conceptually generated from human activity and intuited ideals arising from the very principles that structure perception. He offered notable examples from artists and other prominent religious figures. When a musician immediately intuits an entire composition or a painter a painting, without any effort, where does it come from? These would be examples of artists in closer contact with pure experience and how its activity is uniquely expressed within each individual. In Eastern thought, increased connection with pure experience leads to the grounding of intellectual activity within it, completely unifying it. This marks the exception, where intellectual activity now becomes aligned with primary experience in contrast to remaining secondary. This bottom-up approach contrasts with the traditional Western top-down approach.

We are not solitary within the confines of our own minds. Organicity forms the very bedrock of our intelligence, a sustaining ground for both our being and becoming. Unlike other creatures, we possess the extraordinary faculty to disentangle conscious thought from the immediate press of space and time, stepping beyond our roots. This faculty, while a boon to survival—enabling foresight, deliberation, and strategic response—has also made us peculiarly susceptible to ensnarement by the intricate NETS (i.e., narratives, emotions, thoughts, sensations) of our own making. When you are constantly thinking, the mind is like a bustling city, drowning out the subtler whispers of intuition, the primal sense through which nature speaks to us. To follow the way of nature is not to abandon thought but to harmonize it with deeper attunement, allowing the foundational rhythm of who you are to resonate freely. Nature, ever patient, communicates in gestures subtle yet profound—through the stirrings of instinct, the clarity of a sudden insight, or the pull of an inexplicable knowing. To heed its signals is not merely to listen but to weave its wisdom into the fabric of daily life, to align with the currents of the world rather than swim perpetually against them. Depending on the context, nature's signals may play the role of a muse, advisor, sage, or teacher (MAST):

- *Muse:* Signals may be creativity oriented, providing and inspiring ideas, such as in Mozart and Escher.
- *Advisor:* Signals may come as an advice, a feeling, and/or bodily experience suggesting one decision over another in times of uncertainty.
- *Sage:* Signals are related to morality or the "sacred," such as a moment of feeling moved to tears by admiration of a person's character traits. This points to values and ways of being that are a necessity for you to develop.
- *Teacher:* Signals may also come as a lesson, similar to an aha! moment that comes to a scientist in a time unrelated to work

---

Reflection and Practice

As a general rule of thumb:

Complex and unclear? Trust intuition.

Simple and clear? Trust analysis.

1. What are some moments that intuition has been of benefit to you (e.g., in relationships, work, or play)?
2. What are some moments that it has led you astray?
3. The next time you confront uncertainty, clear your mind through meditation, and once you get into a state without emotional agitation or endless thoughts, pay attention to deep bodily internal signals. What is your experience signaling you toward?
4. As you reflect on a moment in the past that brings you

---

feelings of guilt or shame, try not to ruminate on them; instead ask yourself, *What is my experience as I reflect on what I did? To what action is it leading me?*

5. What are moments where your intuition has acted as Muse, Advisor, Sage, or Teacher?
6. Has your intuition played any other role?

The key is to elaborate on your present experience as a way for novelty and insight to emerge. When we focus too much on a play of ideas already known, we fall into the trap of further intellectualization when what is most needed is to explore the unknown. Allow your intuition to guide you with deeper feelings inherited by thousands of years of evolution.

VII

ORIGINAL NATURE

*"The wise silence, the universal beauty, To which every part
and particle is equally related, Is the tide of being which floats us into
the secret of nature; And we stand before the secret of the world."*
—RALPH W. EMERSON

*"The self is not only the centre, but also the whole circumference which
embraces both conscious and unconscious; it is the centre of this
totality, just as the ego is the centre of consciousness."*
—C.G. JUNG

Image 10: My Grandfather's Painting

My grandfather, a fierce businessman and entrepreneur, became an amateur Chinese painter at age seventy. I grew up with many of his paintings surrounding me: vast landscapes with mountains, lakes, rivers, and forests. Upon closer inspection, one will then notice a human, an insignificant speck meandering within the vastness of nature. Overall, Chinese paintings stand in contrast to Western European style paintings due to their de-emphasis on the individual. In fact, contrary to many other philosophical systems or religions, Daoism views the self as a part of nature, with the goal of harmonizing with nature in contrast to viewing the self as separate from nature with the goal of overpowering it. When the self is viewed as separate, the self follows its own conceptual systems and thinking, resulting in more egocentric perspectives. Unlike the West, the "true self" is not *created* over time but *discovered*,[7] which is why Daoist and Zen writings may refer to it as "original nature." Our original nature is a primordial melody, and to hear it, one must silence all the extraneous noise. Self-cultivation facilitates the process of discovery, which is of prime importance. This is why in Chapter 33 of the Daodejing, it is said, "Knowing others is wisdom; Knowing the self is enlightenment."[36]

Daoist thought is deeply embedded in the cultural fabric of China. Humility is a core value in many collectivist cultures. In Daoism, the self (Ji 己, wo 我) is considered being insignificant compared to our natural disposition, as well as a potential barrier to aligning with it. That is because the self involves the layering of conceptual structures, which filters the natural flow of experience. The development of identity, preferences, and distinctions keeps us blinded by a figure on an indefinite background. Zhuangzi's perspective is that to harmonize with nature, one must experience no-self (Wuji, 無己) by emptying one's mind of all that it identifies with. This leads to experience that your body and everyone else's can be united by nature. This unity leads to unselfishness, and unselfishness leads to stillness (Deng Ming-Dao, personal communication, 2024), whereas selfishness depends on and continues to cling to objects and experiences.

In Chinese, two highlighted states of being are the narrative self (Ziji, 自己) and spontaneous natural feelings of ease (Ziran, 自然). Ziran has also been translated to self—being in tune with one's original nature.*7

It is original because it is our earliest experience of being, prior to the complexities that more recently evolved areas of our brain introduced (categorizing, language, meta-cognition). Not being separate from anything else, it is attuned to the natural world. Of scientific interest, the self might be initially viewed as a feeling, which serves as the ground for narrative selves. This is found in the work of Panksepp.[94] Grammatically, "zi" is a spontaneous, original self from which pure life flows, hidden among layers of mental filters. As such, it is always placed before any verb. "It is reflexive, indicating that the subject performs the verb upon themselves. Sometimes it can even be connected to performing a verb 'for oneself'" (e.g., in Laozi 7 以其不自生，故能長生: it is because they do not live for themselves that they are able to live long") (Larson Di Fiori, personal communication, 2024). Interestingly, "zi" also refers to a Chinese character that displays a nose.[8(p193)] Instead of pointing toward the heart or chest when referring to "me," many East Asians may point to their noses. Coincidentally, our sense of smell is the only sense that does not pass through the thalamus but has a direct pathway to the limbic system. This means that it has a direct relationship with more primitive regions in the brain related to functions such as homeostasis, memory, and emotion.

"Ji" (己) refers to "an organized structure, something one can see on the outside, something that can be manipulated and controlled."[8(p192)] One can use the metaphor of a concerto that is playing as one's original nature and the narrative self as an extra instrument that may either play in tune or out of tune with the orchestra. In The Zhuangzi, the narrative self can be filled up or emptied. When filled up, nature does not take its course fluently, but emptied, nature can express itself most clearly. Emptied, we arrive at the no-self (Wuji, 無己). There is nothing mystical about no-self; it is very practical. When narratives are cleared, the self is open to its natural expression without hindrance. The self is a process, not an entity, that can either align with the current of natural change or work against it.

Importantly, Zhuangzi does not entirely negate the existence of a phenomenological self. Advocating for the complete annihilation of the self may only be possible for the dead. According to Wang,[119] Zhuangzi's dialogues suggest that "forgetting the self" opens the closure, resulting in self-other distinction and enabling us to be free from the confinement of a single perspective. Perhaps it may be better understood as "for-getting the self." With these boundaries dissolved, we become more whole and thus more genuine. He asserted:

> Forgetting self is not an annihilation of conventional self, but merely a radical transformation of the latter. Transcending the distinction...does not mean abandoning the world...rather makes one open to the dynamic relationship of self-other, to the relativity and mutual involvement of self and other, and to the infinite transformations of the world.[119 (p355)]

Thus, the Sage relies on their wholeness when making decisions. Through self-cultivation, the sage takes on what is needed for their vitality and lets go of anything excessive that may lead to dependence. They do not rely on objects independent of themselves for their well-being. They are not swayed by desires of the narrative self, unless it resonates with the natural self.

Image 11: Rio Celeste in Costa Rica. Two rivers (Rio Buena Vista "Good View" and Quebrada Agria "Sour Creek") meet and the acidic nature of Sour Creek, alongside the aluminosilicates in Good View converge, allowing them to grow. Sunlight scatters off minerals (i.e., Mie Scattering) creating a heavenly celestial color.

The nine-mile-long river called Rio Celeste ("Celestial River") in Costa Rica is a perfect metaphor for the harmonious interaction between the original self and the narrative self. While the original self carries the potential (aluminosilicate), it is in interaction with the narrative self that allows it to be realized.

How does this concept intersect with neuropsychology? There is agreement that the narrative self is not a static and enduring *entity* but a dynamic *process*. The former perception may lead people to attach rigidly to behaviors and identities, consequently increasing their fear or difficulty of change. One hypothesis coming from Gerald Edelman[120] is that the stability of self is experienced because of a process whereby autobiographical memories are continually tested against perception. This theory provides an evolutionary basis for the self, given that this dynamic improves our chances of survival. Notably, autobiographical memories are unreliable (e.g., we mainly remember the gist, they are easily influenced by others, they are altered every time they are remembered, and they may exist for predicting the future). The best theoretical match for Daoist thinking would come from Northoff and Panksepp[121] who postulate the existence of an affective self, linked to the subcortical midline structures in the brain (i.e., brain stem and limbic system), and narrative selves, correlated to the Default Mode Network (DMN, Central Midline Structures). These two systems are connected; they hypothesize with the subcortical systems expressing the organism's goal pursuits through internal experiences (e.g., needs), and the DMN involved in facilitating the coordination of what is important in the environment through self-referential processing (i.e., identifying information relevant to the organisms self-preservation and flourishing). While the affective self may relate to the experience of *feeling* to perception, it would be void of narratives. The narrative self, as I have argued,[19] is likely composed of multiple self-processes competing and/or working together. In support, studies find that states of flow, or heightened states of meditation, are accompanied by a quieting of the DMN, though not its complete disappearance.

It is important to remember that Zhuangzi uses hyperbole as a literary device (alongside many others, e.g., paradox, wild imagery, and absurd scenarios) to disrupt conventional thinking, prompting readers to step outside fixed notions of self and reality. In this context, his idea of forgetting the self is not about annihilating it, but opening up its borders to join its original nature. Paradoxically, this allows one to inhabit even more perspectives, as opposed to being trapped by a single perspective narrowed by narratives.

What is it, then, that remains stable? I've argued that we conflate the narrative self with consciousness.[19] Although the self continually changes through time with our experiences, memories, and projections of the future, our *sense* of self remains stable. Consciousness may be seen as this *sense*, a mirror reflecting all experience perceived. Indeed, in Daoism, the sage is described as a mirror of nature. The distinction I would make between the affective self and consciousness is that the affective self is primarily a feeling, whereas consciousness is the awareness of that feeling—awareness that gives it a quality of experience or a "likeness."

The Neiye[7(p72)] has a revealing passage that is worth reviewing:

> By means of the mind you store the mind:
>> Within the mind there is yet another mind.
>> That mind within mind: it is an awareness that precedes words.
>> Only after there is awareness does it take shape;
>> Only after it takes shape is there a word.

In it, we find the narrative mind (the mind), original nature (the mind within the mind), and awareness, which gives it shape. The self emerges from and returns to nature. It is an enclave, populated by ever-changing narratives and bordered by our faculties of discrimination. Its function is to distinguish itself from the undifferentiated ground of nothingness, thus advancing creativity, and to select what is important to its survival and flourishing. In terms of its survival, the narrative self is thrust into an infinite loop of dissatisfaction and desire to keep the individual from perishing. While this is an ingenious design to keep us going, it is of no use to achieving peace of mind. Western civilization has generally reached the point where most people have a surplus, and the surplus is hindering our well-being. It seems humans have long struggled with excess desires, as Zhuangzi's ideas were in revolt against this problematic human tendency. From the perspective of neuroscience, Zhuangzi emphasized a life related to the flourishing of so-called *here and now molecules* such as oxytocin, endocannabinoids, endorphins, and serotonin.[123] This translates to appreciating and fully engaging the present moment, which would stand in opposition to dopamine circuitry specifically involved with motivation and anticipation, focused on the future, unrealistic expectations, and the incessant craving for reality to be other than it is.

When one identifies the essence of their being with the Dao, the narrative self becomes a transparent and open process. That being said, its function is necessary to operate in the world, but it need not define the world. We become "companions" of the way. What it negates is the identification with the self as a static entity in charge of directing all actions. Daoism views the self as a process that, when emptied, can be in a genuine relationship with the Dao. This leads to a unique expression of "De" in each person. The unique combinations of distinction and connection with organicity stimulate creativity. Guided by nature, the self may inform, execute, and facilitate creative potential. Intuition acts as our compass while our analytical self fulfills the act. In alliance with wisdom from small band hunter-gatherers, Narvaez describes the self as such: "…one cannot separate the individual from her community. There is no solitary self, but a sense of self as part of a larger common self shared with all entities. All things (wind, mountain, animal) are aspects of the common self. In fact, reality is a set of shifting selves, massive energies that emerge as particular animals or people but that continually reintegrate with the larger Common Self. Death is a temporary transition before transformation into another lifeform. Although nothing is constant, everything is eternal…"[102, (p236)] It is of great interest that this description resonates well with Daoist thought.

An individual experiences their ego as secondary to pure life. Now fully aware of potential and possibility as its fundamental ground, interconnection becomes an organic feeling. One treats all others as a part of oneself, and the world becomes their home, no matter where they are or who they are with. This is why Zhuangzi asserted, "The man who has forgotten self may be said to have entered Heaven."[9(p89)]

Theory and Practice

What is the benefit of "forgetting" the narrative self? It is someone who:

1. identifies others as important.
2. releases fixed ideas, resulting in less-biased decisions and thoughts.
3. increases openness and tolerance of others.
4. may become more adaptive and psychologically flexible.
5. may have an enhanced mood due to feelings of belonging, connection, and present orientedness.
6. may be less reactive when nothing is taken "personally."
7. no longer clings to desires or any identity, thus feeling at peace as they flow with the tides of becoming and change.

How would you navigate your life differently if you achieved such a condition of mind?

How might your relationships, with yourself and others, change?

Endnotes

* According to scholar of Daoism Larson Di Fiori (personal communication, 2024), "The identification of 'nature' with 'natural world' (大自然 in modern Chinese) is fairly recent historically. So although the idea of humans existing in the natural world is important to the early texts, being Ziran (自然) means being in tune with one's innate, authentic, or original nature, which, because it is not separate from anything else, is ultimately the same as being in tune with the natural world as well."

VIII

WUWEI AND FLOW

"'Spontaneity,' said Old Shu, 'is myself being itself.
When I release to my inner nature, I enter the freedom of who
I am. Then my thinking and my doing arise from the nameless
place that's their own home… When this wholeness is itself—
when it's unbothered and unaffected by things that don't belong
to it—then my spontaneity is undivided and pure.
That's when the differences within me disappear and I
move with an ease and a grace that's effortless.'"
—RAY GRIGG

"Enter the fullness of the present,
become one with its unfolding wholeness, and
then move with each moment's urging."
—RAY GRIGG

We stand as creatures of dual allegiance, tethered to the primal currents of our original nature, and yet as the constructed architectures of our narrative selves. Intuition whispers to us of an inner source, an unmediated truth that speaks in tones unclouded by deliberation. Yet, our conscious mind can obscure this quiet voice, erecting boundaries between what we are and what we construct ourselves to be. To reconcile these realms, to achieve a wholeness that honors our original nature and intellect, we must turn to practices that dissolve these barriers: meditation, which invites stillness and reawakens the intuitive; and *wuwei* and flow, which bring about a seamless state where thought and action merge into one harmonious rhythm. These are not separate pursuits but twin aspects of a single journey toward reintegration, each illuminating the path to a life more fully lived.

Wuwei (無為) and flow are related but not the same. *Wuwei* is a more encompassing term referring to an ideal way of life whereby the individual is completely attuned to any given situation leading to an optimal expenditure of energy and efficacy in activity. Someone who achieves this way of being would move through life as naturally as a cloud drifting through the sky. This appears as "effortless action," a way of being that is in perfect harmony with nature. Zhuangzi typified two types of thinking, one which he called weishi (為是) which Graham translates to "that which deems" and yinshi (因是) "that which goes by circumstance." Roth[67] labeled the latter as flowing cognition, because it is inherently adaptive and free from the clinging of the self. This construct stands in contrast to the former, which he referred to as "fixed cognition." *Wuwei* and flow are primarily a state of mind, yet the mind is also encompassed in the body.[23, 24, 25, 26] Yinshi is not blind, but contextually aware, and the awareness of context is recruiting frontal regions of the brain, albeit in the right hemisphere.[60] This is of interest because while we speak of original nature as being primarily the subcortical midline structures, it is a unique integration, not negation of any brain region.

Most neuroscientists, psychologists, and mental health professionals would agree there is far more non-conscious activity occurring in the brain and mind when compared to conscious activity. Aside from the obvious complexities involved with functions such as sensation, perception, homeostatic regulation, and emotions, part of the question becomes whether there is intelligence in activity that we are not aware of in the moment. The following studies offer support that organic activity can be intelligent:

- Participants can learn grammar rules and patterns without being aware of them.[124]
- People can improve perceptual and discrimination abilities through repeated nonconscious presentations of stimuli.[125]
- Task irrelevant perceptual learning: individuals may learn information outside a goal-directed task simply by being exposed to it throughout their performance. Importantly, individuals are not attending to this information or aware of it.[126]
- Priming: Nonconscious exposure to a stimulus can influence behaviors that follow.[127]
- Implicit memory, for example in the form of procedural memory, is well documented. Complex motor skills can be performed without conscious awareness (e.g., riding a bike).
- Tacit knowledge refers to knowledge that one can't express or transfer verbally because it is acquired through experience and practice. It is knowledge of how-to versus what is. This type of cognition occurs outside of language. An example would be asking an artist how they express creativity with precise details. It would be very difficult to do so. There is an intuitive understanding of what gets done and how, but most are not consciously calculating the precision of how a color would blend with another, or how a musical tone would harmonize with another. They just know.
- Bandura[128] asserted that social learning and imitation may occur without awareness. We may imitate others and acquire social norms and customs without intentionally trying to.

Is there any proof that spontaneous activity may *outperform* conscious activity? Here we acknowledge the work from Bruya and Csikszentmihalyi. "Flow," a term introduced by Csikszentmihalyi,[129] refers to the experience of deep absorption and engagement with the moment. In states of flow, one may be disconnected from time, lose one's sense of self, and dissolve the boundary between doing and thinking. One entirely merges with the moment. While at first glance they may appear to be synonymous, it is more accurate to say flow is an aspect of *wuwei*. While *wuwei* is an aspirational way of being in the world, flow is a psychological construct that is used to understand peak performance. Many of Zhuangzi's stories refer to this ideal, such as a butcher whose movements are so refined he can effortlessly slice through ox without dulling his blade or running into bone, or a man who dives into a dangerous river yet emerges unharmed because he swam with the currents. Both emphasize following nature's patterns and rhythms.

Flow states may arise when one cares about what they are doing (intrinsic motivation), are deeply absorbed, and when there is a balance of challenge and skill. Flow activities have been associated with enhanced functioning, well-being, and life satisfaction.[130] Tse and colleagues[130] could demonstrate that flow is positively associated with well-being, and people with higher autotelic personalities enjoyed more frequent flow experience. People who know flow activities (i.e., exercising, creating art, playing an instrument, etc.) facilitate long-term happiness. However, findings suggest there is still a preference for passive activities. This has been called the paradox of happiness. Much of this is related to the amount of energy that must be invested in initiating flow activities. In addition, results indicate that affective forecasting (predicting how one will feel in the future) played a role in participants' inability to engage in flow activities as frequently as passive activities.

There has been much research concerning flow. Flow is a universal. Anything that is universal is important, as it is a condition of mind conserved through evolution. One axis of the brain that flow may target is the vertical axis, which means from the subcortical areas of the brain (i.e., bottom, deeper layers of the brain) to the cortical (i.e., up, outer regions of the brain). To begin with, neuropsychologists divide cognition into "hot" and "cold" cognition. Hot cognition involves rapid bottom-up processes, such as emotions and other cognitive faculties occurring below conscious awareness. Cold cognition is based on top-down processes, such as executive functions, which are much more deliberate, effortful, and slow. Slingerland[131] speculated that *wuwei* is achieved by cold cognition releasing its control to allow hot cognition to take over. To support this idea, he cited a study by Limb and Braun,[132] who investigated jazz pianists engaging in both improvisation and scales. For reference, areas of the brain such as the dorsolateral prefrontal cortex (DLPFC) and the anterior cingulate cortex (ACC) are highly active during goal-directed activities. The ACC can be considered the "oops center" of the brain, given that it monitors potential conflicts, whereas the DLPFC correlates to the execution of the activity accordingly. During improvisation, many areas of the PFC were deactivated, including the dorsolateral prefrontal cortex. However, during improvisation, there was also focal activation of the frontal polar medial prefrontal cortex, relevant areas in the sensorimotor regions, and the ACC, besides reduced limbic activity. Interpreting this finding, areas of the prefrontal cortex, especially the dorsolateral prefrontal cortex, become highly active during activity. However, in improvisation, spontaneity required the attenuation of that activity, as well as reductions in areas of the limbic zone related to fight or flight, while still monitoring for potential errors (i.e., the ACC). Thus, flow states tap into evolutionarily older systems that operate at time scales much more rapidly than voluntary systems. It is the fast system, not the slow system, and it operates as a parallel processor, not a serial processor.

These findings were similar to another study conducted by Liu and colleagues[133(p1)] examining the brain of people engaged in freestyle rapping. Under functional magnetic resonance imaging (fMRI), they encountered "dissociated activity in medial and dorsolateral prefrontal cortices, providing a context in which stimulus-independent behaviors may unfold in the absence of conscious monitoring and volitional control" and "widespread improvisation-related correlations between medial prefrontal, cingulate motor, perisylvian cortices, and amygdala, suggesting the emergence of a network linking motivation, language, affect and movement." What this means is they found support for the bypassing of executive systems that monitor and produce conscious control.*

The flow state requires a moderate level of arousal, described as optimal intellectual stimulation and emotional gratification. Not enough or too much arousal in the brain leads to task exploration, which may lead to procrastination. Too little arousal leads to boredom and fatigue; working on a task that is too easy and does not require much effort causes us to explore other options. Too much arousal can cause a person to become frustrated and stressed, leading us to task exploration, but now we must find more manageable tasks that do not require too much effort. When we're mildly excited, we can focus better on things we enjoy.

There are many ways that a flow state can be achieved; musical improvisation and freestyle rapping are just a few examples of how skill and spontaneity may result in flow. In a sense, closely related Daoist practices, such as Taijiquan were designed to engage flow states. It does this by integrating mind and body harmoniously. Movement is perpetual, calm, and balanced, similar to the movement of time. Large circular motions of the arms may mimic magnetic fields, and many movements reflect nature or engagement with it (e.g., cloud hands, the white crane spreads its wings, grasp the peacock's tail, open the window and gaze at the moon, etc.). It is an embodied expression of many Daoist ideas (Sam Wuest, personal communication, 2025). As an example, the first two positions in traditional 108 form are Primordial Chaos and the birth of Yin and Yang. While the movements may initiate as effortful, they soon become automated as they transition into our long-term memory. Movement becomes fluid and seamless. When complex motor movements are paired with regulation of the breath, the mind naturally becomes still. As expected, when practice matures, moments of total immersion increase.[138]

Practice

We can engage in many activities to help cultivate our comfort and confidence in being spontaneous. The following are examples.

1. Join an improv class.
2. Try freestyle singing, rapping, or dancing with friends (or alone). Let your body lead.
3. If you are presenting, and you are typically very structured, try adding unstructured moments throughout.
4. If you journal with intention, try "stream of consciousness" journaling.
5. If you are a musician, try improvisation.
6. Play games that emphasize spontaneity. Sometimes with children and groups of friends around the dinner table, we play a game where everyone makes up a line to a story and the next person continues it.

Wuwei: is considered a valued condition one can attain in daily life.

1. If you are engaged in a mundane activity (likewise with a complex one), be fully present with what you are doing, continually tethering yourself to the present with your breath, if needed.
2. Try Taiji, QiGong, and other types of still or moving meditations.

Flow: The following are factors from Csikszentmihalyi[139] that improve your chances of attaining a flow state. In flow states, people

---

inherently experience, a loss of self-consciousness, an altered sense of time, and a heightened sense of clarity.

1. Intrinsically motivated: engaging activities for the joy of it.
2. Skill level matches the challenge.
3. Total immersion: Complete presence with the activity.
4. Autotelic nature: refers to individuals who possess a natural tendency to seek out and engage in activities for their own sake. There is no reward or goal, but a clear goal can also be effective.
5. Immediate feedback: provides the ability to rapidly adjust.
6. Concentration and focus: the optimal condition is one where possible disruptions are minimal.
7. Control and agency: feeling in charge is important.

Kotler and colleagues[140] from the flow research collective suggest the triggers for flow include:

1. Clear goals, immediate feedback, and challenge/skills balance where both the task's challenge and an individual's skills are high (aim for > 4 percent of current skills).
2. Novelty, complexity, unpredictability, and insight.
3. Risk.
4. Deep embodiment or the hyper-awareness of cross-sensory modalities with major intrinsic motivators, such as curiosity, passion, purpose, and mastery.

Other factors to consider:

1. Complete concentration lasts for about 90–120 minutes.
2. Optimizing autonomy requires quality sleep, and exercise brings about alertness and energy.
3. Make creativity a value (or as I would say, open up to the creative principle of nature).
4. Improve pattern recognition.

Excluding the challenge/skill balance, the evidence for nearly all these triggers is correlational. Therefore, the causal role of these triggers remains uncertain.

Endnotes

* Naturally, diminished self-referencing often accompanies flow states. Studies predictably identify the deactivation of the DMN in flow states because this network has been associated with self-referential processing.[134, 135] From a neurochemical level, researchers Espana and colleagues[136] and Linden and colleagues[137] have hypothesized that the locus coeruleus-norepinephrine (LC-NE) system may play a part in achieving flow. LC-NE is responsible for releasing central norepinephrine, which plays a pivotal role in the brain's arousal levels. LC-NE also regulates decisions related to task exploration versus exploitation (i.e., gathering information versus using information to achieve a goal) based on the trade-offs between task rewards and the cost of doing the actual task. Without the necessary LC-NE output, it may be impossible to perform activities that need a high concentration level in a flow state.

PRINCIPLE III

RELATIONSHIP

One can trace the life of a tree back to rain that nourished it, to the cloud the rain came from, and to the water from which the cloud arises; the story goes on ad infinitum. Nature is a relational process. Every human is born through interaction, and develops continuously in relationship to others. There is no such thing as a purely isolated, fixed, self-subsisting being. Being itself is constituted by becoming, which is why I prefer the term *transformation*—a more stable process of relationships interacting. Humans are no different. We cannot survive without consuming materials on this earth. The elements that compose our bodies can be identified in the periodic table. In fact, there are many elements that do not compose who we are, reminding us that nature is a process that encompasses who we are, and much more.

The principle of relationship in being is to learn how to relate differently, more intentionally, and more authentically with oneself, others, and the world. Intention allows us to return to the path once we have strayed, and with time, intention returns to intuition. One purpose of thinking is to help us re-align, and when we are, we no longer need to think about it.

Paying attention to how you relate to your feelings or thoughts is a nice place to start. This then spreads—how do you relate to others around you? how about animals, objects and the environment? How can you shift how you relate so that it is closer to truth?

The principle of relationship in attending is to attend to the other as an individual with their own thoughts, feelings, and aspirations. It is to attend to them and the world through what Buber famously coined the "I-Thou" vs. an "I-It" relationship. People are not objects to be manipulated, nor is the world. How you attend to the world may influence the kind of world that emerges for you.

The principle of relationship is to embody the realization we are deeply connected to the world around us. This includes other human beings, as well as plants, animals, and fungi. If we know it is true that humans are deeply connected with the world and others, how does that change your actions? Might you be more community driven? More kind to the environment? More patient with yourself or others?

Hunter-gatherer communities are close-knit, with daily engagements with each other and every member joining for communal activities. For hunter-gatherers, alloparenting, or the idea of a child, having multiple parents is critical. Children are always monitored. Children of the Efe of the Democratic Republic of Congo, spend 60 percent of their time with an alloparent and many are nursed by multiple females.[141] This provides a host of benefits, such as preventing insecure attachments should the primary caregivers be abusive or neglectful, improving social cognition as well as assisting with the efforts of raising a child, which can quickly deplete two parents on their own.[50] The connection hunter-gatherers have with nature is far deeper than many of us living in WEIRD societies. The enslavement of nature is not "human nature," as found in hunter-gatherer literature.[142] As Ingold puts it:

Hunter-gatherers do not, as a rule, approach their environment as an external world of nature that has to be "grasped" conceptually and appropriated symbolically within the terms of an imposed cultural design, as a precondition for effective action. They do not see themselves as mindful subjects having to contend with an alien world of physical objects; indeed, the separation of mind and nature has no place in their thought and practice.[142 (p42)]

The worldview is far more interdependent, viewing nature as a mother or father. This is also not seen as a mere metaphor but lived in accordance with (e.g., sharing, parental care, empathy, keeping in touch with it).

The principle of relationship comes alive in the science of interconnection and the wisdom of the right hemisphere. Modern insights into interconnection unveil the web of life, where no part exists in isolation, while the right hemisphere's holistic perception allows us to see the world as an integrated whole, alive with relationships. Together, they reveal that meaning and being emerge not in separation but in the threads that bind us to each other and the cosmos.

IX

INTERCONNECTION

"Cavernous and undifferentiated heaven and earth,
chaotic and inchoate Uncarved wood, not yet created and
fashioned into things: this we call the 'Grand One.'
Together emerging from this unity, so that each acquired its
distinctive qualities, there were birds, there were fish,
there were animals: this we call the
'differentiation of things.'"
—THE HUAINANZI

"I can at times feel strongly the beauties you describe,
in themselves & for themselves—but more frequently all things
appear little—all knowledge, that can be acquired, child's play—
the universe itself—what but an immense heap of little things?—
I can contemplate nothing but parts, & parts are all little—!
—My mind feels as if it aches to behold & know something great
—something one & indivisible—and it is only in the faith
of this that rocks or waterfalls, mountains or caverns
give me the sense of sublimity or majesty!
—But in this faith all things counterfeit infinity!"
—SAMUEL TAYLOR COLERIDGE
from "The Eolian Harp"

While empathy is the awareness of an emotional connection with another and the attempt to understand what they are feeling, compassion incorporates this alongside the ensuing desire to help. Chapter 27 of the Daodejing has clear passages supporting the sage as someone who does not abandon others, who actively helps others in need, and who naturally finds it their responsibility to be a potential guide to those who have lost their way. This is due to their connection with nature and the transparent boundaries between themselves and others. Is the deep experience of interconnection felt and described in Daoism supported in science?

SOCIAL EXPERIENCES AND THE EXPERIENCE OF SELF

Amsterdam[143, 144] developed the rouge mark test in which a baby's nose would be marked, and when presented with a mirror, the baby either recognizes himself/herself and removes the mark or does not. These experiments have been replicated,[145] suggesting that self-recognition begins around twenty months, or two years old. Rochat and Zahavi[146] argued about the extent of what this means, further noting that before this time, there may be an earlier experiential self (i.e., ecological self) of infants at three months old, demonstrated by their ability to discriminate between themselves and others, alongside other lines of evidence like children from different cultures who do not remove the mark until the age of six or seven. There may exist an implicit primitive feeling of phenomenal experience detached from memories and higher order cognition, which would also be supported by the work of Panksepp.[94] It is important then to distinguish between having an experience of a self ("I am") and the experience of a sense of self ("I know I am"). Irrespective of the exact timing of when the sense of self begins, the very first experience anyone has is always in relation to the environment.

For many of us, our first memories begin around the age of three,[147] which coincides with our capacity for theory of mind, the ability to know that another person has a mind of his/her own.[148] Even the action of self-reflection triggers the activation of mirror neurons[149] that fire when another individual performs an action. It is hypothesized that these neurons enable a subject-object distinction, meaning we view people as separate from ourselves. This also means mirror neurons make it possible for us to view ourselves as an object through self-reflection. The sense of self and other may emerge at the same time.

Self-awareness involves the integration of external and internal bodily signals to provide a coherent multisensory experience of one's body. Interoception is, therefore, one aspect of self-awareness, as it is the perception of internal bodily sensations. The ability to accurately detect internal bodily sensations is known as interoceptive accuracy (IAcc). Studies have shown that IAcc can increase when one's attention is directed to self-related information, such as viewing one's reflection or picture. One study[150] considered how focusing on a romantic partner can enhance IAcc, similarly to viewing one's self. This assumption is based on the idea of the relational self, a distinct self-experience evoked in the presence of significant others (SOS). SOSs are crucial for shaping our self-perception because they act as social mirrors. The relational self is also linked to affective, behavioral, and self-regulatory responses activated by the presence of an SOS. Optimal emotion regulation requires one to be aware of their current emotional state, which in turn is closely linked to interoceptive awareness.

To measure IAcc, participants were asked to count their heartbeats without taking their pulse. The study found that viewing one's partner improved accuracy in the low baseline IAcc group, but viewing one's face did not improve accuracy. Focusing on a romantic partner seemed to function as a more relevant cue to interoceptive awareness than self-face observation. These findings are supported by studies on locating the brain area activated during interoceptive processing. The insula has been shown to play a key role in awareness of internal sensation and emotion regulation. It is also activated when viewing one's own face and also viewing a romantic partner's face.

Questions to contemplate:

Who were you before the age of two or three? Who were you within gaps of memory?

In Daoism, the underlying substratum of the universe is undifferentiated, meaning unified without any distinction. Prior to multiplicity exists a fabric where everything is unified. Other and self, hard and soft, good and bad, beautiful and ugly, hot and cold, all exist together, separated only by the intellect, which divides and categorizes. So, too, the brain begins to be undifferentiated, and it continues to differentiate as it evolves through time, just as the singularity point preceding the Big Bang. Things are undifferentiated before they began to differentiate. This is a pattern in nature.

THE BRAIN IS A RELATIONAL ORGAN

When a child is born, about 65 percent of their brain has developed.[151] Immature circuitry, which makes up the other 35 percent, develops in relationship to their environmental experiences, especially those with their caregivers. Beyond brain development, levels of maternal care affect epigenetic mechanisms.* As children learn, the development of their caregivers' capacity to regulate themselves becomes encoded and embedded into the neural circuits of their children. The idea that we develop executive functioning skills and relational models from early childhood has found ample support in attachment studies.[22, 27, 153] In fact, the best predictor of attachment in children is the coherence of parental narratives when using the Adult Attachment Interview (a tool used in psychotherapy to help determine an attachment style). It can correctly identify childhood attachment styles in 75 percent of cases.[154]

Children often mimic the behaviors of their parents and others around them. As they get older, they learn from the mistakes of others. An adult may accidentally touch a heated stovetop and retract in pain; consequently, the child knows the adult has done something dangerous and will not likely commit the same error. Mimicking and learning through observation triggers mirror neurons. Our brains continually encode activities of those around us. The reason why we do not feel the pain of the adult who has touched the stove top is because we have skin receptors that signal our brains that it is not us who has touched the hot stove, but someone else. Yet, when these receptors are anesthetized, we can actually feel what we are directly observing, as discovered in experiments by V. S. Ramachandran.[155]

NATURE SELECTS TRAITS THAT ARE BENEFICIAL TO THE GROUP AS WELL AS THE SELF

When we think of evolution, we think about natural selection. Many of us were taught that natural selection only happens at the individual level and that genes are propagated via survival of the fittest. Today, however, we know this is only half of the story. David Sloan Wilson[156] has championed the idea of multilevel selection, which has been increasingly gaining scientific support. He found through many studies that traits beneficial to the group may be selected over a trait beneficial to an individual person. This selection process is multi-tiered and may extend beyond the immediate social group to countries and nations. A trait like altruism, which may be counterintuitive for an individual person, may still be selected because it benefits the society in which that person lives. This phenomenon emphasizes the importance of survival and groups. If we are to compare the success of an altruistic society with one that is selfish, it is more likely the altruistic society will flourish. There is then a balance of selfish and selfless actions throughout society and within each individual.

OUR BRAIN WAVES ARE SYNCHRONIZED WITH THE ENVIRONMENT AND OTHERS

Social neuroscience has advanced with a technique called hyperscanning, which measures inter-brain coupling using electroencephalograms (EEG) which measure brain waves, functional magnetic resonance imaging (fMRI) which measures brain activity through blood flow in the brain, or functional near-infrared spectroscopy (fNIRs) which also measures blood flow through near-infrared light. Synchrony between brains depends on the activity, but has occurred among a variety of regions during different tasks, such as in personal social interactions, coordinated movements, and creative/collaborative group activities.[157]

Neural entrainment refers to the coupling of neural oscillations (i.e., brainwaves) between a person and their environment. Brain waves will synchronize with the rhythmic activity of external stimuli. For example, lights, speech, music, or tactile stimuli elicit responses from our sensory receptors, resulting in neural oscillations that will synchronize with them. Neural entrainment and synchronization may also constitute a key factor in language comprehension and interpersonal communication. A study by Pérez and colleagues[158] used electroencephalogram (EEG) imaging to measure the neural activity of fifteen pairs of individuals engaged in conversation for the first time. The results showed that the rhythms of the neural oscillations of both the speaker and the listener synchronized during the conversation, demonstrating the existence of brain-to-brain entrainment. Results showed the entrainment was not merely an epi-phenomenon of the auditory processing on the part of the listener, but was induced in part by an interactive communication process that took place in the actual conversational situation, without being mediated by the physical properties of speech. This finding highlights the potential significance of neural entrainment in the context of interpersonal communication. Entrainment may also constitute an important factor for understanding different states of consciousness, given that various brainwave frequencies (e.g., gamma, delta, theta, etc.) correspond to different mental states (e.g., memory, moods, etc.).

The fact the brain is an electromagnetic organ often receives less emphasis. In Georg Northoff's[159] neuroecological approach, he identifies electromagnetic currents nested within each other, which he refers to as temporal activity, with spontaneous brain activity characterized by blood flow as spatial. At the deepest level are neural waves synchronizing with electromagnetic frequencies in the world, which he terms the neuroecological layer. They continue synchronizing in different ways as we engage in different activities. As examples, he notes clinical studies whereby individuals suffering from conditions such as early childhood trauma, schizophrenia, depression, anxiety, and bipolar all demonstrate unique electromagnetic signatures as they continuously synchronize and desynchronize with the world.

He asserts that space and time are "the shared currency" among humans, and humans with the world. In fact, many noted conditions present with common phenomenological experiences, such as slowed time in depression (slower waves), entropy in waves in trauma, and waves characterized by uncertainty in anxiety. Space and time are two territories where classical Daoism does not elaborate much on, yet it is another one where interconnection can be found.

THE ENVIRONMENT DIRECTLY AFFECTS OUR BRAINS

One of the highest risks for developing Alzheimer's disease is pollution. The quality of the air we breathe interacts with our biological systems and may predispose us to this neurodegenerative disorder. Several studies have shown the effects of pollution on our cognitive abilities and overall health and well-being. De Prado Bert and his colleagues'[160] review of research concluded that in the general population, traffic-related air pollution exposure has been associated with negative effects on cognitive, behavioral, and psychomotor development in children, and with cognitive decline and higher risk of dementia in the elderly. An examination of the impact of long-term exposure to air pollution on the brain via neuroimaging found that cerebral white matter tracts, cortical gray matter, and the basal ganglia might be the prime targets of air pollution, and damage to these areas is suspected to be involved in cognition changes.

Another study tested the association between exposure to outdoor air pollutants and domain-specific cognitive performance, finding that significantly poorer cognitive performance was associated with exposure to outdoor air pollution, even at low levels of exposure. Specific areas of cognitive performance that suffered included semantic fluency and domains of executive function.[161]

DISTINCTION

In science, humankind shares a staggering 99.9 percent of its genetic composition. Yet that 0.1 percent difference equates to around three million base pairs. This interplay of unity and variation forms the essence of our shared reality—a paradox of sameness and divergence that shapes our relationships with one another and the world.

What strikes us most vividly is not merely the thread of interconnection binding us all, but the ways in which our peculiarities and perspectives break forth, claiming their rightful place in the mosaic of existence. This is particularly made clear in the work of Zhuangzi; in fact, he would revise the golden rule of "treat others as you would like to be treated" to "treat others as *they* would like to be treated."[8] This is quite evident in two parables:

1. Two emperors would meet in a territory called "Hundun."
   They regarded Hundun as very generous. In recompense,
   they gifted Hundun with human qualities, such as the senses.
   They drilled holes into Hundun to provide him senses, and
   on the last day, Hundun died.[10(p59)]
2. There was a beautiful sea bird that the Marquis of Lu
   entertained. He played music for it and gave it meat, but the
   bird remained unimpressed and confused. The bird did not
   eat or drink, and in three days, it was dead.[10(p143)]

Both parables include characters who make assumptions about others based on their own preferences. Consequently, both beings died. This is further reminiscent of another colloquial saying in the West, "One person's trash is another person's treasure." This, of course, can just as easily be reversed. The parables speak of the necessity for humans to respect each other's differences and step out of the egocentric framework when treating others. Diversity is required for flourishing, and it is an expression of nature's creativity. Following this line of thinking, we could say that one strives to be moved by unity, while respecting individual differences. It is a call to understand, to attend, to acknowledge the diverse textures of human experience not as deviations from a norm, but as vibrant expressions of our collective potential. In this, Zhuangzi invites us to embrace the unending dance of likeness and difference, not as a problem to be solved, but as the essence of what it means to live a life enriched by the other.

Reflection and Practice

For most of us, it will take time and practice to root ourselves in the experiential foundation of interconnectedness. Meditation and activities that engage flow are prime techniques. Yet from the science of psychology, we also know that people can change from the outside in, and by this, I mean that changing our behaviors can change our emotions and thoughts. What might experiential interconnectedness look like from the outside in?

With other humans:

- ▶ Try following the motto: treat others as they would like to be treated.
- ▶ Engage in more group activities that involve teamwork and a common goal.
- ▶ If you are a parent, learn from hunter-gatherers and consider alloparenting, which may help protect children from insecure attachments and build communal bonds.
- ▶ Engage in activities that involve synchronization (e.g., singing, dancing).

Nature:

- ▶ Learn more about the natural world by taking classes. The more familiar you feel, the more nature will feel like home. Imagine walking into a forest and simply knowing what trees surround you, what mushrooms or plants you can eat, and the lifestyle of animals.
- ▶ Start taking steps toward living more consciously in the world, paying attention to how you might reduce your carbon footprint.
- ▶ Go on a nature walk or to a botanical garden.

Many of these are quite intuitive and rightfully so.

Endnotes

* Epigenetics is how experience modifies gene functioning. Although the genotype remains the same, the phenotype or how the genes are expressed may be altered.[152]

X

DAO AND THE RIGHT HEMISPHERE

*"The conscious mind (which does the thinking) is
supposed to be a servant of the original mind [the Tao or spirit],
but the activity of the conscious mind tends to become so
self-involved that it seems to have become an independent entity.
When 'the sword is turned around'…the original mind retrieves
command over the delinquent conscious mind."*
—THOMAS CLEARY

*"Each thing is a half, and suggests another thing to make it whole.
As: spirit, matter; man, woman; Odd, even; In, out; Upper, under;
Motion, rest; yea, nay. All are needed by each one. Nothing is
fair or good alone; to empty here, you must condense there."*
—RALPH W. EMERSON

In previous chapters, we tackled the brain from the perspective of neural networks, exploring the Default Mode Network (DMN), Salience Network (SN), Central Executive Network (CEN), and subcortical midline structures (SCMS). One way of attuning to nature is meditation, and findings suggest increased interconnectivity between these networks allows for more flexibility and efficiency in their communication.[162]

The brain axis of focus now is the lateral axis, or the right and left hemispheres of the brain. In particular, the right hemisphere-biased functions correspond well with descriptions of sages aligned with nature. It also follows that left hemisphere-biased functions (when used inappropriately) correlate more with discordance.

The earliest studies on interhemispheric differences came from Roger Sperry and his group,[163, 164] winning him a Nobel Prize. They found, for example, that the left hemisphere mediated language expression, whereas the right hemisphere was biased toward visual information. They concluded that each hemisphere houses autonomous perceptual accounts of the world. Since then, many fascinating studies have indicated they also house autonomous *conceptual* accounts of the world.[45]

Gazzaniga[165, 166] conducted research on split-brain patients. In one of his studies, participants were shown a picture of a chicken claw to the left hemisphere (i.e., right eye) and a snow scene to the right hemisphere (i.e., left eye); participants were then asked to choose an appropriate card among an array. With the right hand, participants would choose a picture of the chicken (related to the chicken claw). Yet with the left hand, they would choose a shovel (because they were shown snow), but they were unable to verbalize why. When asked, one of the participants replied, "Oh, that's simple. The chicken claw goes with the chicken, and you need a shovel to clean out the chicken shed."[165(p225)] This is an example of confabulation, which occurs when the brain makes up a narrative to fit what it already knows, rather than admitting to a deficiency. For this reason, Gazzaniga[167] calls it the left hemisphere interpreter as the left hemisphere attempts to verbalize explanations that are not true. The left hemisphere requires certainty and needs to be right. Another example: the word "walk" was presented to the right hemisphere. The person began walking and when asked why, they replied, "I'm going into the house to get a coke." Yet another: "laugh" was flashed to the right hemisphere, and the person started to laugh. The experimenter asked, "Why are you laughing?" and the subject replied, "You guys come up and test us each month. What a way to make a living!" This emphasizes the unreliability of our internal narratives and provides support to Daoist skepticism. Our left hemispheres are literally making up responses, and this is why I say confidence does not necessarily correlate to accuracy.

The work of Allan Schore[168, 169, 170] supports the idea that the right hemisphere plays a dominant role in capturing unconscious nonverbal communication, slight changes in emotional expression, and intuitions related to variations and facial expressions, ultimately connecting with the patient's unseen world. He speculates a right-hemisphere-to-right-hemisphere linking in psychotherapeutic engagements. This empathic attunement facilitates the establishment of an emotional bond, which may further facilitate the regulation of emotional experiences that arise in the session. The benefit of this connection is the establishment and internalization of a relational process that may facilitate emotional maturation.

Iain McGilchrist[45] asserted that the dominance of language and intellect has led to the illusory control of the left hemisphere over the right hemisphere. This has affected our cultural evolution such that it focuses on productivity, objectification of others, loss of present-orientedness, and a society wracked with anxiety and depression. After detailing differences between how the two hemispheres conceive the world, he concluded the right hemisphere should assume its rightful place as *master* and left hemisphere as its *emissary*. Importantly, one must not assume the hemispheres work in isolation, rather that there are biases or increased activity that occurs in relationship to the following functional distinctions.

Right Hemisphere	Left Hemisphere
Present oriented, presentation of the world	Representation of the world
Understanding of the world and how to relate to it	Manipulation of the world
Focused on global	Focused on details, the local, the central in the foreground, easily grasped
On the lookout for novelty (an anomaly detector according to V. S. Ramachandran) and dealing with it, also plays "Devil's advocate"	On the lookout for what is known and what is predictable, emphasizes routinized and mechanized behaviors
Opens up possibility	Narrows things down to certainty
Sustains ambiguity and holds together information that may be contradictory	Makes it the decision
Views the world as a whole	Views the world as isolated, discrete, fragmentary
Change and flow	Fixity and stasis
Implicit and embedded in context	Explicit and decontextualized
Animate (both hemispheres, preferentially right)	Focus inanimate (machines and tools, coded in LH)
Understands narrative	Prefers to categorize
Reference to unique exemplars	Categorize based on presence or absence of features
Body image, embodied, less abstract	Fine analytical sequencing
Superior at reading body language and emotional expressions/prosody, meaning pragmatics	Linguistics, syntax
Preconception, as they present us	Represent
Realistic, pessimistic	Optimistic
Empathy, theory of mind, primary process is emotion	Superficial emotions, representation of observed emotions (affect)
Music	Simple rhythms, technical aspects

Table 6: Right and Left Hemisphere Functions

The right hemisphere's perspective is further described by the well-respected neuroscientist Jill Bolte Taylor,[171 (p42)] who suffered a stroke to her left hemisphere:

> By this point I had lost touch with much of the physical three-dimensional reality that surrounded me. My body was propped up against the shower wall

and I found it odd that I was aware that I could no longer clearly discern the physical boundaries of where I began and where I ended. I sensed the composition of my being as that of a fluid rather than that of a solid. I no longer perceived myself as a whole object separate from everything. Instead, I now blended in with the space and flow around me. Beholding a growing sense of detachment between my cognitive mind and my ability to control and finely manipulate my fingers, the mass of my body felt heavy and my energy waned.

She further described the right hemisphere in this way:

To the right mind, no time exists other than the present moment, and each moment is vibrant with sensation. Life or death occurs in the present moment. The experience of joy happens in the present moment. Our perception and experience of connection with something that is greater than ourselves occurs in the present moment. To our right mind, the moment of now is timeless and abundant.[171(p30)]

Alignment with the Dao	Observing its manifestations
Non-duality/original oneness	Duality, "The Ten Thousand Things"
Desirelessness	Desire for the present to be other than it is
Freedom, aligned with the process of becoming	Clinging to self, identity, memories, things
Undivided, whole	Divided
Integral awareness and wisdom	Worldly wisdom
Unconditioned	Conditioned
Nature, pure life	Human nature, ego, self-process
Spontaneous	Labored
Ineffable, pure experience	Words, symbols, language
Stillness	Change, fluctuation of thoughts, emotions
Formlessness	Form or "The Ten Thousand Things"

Table 7: Primary and Secondary Way

There are many similarities between right hemispheric specialties and descriptions of what it is to be aligned with the Dao. You may also notice left hemispheric specialties related to the experience of the manifest world. Attunement to the Dao appears to be more right-hemisphere mediated, leading to qualities such as an intimate connectedness with the living, empathy, embodiment, living in the present, remaining open, unbiased, experiencing the world as a process of change, and the self as one with Nature.

Reflection and Practice

Now that you are aware of these hemispheric differences and how the right hemispheres have a particular affinity with the Dao, you can begin cultivating a deeper awareness of the origins of some of your thoughts and decisions. Experiment with your decision-making process by identifying whether they are more aligned with right or left hemispheric operations. Remember, the right hemisphere has no ability to speak; rather, it is governed by nonverbal experiences. You can view these comparison questions as left hemispheric symbols attempting to point toward inner experiences.

The following are some examples:

1. Am I seeing the forest for the trees? (left-hemisphere, LH), or am I focusing on the whole and the details? (right-hemisphere, RH)
   a. In relationships: Am I judging someone based on a single attribute or behavior without considering the rest of who they are and how they have been like with me?
   b. In work: Am I judging a criticism of my performance too harshly? Am I ignoring positive feedback and generalizing this criticism too much?

    c. Relationship to body: Am I too focused on a particular area of insecurity, and ignoring what I look like as a whole?

2. Am I being present (RH)? Or is my mind lost in thought (LH)?

3. Am I treating someone as an object to be manipulated (LH)? Or as a fellow human with thoughts, feelings, and aspirations (RH)?

4. Am I really considering another person's perspective (RH)? Or am I basing it on a superficial judgment of a facial expression (LH)?

5. Am I being open to change (RH)? Or am I rigidly trying to keep things the same (LH)?

6. In uncertainty, am I being open to possibilities (RH)? Or am I obsessing about the need for certainty (LH)?

7. When I am listening to music, am I appreciating and feeling the piece (RH)? Or am I trying to understand the notes and technical abilities of the musician(s) (LH)?

8. Am I being realistic or pessimistic (RH)? Or am I being optimistic (LH)?

9. Am I basing a decision on intuition and being spontaneous (RH)? Or am I being calculated (LH)?

10. On a hike, am I taking in the full beauty of the world without thought (RH)? Or am I categorizing and actively thinking about it (LH)?

11. Am I fixated on the narratives of who I am (LH)? Or am I open to feedback and change (RH)?

12. Am I excessively drawn to the virtual world, technology, and mechanical things (LH)? Or am I more drawn to the living world as it is (RH)?

WHOLENESS

Nature consents to all. Nature houses beautiful mountains, cloud forests, and vast oceans, as well as rotting carcasses, moldy food, and venomous snakes. The sun rises for you whether you are considered "good" or "bad"; the rain will get a hero and a villain wet; good things will happen to sinners and bad things will happen to saints. Nature does not discriminate; it is fully open and gives existence to all things. Wholeness is an attitude whereby one perceives the world in all its glory and gloom. One does not overemphasize one side over the other. This translates into our own psychological dynamics. As humans, every one of us has aspects of ourselves we like as well as parts of ourselves we dislike. Part of our journey is reconciling these differences.

At the level of being, the principle of wholeness is about integrating all parts of yourself, without neglecting or suppressing them. The "good" with the "bad." In relationships with others, we might consider the distinction between psychological facts and truths. Facts may be partial, whereas truths consider the whole. It may be a fact that you are having a feeling or narrative related to an incident, but that need not mean it is a truth.

It can be partially, if not completely fictional when considering the truth. The truth considers all sides. This consideration may lead to revisions to the original response. The acceptance that narratives are incomplete may give way to curiosity, as defensiveness or agitation subside.

This might mean holding on to ambiguity until more information surfaces (which is a right hemisphere function) or accepting paradox. It is to open yourself up to the possibility of the positive in the negative and the negative in the positives.

At the level of attending, the principle of wholeness is about attending to the widest field of possibilities, while taking into consideration what your salience network (i.e., director) has determined to be of most importance to you. If we follow through with the idea that there's a mismatch between what our brains evolved for and our current environment and culture, then we must engage other cognitive systems nature endowed us (e.g., meta-cognition, alternating attention, divided attention) to re-orient ourselves when necessary.

At the level of doing, the principle of wholeness is about finding effective ways of expressing what has been psychologically recognized, accepted, and integrated. Anger might turn to assertiveness, sadness might turn to self-reflection, and anxiety might turn to productivity. It is about embodying the best possible adaptation to any environmental context in relationship to the unique topography of your inner life.

Hunter-gatherers are well aware of the cyclical nature of the world, and they adapt their lifestyles accordingly. They stay close to their immediate experiences, and accept when something is not working. Is it possible for us to maintain our expectations at a minimum? To accept the darkness with the light?

Under the principle of wholeness, we explore experience and paradox. Experience, rich and varied, teaches us that life's truths are not always linear but encompass the contradictions of simplicity and paradox. Paradox opens the door to deeper wisdom by showing us that opposites coexist and reveal one another. Together, they remind us that wholeness is not the absence of complexity but its harmonious integration.

XI

EXPERIENCE

"What you speak of now is still the footprints, and the footprints
are where the shoes pass, they are not the shoes!"
—THE ZHUANGZI

"All teachings are mere references. The true experience is living your
own life. Then, even the holiest of words are only words."
—DENG MING-DAO

Daoist writings emphasize the limitations of language and concepts. The sage enters like a bulldozer, demolishing the certainty of conceptual systems. Our strong identification with our thoughts detaches us from the present moment. Grammatical rules, lexicon, and other semantics in languages may also influence cognition. The English language is biased toward phrasing things as static, isolated entities, as opposed to dynamic processes (which are closer to the facts). Arbitrary distinctions within our minds create borders that narrow our experience of reality.

When the people of the world all know beauty as beauty,
     There arises the recognition of ugliness.
     When they all know the good as good,
     There arises the recognition of evil.[4 (p101)]

Making a particular judgment creates an imaginary boundary, boxing in an experience and separating it from other possible viewpoints. When we determine something is beautiful, it makes a simultaneous judgment of something else as being ugly. The same occurs when we judge someone as good; it creates a bin for what is bad. Bad defines good, and vice versa. To emphasize the point, nature has no preference and contains all experiences. For this reason, in classical Daoism, nothing is sacred, and at the same time, everything is sacred. Nature holds all things, from manure to a beautiful vista, with the same regard.

> Men claim that Maoqiang and Lady Li were beautiful; but if fish saw them, they would dive to the bottom of the stream; if birds saw them, they would fly away; and if deer saw them, they would break into a run. Of these four, which knows how to fix the standard of beauty for the world? [10(p15)]

To elaborate on this concept, Zhuangzi points out that we assume humans behold the standard of beauty. Yet the standard is challenged when one attempts to inhabit another viewpoint, such as that of another animal. The universal standard or consensus of beauty, even among humans, has not been established. There is still controversy about whether individuals find symmetrical faces more attractive than asymmetrical faces.[172] More personally, have you ever had a disagreement with a friend about the physical attractiveness of an individual? Although there is variation in the judgment of superficial beauty, a virtuous character is more invariable through time and space. In fact, the very idea of beauty challenges the notion that evolutionary variations can be reduced to fitness in some respect. Where, for example, is the evolutionary benefit in seeing beauty in the vast, empty dunes in a desert, or an abandoned building in the rain? Neither of these confers any survival advantage; in fact, the opposite is true.

Distinctions made by the intellect are not necessarily bad. In one parable from Zhuangzi, he discusses the skill of a butcher as demonstrating an ideal state. Of interest, butchers were seen as very lowly on the social hierarchy due to the nature of their profession (i.e., killing and butchering animals). Yet in this story, he speaks of the butcher as a paragon of sagely activity, and butcher Ding shares his process of butchering. When he is engaged, he is in a state of flow, knowing exactly where to cut, what to cut, and how to cut, allowing him increased efficiency and a knife that never seems to dull. Of importance, where he cuts are areas that are empty of interfering parts, such as bone. This simultaneously emphasizes how the sage reaches maximum efficacy when moving through spaces defined by absence. Thus, distinctions are necessary to help us learn, and although learning begins as effortful, it soon becomes effortless. Thus, it is not that effort is shunned in the context of learning, but that effortlessness is extolled.

The problem with discrimination is that we are constantly reducing a whole that is greater than the sum of its parts. The following passage exemplifies this conundrum well:

> There is "beginning," there is "not yet having begun having a beginning."
> There is "there not yet having begun to be that" "not yet having begun having a beginning."
> There is "something," there is "nothing."
> There is "not yet having begun being without something."
> There is "there not yet having begun to be that" "not yet having begun being without something."
> All of a sudden there was nothing, and we do not yet know of something and nothing really which there is and which there is not. Now for my part I have already referred to something, but do not yet know whether my reference really referred to something or really did not refer to anything.[11(p55)]

As Graham indicates, this passage is a "criticism of describing in words the whole out of which things divide. Analysis always leaves an overlooked remainder, and that the whole cannot be recovered by putting the parts together again."[11(p55)] Experience will always be greater than what words can capture. According to Wang,[173(p350)] "As Zhuangzi observes, everything has a 'this' and 'that.' When we identify a thing as 'this,' we suppress it's 'that' within it. By discriminating something, we conceal something."

This limitation of language and analysis becomes particularly evident when we consider emotional experience. One of the most common pitfalls I encounter in my work with patients is the tendency to latch onto a narrow, fixed viewpoint of a situation as if it was the whole truth. This is evident in the realm of emotional experience, where people often confuse emotional facts with emotional truths. Emotional facts, in my terms, are the immediate, raw feelings one is experiencing, regardless of the objective reality of the situation. For instance, a person might feel an overwhelming sense of rage because they believe their partner is betraying them. This feeling of rage is an emotional fact—it is a real experience, an undeniable part of their consciousness. But this emotional fact does not necessarily reflect the truth of the situation. The emotional truth, on the other hand, is the objective reality of what has actually transpired. It may very well be that, upon further reflection and perhaps through seeing the situation from the partner's perspective, the girlfriend realizes that her belief was based on a misinterpretation or misunderstanding.

What I am pointing to here is the dynamic interplay between emotion and cognition—how our immediate emotional experience shapes and sometimes distorts our perception of objective reality. Just as in our broader experience of the world, where language and analysis cannot capture the entirety of our lived reality, so too does emotional experience often present us with a fragmentary understanding. The raw emotion we feel is real, but it is not the entire story. Only by stepping back and incorporating other perspectives—by transcending the narrow view shaped by our emotions—can we hope to approach a fuller truth. This is why emotional experience, like all experience, demands a delicate balance between acknowledging the immediacy of our feelings and seeking a more comprehensive understanding of the situation that goes beyond them.

When we attempt to grasp what experience truly is, we are confronted with a complexity that defies measure, an intricacy that lies far beyond the capacity of any single analysis. And yet, in its manifestation, experience seems deceptively simple, immediately present to us as a coherent whole.

Simplicity is another major theme and value in Daoism for which many people strive. To be simple means to be direct and clear, not dumb or naïve. It means to stay true to the present experience and not fall sway to lofty ideas that may occlude reality or seductive temptations that may complicate well-being. In this age of technology, we have become increasingly attached to external goods. The paradox here is we do so because we believe they may bring us more joy, but they do not in the long run. A new car loses its novelty and excitement in a matter of weeks, just as a child may lose interest in a new toy within a day or two. We run on the hedonic treadmill, straining forward but ever stationary. Addiction to substances is another example. Addictions blunt all other pleasures as the progression ensues. One way to reignite our joy for life involves surrendering these illusory wants to stabilize our levels of dopamine. In other words, we must return to simplicity.

Differentiation can achieve clarity in psychotherapy. Light is shed over hidden dysfunctional patterns, and with this newfound awareness, the individual has an increased ability to change. After a dysfunctional dependency on an object, a narrative or statement is made aware of and subverted, and newfound freedom inevitably finds its way to new sources of creativity. From the Daoist perspective, clarity is achieved through a process of "darkening," which can facilitate therapy. Darkening refers to the conscious dissipation of mental activity. To engage in this process, one must develop psychological skills that improve one's mindsight. In the process of darkening, one learns to recognize the quality and quantity of their thoughts and feelings, cultivating the ability to detach their emotional investment in them, and become lodged in silence and mystery. A still mind is a peaceful mind. Darkness stabilizes the mind, enabling an individual's fundamental nature to shine forth. This process may help an individual find their way through limiting conceptual schemes and narratives that have been driving them for years.

Reflection and Practice

"The sage dwells in the formless,
moves in the traceless
and wanders in the beginningless"
—*from The Huainanzi*

"Simplicity is the ultimate sophistication."
—*Leonardo da Vinci*

"Nature is what we know—
yet have no art to say—
So impotent our wisdom is
To her simplicity."
—*Emily Dickinson*

1. Language may *Fragment* the whole, *Exclude* components, and lead to *Narrow-mindedness* due to *categorization* and incongruence with *experience (FENCE)*.
2. Reflect on an interpersonal challenge you have recently faced. Consider what might be the emotional facts vs the emotional truth.
3. Zoom out from your current perspective, until you are considering a problem or question from the perspective of the

---

universe itself. How does that change your feelings toward it, and/or your perspective?

4. If you are holding unreasonable standards for yourself, try relativizing your experience by adopting the perspective of other animals or objects in the world.

5. Do any of your beliefs conflict with your behaviors? If so, what are they? What are other perspectives that might also be true? If you can't think of one, try consulting with a friend or a therapist, and remember that your perspective is simply one.

6. Is there anything internal that you find yourself relying on too much? Perhaps it is the belief you are "not good enough." Try spending a full day acting as if this belief was nonexistent. How does that change your decisions and actions?

7. Is there anything external you rely on too much? Perhaps it is your phone. Try reducing its use, or even going a full day or more without using it. Journal about how you felt and how your day went. Were you more present in your interactions? Or perhaps you realized you have become so reliant on it that without it you suffer from cravings or the "fear of missing out." Is this the person you would like to be?

XII

PARADOX

The tension between "opposing" forces in a paradox is a unique relationship. It can create, or destroy, balance or disrupt. Without our abstract minds creating categories, there would be no paradox. It would simply be the wholeness of experiences binding all things in equilibrium.

The world in which we live is a paradox.* The world is both meaningful and meaningless. It is meaningful if our lives and quality of existence matter to us. It is meaningful when we are drawn to truth, morality, and beauty, and yet struggle with them in the face of temptations that may lead us astray. It becomes less meaningful when we consider the impact of each individual life in the vastness of time and space. It is meaningless when we consider the mere fact of existence with no direct knowledge of purpose. Yet if we view humans as a meaning-making species, and humans as a part of nature, then nature itself becomes a meaning-making process.[19]

From another perspective, death is necessary to sustain the living. In our everyday lives, cells die; indeed, their death is necessary for life. Apoptosis, or selective cell death, is a developmental process that occurs throughout our lives, especially in the initial stages. One of the primary risk factors for developing autism is the failure of apoptosis. This also reflects psychologically in our aging; certain behaviors must "die" before new psychological structures and behaviors can emerge. Alternatively, too much life can bring death. In adulthood, cells continue to proliferate, and when there is not the added component of death or apoptosis, cancer emerges. Psychologically, manic states in bipolar disorder may bring much joy and energy to individuals experiencing them, but may threaten their lives (e.g., risk-taking behaviors) and negatively affect those around them.

Thinking is linear, and accepting paradoxes is a nonlinear experience. The thinking mind is driven in circles as it attempts either/or dichotomies. Try this logic-based paradox:

The succeeding statement is correct. The previous statement is false.

The preceding logical paradox leads to circular reasoning. Language limits the nature of thinking and can never convey the entirety of your experience. The best it can do is select a figure from an indefinite temporal and spatial background. Such parameters do not bar the world outside of thinking. As an example, the dreamscape can bring together what linear thinking cannot, binding inner harmonies and discordances—paradoxical truths, as the integrity of sense is dissolved in its wake.

Nonlinearity is more encompassing, and this mode of experiencing the world is available to us.

Wuwei and its western counterpart *flow* embody paradox—effective activity and quiescence. In the Daodejing,[4] one encounters many passages that are paradoxical. For example:

> Being and nonbeing produce each other; Difficult and easy complete each other.[4(p101)]
>
> To yield is to be preserved whole, to be bent is to become straight. To be empty is to be full. To be worn out is to be renewed…he does not show himself; Therefore he is luminous. He does not justify himself; Therefore he becomes prominent. He does not boast of himself; Therefore he is given credit. He does not brag; therefore he can endure for long. It is precisely because he does not compete that the world cannot compete with him.[4(p139)]

Particular pairs with paradoxical themes found throughout Daoist literature include but are not limited to being/nonbeing, action/nonaction, individual/universal, serious/playful, effortful/spontaneous, male/female, full/empty, appearance/hidden, useful/useless, hard/soft. Daoism stresses oneness, which incorporates the unification and transcendence of opposites. Pairs that appear to be opposites are complementary. Laozi stresses their mutual causation and non-duality, whereas Zhuangzi elaborates on the nonduality of duality and non-duality, which can be captured because there is the being of being and nothingness, and beyond it, the nothingness of being and nothingness. McGilchrist[60] arrives at this conclusion in his two-volume book *The Matter with Things*. We cannot intellectually grasp some paradoxes, but the mind can open up to them, and experience can digest paradoxes. Perhaps my favorite painting of dragons comes from Chen Rong's *Nine Dragons*. In it you will find the play of being and nothingness. Areas that are partially hidden refer to the mysteries inherent in nature.

Image 12: A dragon from *Nine Dragons* by Chen Rong (1244)

One example in small-band, hunter-gatherer societies is giving and receiving. Narvaez[102] stresses that in primal societies, Western thought separates giving and receiving, but these acts are connected. As an example, "the sharing of a life is a gift and must be treated as such…animals and plants are asked permission for their use in feeding and comforting human beings…for successful hunting or capture of the gift of life, one must lose self-consciousness and merge one's identity with the larger domain of being…harming others is forbidden except killing for food, which must be performed with respect for the life taken."[102(p238)] This resonates with Daoism and the principles of Yin and Yang, of seeming opposites being collapsed into one.

Zhuangzi examines many paradoxical parables through perspectival relativity. For example, in one of his parables, we encounter a carpenter who, upon seeing a crooked tree, views it as worthless. To try to use this tree to create boats would cause failure, coffins would rot, vessels would break, and beams would be impossible to make. The story continues, however, when the carpenter dreams the tree is speaking to him.

It proclaims that it is precisely because of its "uselessness" to humans that it has survived so long. Because of its shape, it can provide shelter to thousands of animals. Because of its appearance, it is considered a sacred tree, and this is why a village shrine was built around it. The trouble with being useful from the perspective of humans is the increased potential for exploitation. The term "useless," therefore, becomes reduced to a matter of perspective. The following two quotes offer further examples countering the ideas of usefulness and uselessness from The Huainanzi:

> There is nothing that does not have some use. Tianxiong and wuhui are the [most] virulently poisonous of herbs, but a good physician uses them to save people's lives. Dwarves and blind musicians are the troubled invalids of humankind, but the ruler of men uses them to perform music. For this reason, the sage prepares even the shavings from the timber. There is nothing that he does not use.
>
> The myriad things all have some use. Nothing is so small that it is useless. If you view things from the perspective of their uselessness, precious jades are [no different from] manure.[13 (p355, 378)]

The critique targets one-sided thinking. Statements that are true usually require multiple perspectives and precision of degree. The problem is that experience is so encompassing that language cannot account for wholeness. One-sided thinking further extends to the biases of our preferences. People are often quick to judge based on first impressions, yet we must remember that many variables may uproot these opinions. In the following quote, Zhuangzi exemplifies the relativity of perspectives: "Mr. Lame-Hunchback-No-Lips talked to Duke Ling of Wei, and Duke Ling was so pleased with him that when he looked at normal men, he thought their necks looked too lean and skinny."[9 (p40)]

In the preceding passage, we find that the Duke, after being swayed by a paragon of the Way, suddenly has a shift in his perspective of what the standard of appearance ought to be. This translates to superficial appearances, just as an individual may appear more attractive or unattractive after an initial encounter. There is some flexibility for superficial experiences, and a person is not complete until they are known. We only ever know a fraction of each individual we meet, even those with whom we are intimate. This is fortunate because continual novelty exists in everyone's process of becoming. It is also often forgotten with people we believe we know well. The problem with "boxing" people in is it can result in harmful predictions, inferences, boredom, and resistance.

"Men eat flesh of grass-fed and grain-fed animals, deer eat grass, centipedes find snakes tasty, and hawks and falcons relish mice. Of these four, which knows how food ought to taste?"[10(p15)] In this quotation, human preferences are but one among many. It is common for us to use our own perspective to judge a situation, less common to attempt the adoption of perspectives of other people, and rare to consider the perspective of other natural processes. Yet, all these perspectives are important to consider when attempting to grasp at truth. We take our preferences for granted, believing our tastes to be superior, yet when we incorporate other views, our judgment of taste loses its validity.

Daoism usually evokes the image of the famous *Taijitu* (i.e., the Yin-Yang symbol). In this symbol, opposites are symbolized as complementary. Nature has no preference and unifies all things that appear to be contrary. Without the good, there cannot be bad. Without soft, there cannot be hard; without beauty, there cannot be ugliness. These are all human constructs that rely completely on one another for their existence, meaning they are two sides of the same coin. Nature houses all things without discrimination. Sometimes, "good" people suffer tremendously, whereas "bad" people reap the glory. Every day, the sun rises and sets for everyone, regardless of who they are and what they have done. The self-generating spontaneous universe is thus considered to be impersonal.

One paradoxical notion in Daoism is that one grows and develops to return to purity like that of an infant (though not naivety). Rather than a linear evolutionary progression, the trajectory is like a spiral. The end eventually incorporates the beginning, though it also extends beyond it. One unlearns to learn, and by letting go, we gain.

The most popular paradox in Daoism is *wuwei*, often translated as action through nonaction. The Western parallel to this construct is flow (although it transcends it). How is it possible for one to act without action? Many times, especially in sports (basketball players refer to this as being in "the zone"), painting, music, and other performing arts, individuals share the feeling of complete immersion into the experience. The body flows with the passage of time, yet many would describe the experience as "timeless." The self is in action, yet the experience is that there is no self-acting. In these states, people perform at their peak and, paradoxically, when they become conscious and effortful, mistakes are made. *Wuwei* is best understood as effortless action, and will be explored in more depth in a later chapter. The paradox is that one performs best when they are "trying not to try."[131]

Paradoxes define the universe, making it difficult for our minds to grapple with the limits of logic. We find many paradoxes in nature beyond Daoist literature. Humans exhibit these paradoxes in logical, neurological, and psychological instances.

EXPERIENCE AND PERCEPTION

*"Line in nature is not found; unit and universe are round; in vain
produced, all rays return; evil will bless, and ice will burn."*
—RALPH W. EMERSON.

One point of interest is the difference between what we perceive and what we experience. In our lives, we view the world, certain that our senses are delivering truthful impressions to us. Yet, the work of Donald Hoffman[175] reveals that it is unlikely we view the world as it is. Through experimentation, such as the use of evolutionary game theory and simulated life forms, he developed an interface theory of perception. He shares that (1) it simply takes too much time and (2) energy to perceive anything beyond what suits our survival, (3) there is too much noise and uncertainty to account for our processing constraints, (4) there is no 1-1 monotonic relationship between truth and what we perceive (in fact it can be a disadvantage), and (5) simpler perceptual systems are selected over complex ones because they can evolve more easily. His analogy is that our perception is an interface, like a computer screen designed to be user friendly. Underlying our desktop view is coding, electrical circuitry, and all sorts of other machinations beyond my knowledge. That is analogous to the truth of reality.

Classical Daoists would agree that we can only perceive the Dao through its expressions; we cannot directly perceive it, yet we can experience it. From the Neiye:[7(p52)] "We do not see its form, we do not hear its sound, Yet we can perceive an order to its accomplishments. We call it 'the Way.'" Another revealing passage: "cultivate your mind, make your thoughts tranquil, and the Way can thereby be attained."[7(p54)] The world we see are manifestations of the Dao, which emerge through conceptual activity and interpretative frameworks. When we subvert these interpretations, we are then able to experience the world with more accuracy. But here, paradoxically, "accuracy" in perception is not a matter of precise delineation or clarity of distinction. Rather, it is the recognition that all differentiation is rooted in, and ultimately depends upon, a fundamental undifferentiated ground—a bedrock of non-differentiation which sustains the very possibility of difference. Thus, by overcoming the separations of thought, we return to a deeper unity where distinction and unity are not opposed, but mutually dependent.

Perception itself is anything but straightforward. The perceived world results from reception and production. We receive the world as light streams inward, yet at the earliest level of sensory interpretation, our predictive systems are influencing this information. Sensory information conforms to our brain's predictions. In fact, it is quite clear that our brains produce information even outside any environmental stimuli. Similarly, when we act upon the world, we expect something to be received. What is received will inform our being, creating a loop that builds off preexisting information (i.e., feedforward loop). This fixes our perception, launching a chain of interactions intricately connecting and narrowing the potential of being, attending, and doing, as they feed off each other and co-evolve.

Now, if perception is a construction, we might ask: What guides this construction? What is the deeper principle, the foundational ground, upon which our cognitive processes build their intricate interpretations of the world? We do not perceive it as an object within the field of sense; rather, it is the very condition that makes perception possible. It is not perceived because it is not something that stands apart from us as an object does; it is what enables the act of perceiving to occur.

Why would our experience be more capable of grasping an underlying patterning force like the Dao? We engage the Dao not by seeing it, but by attuning ourselves to the deeper currents that shape all phenomena, recognizing that experience itself is an unfolding of that very principle. Thus, perception requires a comingling between the world and what is produced in the brain, in contrast to the experience within our being, which harbors direct access to the currents of nature. Our direct perceptions may only touch the surface, but our experience, in its richness and depth, touches something more profound, something that lies beneath or beyond the boundaries of direct sensory data. This deeper access is not a matter of seeing in the conventional sense, but of intuitively grasping that which is always there, just beneath the veil of explicit awareness.

PSYCHOLOGY

"The curious paradox is that when I accept myself as I am, then I change… That we cannot change, we cannot move away from what we are, until we thoroughly accept what we are. Then change seems to come about almost unnoticed."
—CARL ROGERS

Many major streams of psychological thought contain paradoxes. Combined with existentialism, we can theorize that the mind as the uncarved wood is a clear mind with the greatest range of potential. Yet, the mind is in relationship to the brain, body, and environment. Each of these dimensions are passageways for the expression of possibility. A passageway is a constraint. As possibility is narrowed, they become probabilities, and subsequently, actualities, as the mind itself is expressed through decisions and behaviors. Every free choice collapses an infinite set of other choices that could be made. In fact, one reason people suffer is precisely this sacrifice. We cannot be everything all at once, and once we choose a way of being, the only direction left is forward. We have to take responsibility for our becoming. Every choice leads to a meeting with an alternate self. Why not consider one over another? When we choose, we also sacrifice.

We are led to a paradoxical relationship between possibility and actuality. As unique degrees of tension are required in stringed instruments for the harmony of sounds, so is the need for a particular tension between possibility and actuality for our natural harmony to eventuate. While we cannot be all potentials at once, we can inhabit the space of potentials by returning to organicity, instead of acting from calcified narratives and scripts. In this state, we allow the combined presence of all potentials to signal us in a particular direction. The tension enabled by the mind as the uncarved wood permits nature's signals to be perceived in possibilities, and then enacted. Otherwise, the tension is replaced by egocentric signals, leading to more obstacles.

One of Freud's lesser-known insights is that humans are inherently contradictory. We aspire to embody values, yet at the same time, we may have impulses opposing their expression. The conflicts that arise among the id, ego, and superego occur within each individual mind. One goal of psychodynamic therapy is called object constancy, which is the capacity for people to hold the good and the bad together, to view people as a whole instead of viewing people as all "good" or all "bad."

Coming from the field of neuropsychoanalysis, we think, so we don't have to. Consciousness is seen as functionally important for problem solving, and once the problem has been solved, information becomes reconsolidated and belief systems are updated. When everything is working in harmony, we don't need to be conscious of it; in fact, this would lead us to a state of flow. Building from the chapter on intuition, much of our thinking begins with an intuited moral expression before we elaborate it in our minds. Once it is embodied, it again becomes second nature, or automated, so thinking is no longer required; that is, until another circumstance presents itself, challenging what we have previously learned, and thus forms the circular nature of intuition and analysis.

Carl Jung developed a deep relationship with Daoism, though he was not exposed to it until later in his life. His relationship with Richard Wilhelm, who he came to cherish and wrote the foreword to *The Secret of the Golden Flower*,[177] helped ignite his appreciation and curiosity for

Daoism. To his astonishment, he found several parallels, leading him to explore Daoist thought even further. In a letter in 1950, he mentions being "a great admirer" of Zhuangzi and further concludes the letter with "the truth is one and the same everywhere and I must say that [D]aoism is one of the most perfect formulations of it I ever became acquainted with."[(p560)] Dr. David Rosen,[178(pxxi)] upon interviewing two famous Jungian analysts and close colleagues of Jung (Marie Louise von Franz and C.A. Meier), both agreed he had a great affinity with Daoist ideas, and Von Franz even stated, "He lived the [D]aoist philosophy." In congruence with Daoist thought, Jung advocated the reconciliation of opposites. He speculated that opposing psychological experiences, if successfully held together for a long enough duration, may propel a shift in the psyche. This shift involves the creation of a new symbol that can unify these experiences. He called this the transcendent function. From the perspective of the brain, mild-to-moderate stress from the suspension of contradictory experiences may stimulate neuroplastic changes that occur. These changes would support a new baseline that can withstand the tension. His ideas of the ego and Self reflect a similar relationship between the self and the Dao (for more see Rosen, 1997[178]).

Jung's Protégé Erich Neumann[179] described how this might translate into practical behaviors in his book *Depth Psychology and a New Ethic*. Nature consents to everything, and the new ethic reflects this idea in practice. The *old ethic* is that of suppressing and repressing that which we consider "negative." Instead, one learns how give space to both the "negative" and the "positive" and through containing them allowing an appropriate expression to emerge. That way, we do not negate one aspect of our nature over another. Repression may lead to inappropriate ways of acting out. An example of this may be somebody torturing animals because of sadistic tendencies stemming from a childhood trauma. What could be the solution? Someone with his inclination, should they also have positive aspirations, may seek to resolve such conflict by taking on an occupation such as a surgical veterinary specialist. On a milder note, an individual may become assertive if they are typically complacent or docile in a condition where they are being mistreated. If somebody in a relationship has an excessive amount of sexual impulses, they may express this through developing a more creative sex life. If they are single, they could use that energy to develop skills that attract a partner. If one is struggling to contain the emotions involved with contradictory impulses, meditation can be of great benefit.

In dialectical behavioral therapy (DBT), rephrasing thoughts about other individuals may facilitate the capacity to bear incongruent feelings and thoughts, prompting a more realistic outlook. Instead of using the word "but," DBT stresses the word "and."[†]

Consider: Doug has been kind to me for most of our friendship BUT he has been unfairly critical toward me, *versus* Doug may have been unfairly critical toward me AND he has been kind to me for most of our friendship. These two statements will likely lead to different sentiments. Many times, people are quick to judge and react, resulting in the complete annihilation of one's history with another person based on a single act.

Boundaries that separate may unify on another level. For example, being and nothingness require each other; being gives definition to the potential nothingness offers. The awareness of nothingness also gives being its significance. Often, so-called opposites are necessary for each other.

NEUROPSYCHOLOGY

"Defects, disorders, diseases, in this sense, can play a paradoxical role,
by bringing out latent powers, developments, evolutions, forms of life,
that might never be seen, or even be imaginable, in their absence."
—OLIVER SACKS

The mind can be understood as having elements of both a parallel and serial processor. First, our brains have nonconscious circuits that process and interpret multiple streams of information rapidly and in simultaneity. It then signals our conscious functioning, which is akin to a serial processor. Serial processors are much slower. In the context of cognition, our minds reason linearly from A to B to C. Complex interactions occur below conscious awareness. Indeed, it is speculated that over 95 percent of brain processing is hidden and up to 60–90 percent of it is unrelated to external stimuli.[180] Thus, a mind that is clear and still is not equivalent to the complete cessation of being. Only death produces that state. A cessation of NETS (i.e., narratives, emotions, thoughts, sensations) may paradoxically bring about thinking and listening at the same time.

Given the vast number of existing paradoxes and my profession as a neuropsychologist, we will focus on paradoxes in neuropsychological literature. Much of the time when neuropsychologists encounter individuals with neurological or psychological illnesses, there is a focus on deficits. Yet there are times when said illnesses may reap certain benefits. These paradoxes increase the awareness of brain-behavior relationships, improving the balance of negative to positive feedback.

What types of paradoxes have been found in neuropsychological disorders? Kapur and colleagues[181] list five:

1. Lesion facilitation: improvements in cognitive performance of neurological patients

2. Double-hit recovery: A second brain lesion suddenly resulting in restoration of normal functioning
3. Hinder-help effects: Interference with performance in a healthy participant becomes helpful to neurologic patients.
4. Lesion-load paradox: The size or presence of brain lesion does not correspond to the significance of cognitive deficits.
5. Paradoxical positive outcome: Cognitive deficits benefit long-term outcome of neurological injury

Table 8 summarizes several paradoxical cases, many of which come from *The Paradoxical Brain*:[181]

	Cases
Lesion Facilitation	
Moscovitch and colleagues (1997)	Patient CK suffered from close head injury, resulting in visual object agnosia (failure to know the meaning of seen objects) and dyslexia. CK performed better than a control group on identifying hidden faces in an activity. Explanation: other objects were less likely to interfere with finding hidden faces.
Etcoff and colleagues (2000), Sacks (1985)	Asphasic (inability to produce speech or understand) patients were better able to detect nonverbal cues in communication.
Warrington and Davidoff (2000)	Reported a patient with visual object recognition difficulties likely related to Alzheimer's disease. This patient was strikingly better at matching mirror representations of objects that she could not identify compared to ones that she could correctly recognize.
Beversdorf and colleagues (2000)	Reduced false-positive responses and false memories in individuals with autism spectrum disorder.
Goodwin and James (2007)	<ul><li>Hypothesized that bipolar affective mental disorder could enhance creativity. Manic patients may have more amplified perceptual processes and may incorporate novel responses to their environment into their thought process. Mania may enhance creativity, including increased energy, positivity, and reduced inhibition.</li><li>Enhanced negative/positive emotional responses could intensify creative expression.</li><li>The duality of bipolar disorder is suggested to offer the added benefit of two creative industry employees for the price of one (both the creator and the critic).</li></ul>
Pring and Hermelin (2002) Baron-Cohen (2008) Göhlsdorf (2020)	<ul><li>Savantism is found more commonly in ASD. Savantism describes a cognitive profile where an individual shows an area of skill that is significantly superior relative to their other skills.</li><li>Without systemizing as the drive (to analyze or build a system), *Homo sapiens* would not have developed new stone tools in the Stone Age.</li><li>Excellent attention to detail may exist in ASD because of evolutionary forces positively selecting brains for strong systemizing, a highly adaptive human ability.</li><li>New inventions, the Temple Grandin Hug Machine, novel conveyor to reduce sensitivity in cattle.</li></ul>
Pring and Ockelford (2005)	Derek Paravicini: blind autistic musician with extraordinary musical abilities. He cannot read sheet music or perform basic tasks, such as tying his shoes, yet he has perfect pitch and can play any piece of music he has heard.
Double-Hit Recovery	
Helm-Estabrooks and colleagues (1986)	Reported a dramatic improvement in stuttering after brain surgery or brain disease—described the case of an ambidextrous man who ceased to stutter after suffering a head injury.
Cohen and colleagues (2009)	<ul><li>American patient developed a distortion in her speech pattern (German accent) after a left temporal-parietal stroke.</li><li>Three and a half years later the patient suffered a second stroke in the cerebellum. Patient recovered her normal American/English accent.</li></ul>

	Cases
Hinder-Help Effects	
Farah and colleagues (1995) de Gelder and Rouw (2000) Rouw and de Gelder (2002)	With face processing, a well-established hinder-help effect has been found in patients with prosopagnosia, a condition where there is a major impairment in the identification of familiar faces. Although normal participants were better at matching upright compared to upside-down faces, the reverse effect was found in prosopagnosic patients, who were better at matching upside-down faces.
Hawley and Joseph (2008)	• Positive changes may be seen in some patients who survive a brain injury or brain illness—"post-traumatic growth." • On long-term follow-up (an average of eleven years) after TBI, around half of their participants showed evidence of post-traumatic growth on a structured questionnaire, responding to items such as "I don't take life for granted anymore" and "I value my relationships much more now."
Lesion-Load Paradox	
Strasser-Fuchs and colleagues (2008)	Patients with benign multiple sclerosis (BMS) had preserved clinical functioning and had less abnormality than expected from a large T2 lesion load. BMS patients were significantly less disabled than secondary progressive multiple sclerosis (SPMS) patients. Neuroplasticity may play a role in functional compensation.
Feuillet and colleagues (2007)	A man with long-standing hydrocephalus showed normal social functioning despite MRI revealing massive ventricular enlargement and only a thin layer of neocortex.
Paradoxical Positive Outcome	
Adler (1943) O'Brien (1993) Gil and colleagues (2005) Bryant and colleagues (2009)	• Patients with TBI may have a lower incidence of PTSD. • The less often patients recalled their head injury, the less likely they were to develop symptoms associated with PTSD. • Longer post-traumatic amnesia (PTA) after mild traumatic brain injury (mTBI) may be associated with less severe intrusive memories. PTSD is common following mTBI, but longer PTA may be a protective factor.
Xavier and colleagues (2009)	The occurrence of solid tumors in children and adults with Down syndrome (DS) is significantly less than those without trisomy 21.
Wekerle and Hohlfeld (2010)	Autoimmune T cells have the potential to contribute to the regeneration of lesioned cells by depositing BDNF or other trophic factors under certain conditions.

Table 8: Brain Paradox Table

This table illustrates just a few examples of ways in which an otherwise unfortunate condition may confer some benefit. However, these examples need to be explored in more depth. The lesion deficit model presents a one-sided view; a more comprehensive approach offers a more complete understanding. For psychological disorders, there is far too little literature on the potential adaptations that they may have provided from an evolutionary perspective. In my previous book, I discussed ADHD and how some of the disorder's "symptoms" may have been potentially beneficial for survival and ingenuity. The autism spectrum disorder may also have similar benefits. These ideas bring me back to the Daoist belief that nothing in nature is ever wasted. Everything has some function and that which is "useless" is only considered so through a particular perspective.

Nesse[206] suggests six different evolutionary reasons we encounter disease: (1) there is a *mismatch* between our stage of biological evolution and modern civilization (this has been posited by Freud and elaborated on by Erich Fromm), (2) anxiety and pain are *defenses* that may be beneficial to survival, (3) *reproduction* is chosen over health, (4) *trade-offs* occur through evolution resulting in benefits and corresponding challenges, (5) there are *constraints* to natural selection, and (6) the evolution of infections (i.e., viruses and bacteria) progress much more rapidly. He further argues that emotions are not present for our happiness, but to optimize reproductive success to serve our genes.

Some potential adaptations for conditions include the following:

- *Bipolar:* As an adaptation to severe climate conditions during the Pleistocene, which began 2.6 million years ago and ended around 12,000 years ago. Depressive states became adaptive for 'hibernating' in caves, and manic was beneficial for hunting and foraging when climate improved.[207]
- *Anxiety:* Keeping hunter-gatherers prepared and alert for threats may also mediate social interests, such as alarming others or eliciting care.[208]
- *Attention-Deficit/Hyperactivity:* Fluctuations of attention may be beneficial for unpredictable environments. Increased

exploration and movement may assist with foraging and defense.[208]

- *Autism Spectrum:* Heighten parental fitness by increasing the necessity for attention and nurturance.[208]

I would also add that individuals on the spectrum enable a very different perspective in life, allowing unique perspectives that may enhance survival of the group.

- *Depression:* encouragement of rest, defense for disease, and minimizing disruption while promoting analysis of complex problems, in particular interpersonal ones.[209]
- *Narcissistic Personality:* Appear more alpha than they are, as a strategy to increase resource allocation and mating opportunities.[208]
- *Antisocial Personality:* In an unpredictable and dangerous environment, to engage in high-risk behaviors to maximize survival and protect themselves from negative future expectations (many ASPD individuals have unstable and possibly violent early-life experiences).[208]
- *Borderline Personality:* Reduce the risk of social abandonment, which our brain registers as equivalent to death for hunter-gatherers.[208]

As a reminder, many of these conditions may have evolved in a particular time and place that no longer exists in modern-day civilization. This leads to a *mismatch.* Many of these conditions may continue to flourish because it takes thousands of years for adaptations to cease or take place. While our brains have barely changed, there is hope in updating how it functions.

To add more specificity to the problem, Darcia Narvaez's[102] work provides substantial evidence showing that modern-day parenting practices deviate from our species-typical rearing (what she terms the "evolved nest") found in modern hunter-gatherers. This has contributed greatly to several psychological illnesses. "Human babies resemble fetuses of other animals until nearly age two" (Darcia Narvaez, personal communication, 2025), and the way we raise our children requires a particular form of parenting to establish "brain rhythms and set points for many systems (e.g., stress response)…early toxic stress seeds inflammation, the source of all dis-ease" (Darcia Narvaez, personal communication, 2025). Her work provides us with actual strategies to synchronize with the proper evolutionary trajectory of parenting and reduce the impact of the challenges we face because of this mismatch.

In other circumstances where individuals are forced to adapt, such as through a grave illness or injury, there also exist many cases that have led to helpful outcomes. Many times, it may present as a "rude awakening" that leads to a deeper appreciation for life. For example, a football player who lost a limb now finds his identity expanded and experiences happiness in intellectual pursuits, or an attorney suffering cognitive and physical decline becomes more spiritual and finds life to be more meaningful than it ever had been before. Sometimes, great meaning can emerge from traumatic experiences, such as an abused child who grows into a psychologist that helps thousands of other victims recover.

Reflection and Action

Opening your mind to paradox is an attitudinal shift, an acceptance of the limits of rationality, and the experience of humility and awe that resides outside of it.

1. Create a list of paradoxes you have encountered in your own life. Reflect on them and track how your experiences might change your attitude toward life.

2. While it would be beneficial for you to be under the guidance of an experienced Zen practitioner, the practice of koans may be greatly beneficial. One of the most popular methods that opens the mind to paradox and attunement to one's original nature is the infamous Koan. Koans are often used in Ch'an and Zen to assist with the subversion of logic. Try meditating on some of these popular koans:
   a. "What is the sound of one hand clapping?"
   b. "What was your face before you were born?"
   c. "Mu."
   d. In typical Zen practice, individuals are provided with these types of koans to meditate on, and if at any point they return to a master with a logical answer, they can get whacked with a stick and sent back. Koans create great doubt because they defy linear and logical thought, leading to unfamiliar internal experiences for students.
3. Experiment with Neumann's *New Ethic*. Hold on to "inappropriate" desires in proximity to your aspirations. See what creative response emerges from this dynamic.
4. If you are a parent or plan to be one, find out the myths of modern-day parenting, and synchronize your ways to how we can raise our children. More information can be found here: https://evolvednest.org.
5. If you or your child has been diagnosed with a particular condition, find balance in your views and actions. What advantages might the condition provide?

Endnotes

* According to Sainsbury, "A paradox can be defined as an unacceptable conclusion derived by apparently acceptable reasoning from apparently acceptable premises."[174(p1)] They often appear contradictory, yet when analyzed at a deeper level, they can make sense. Paradoxes vary in their complexity and gradation of difficulty to "solve."

† The Hegelian dialectical process: thesis, antithesis, and synthesis.

EQUILIBRIUM

Nature consists of multiple parts working together in harmony. This harmony produces synergy, allowing it to be self-generating. The whole becomes greater than the sum of its parts. Change occurs when an imbalance is detected because a part no longer functions fluidly with the whole. Error signals trigger signals for error correction, and changes are made. Changes provide feedback signals to show whether more changes are needed, or if the changes made are satisfactory. Balance is preserved. An example is shown in the ecosystem of an old-growth forest, where all the basic and complex elements of nature cooperate in service of its great equilibrium.

Why does nature continue to change rather than preserve its structure, conserve its energy, and remain in stasis? An asymmetrical balance whose process allows for movement, creativity, and advancement prevents the rigid and sterile condition of stasis. With a "balanced imbalance," however, novelty becomes necessary. For example, contrasts play a major role in our experience of pleasure and well-being. This means because we have points of negative comparison, we can experience heightened positivity.

In being, the principle of equilibrium is about an attunement to these asymmetrical balances that drive you forward and keep you living with vigor and vitality. It is about finding connections between different domains in your life, and how to balance them so that we find the ideal experience between excess and deficiency.

In attending, the principle of equilibrium is about distributing your attention with intent toward the domains that may be imbalanced in your life. Attention may nurture or neglect. Importantly, it is a finite resource and has a bandwidth. As such, whatever one places their attention on will also lead to the disregard for another.

In doing, the principle of equilibrium is about engaging in the activities required to achieve optimal dynamic balance. If you are working too much, you integrate more play and less work; if you are feeling isolated, you find a community. It is as simple as that.

Hunter-gatherers live a balanced lifestyle, with their cultures surrounding their spirituality, social practices, and survival strategies—all working together in harmony. Their view of the natural world and community is interconnected. This contrasts with the difficulties that WEIRD societies encounter. While we may strive to be more eco-conscious, the majority of products being sold have adverse effects on the environment, to the workforce (e.g., child labor, or conditions), or to animals. It is hard to live a life when our values are not clear, and even if so, our actions may produce unintended outcomes. We may not support poor conditions for animals, yet foods are cheaper, and income may not be amenable to supporting fully organic, unprocessed, free-range diets. All these are complexities that come along with living in such a large community: when communities grow to a size greater than 10,000, problems with subsistence, meaning the amount of food required to feed such a great population, will depend on mass production and technologies related; a lack of interconnection, since we cannot all sit together as a community and discuss problems; the need for leaders, whom we may or may not agree with, because there will be too many voices and opinions to consi er.[1] It is very easy to lose balance in our lives and live in perpetual contradictions.

The principle of equilibrium finds its expression in balance and stillness. Balance is the dynamic tension between forces that sustain life's harmony, while stillness is the fertile pause, the quiet within which balance is restored, and the world recenters itself. Together, they teach us that equilibrium is not stasis but the poised dance of life's forces in continuous interplay.

XIII

BALANCE

"The human race was created from Yin and Yang. We are both.
If we had no tension and interplay between polar opposites,
there could be no movement within us or in the universe.
There would be complete stagnation, a supreme stasis.
Sterility would be the sole reality. Thus, we must accept relativity.
We must accept good and evil, because they are part
of the fundamental process of creation."
—DENG MING DAO

"The nature of human beings has no depravity; having been long
immersed in customs, it changes. If it changes and one forgets the route,
it is as if [the customs one has acquired] have merged with [one's]
nature. Thus, the sun and the moon are inclined to brilliance, but
floating clouds cover them; The water of the river is inclined to purity,
but sand and rocks sully it. The nature of human beings is inclined
to equilibrium, but wants and desires harm it."
—THE HUAINANZI

Our body strives to return to homeostasis, an optimal state of stability among all the interdependent systems that compose who we are. From the level of our brains, an excess of a neurochemical may cause imbalances that may lead to dysregulation. From a psychological perspective, an excess of a particular emotion, or deficiency of adaptive thoughts, may lead to a clinical diagnosis. From an existential perspective, too much chaos can lead to self-destruction, whereas too much order may lead to rigidity and stasis. Wash your hands for too long and they dry out. Don't wash your hands and you can get sick. Daoists use yin and yang to describe opposing forces that set into motion the world of experience.

A concept I've used, inspired by Whitehead,[210] is the term dipole. A dipole is a single pole housing two forces that are related through their opposition to one another and simultaneously their need for one another to function. A simple example would be a positive and negative charge. Dipoles need not be equivalent. There are both symmetrical and asymmetrical balances. It is overly simplistic to think of equilibrium solely as two quantities of equivalent weight balancing a scale. Balance does not signify neutrality; a biological system's equilibrium is equivalent to the flow of life in all its glory. Asymmetry is fundamental in producing movement. The resting state of a neuron, for example, is not at 0 mv, rather −70 mv, and only once it is increased to −55 mv would there be an action potential. From an existential perspective, a certain level of anxiety is required for us to progress and advance. Anxiety may motivate us to work through whatever obstacle we are facing, including the introduction of new insights and strategies. While many might argue the world is more antisocial than prosocial, the fact that human civilization has continued to flourish is a sign that prosocial tendencies still outweigh the antisocial. We have yet to annihilate ourselves. A prosocial term such as love outweighs hate in its encompassing nature. A person can learn to love someone they hate, whereas a person who hates someone would not be capable of loving them.[45]

Balance is a natural law that exists in some form in all living and non-living entities. There is no hierarchy, but balance.[57] All possess equal significance in the grand scheme of nature. Nature is interdependent; every entity plays a role and contributes to harmony. Balance is perpetually dynamic, not static. Seasons change, as do relationships. Predators become prey as prey may become predators. There is an infinite number of entities that can be described in terms of balance. Within and beyond smaller entities, in Daoism, there exists a *primordial equilibrium*, with asymmetrical dipoles that include nothing/something, unity/multiplicity, and stillness/movement.*

"No-thingness" precedes the emergence of all things and is the "fabric" where all things exist. It is fundamental in Daoist cosmology. It is discordant movements in our minds that hinder our growth. In stillness lies the path to equilibrium, not in excessive movement. Importantly, stillness does not mean the absence of movement. When our bodies are still, there is movement, but it is tranquil or calm. Even when we peer into empty space, while we may not perceive it, there is movement at the atomic and subatomic levels. Movement cannot be perceived without the background of stillness; similar to how silence is the canvas for sound, and without silence, there can be no sound. Stillness and movement permeate every layer of existence. The primordial equilibrium penetrates, contains, and extends beyond all dipoles. In it, there exists a dynamism that is spurred by asymmetrical balance.

Practice

Find a quiet space.

1. What feels out of tune in your life?
2. What asymmetrical and/or symmetrical balances do that express?
3. What would you determine as your optimal ratio in different domains of your life?

What can you do to restore balance?

The introductory quote from The Huainanzi in this chapter signals that the development of culture may lead us farther away from our connection to nature. Working against nature is like trying to calm gusts of wind with a fan. Interestingly, Freud[211] reached a similar insight into *Civilization and Its Discontents*. Our evolutionary inheritance diverges from our sociocultural development, and this rift leads to further imbalance.

In Daoism, imbalance stems from a misalignment with Nature, which could be elaborated as the disruption, stagnation, or turbulent expression of nature's principles in each individual. This can be understood in the context of balance and imbalance. For example, "negative" emotions (energy in motion) without stillness result in agitation and acting out. This is an example of the imbalance between stillness and movement. At another level, someone may be agitated because they are taken away by turbulent thoughts independent of experience. This may result in self-inflicted distress. This is an example of the imbalance between the self and organicity. When the conceptual world of the intellect acts as a gravity well, it collapses the present moment into duality, which is not the actual nature of experience. We start to live farther away from the facts, resulting in a narrowing of vision, further concealing truths that may not benefit from being hidden.

> Whoever thinks what matters is to get rich is incapable of renouncing salary. Whoever thinks what matters is to get famous is incapable of renouncing reputation. Whoever is too fond of sway over others is incapable of letting another man take the controls; while he holds on to them he trembles, when he loses them he pines; and one who has no mirror in which to glimpse the source of his unease is a man punished by heaven.[11(p130)]

Identifications coming from the ego are selfish in nature, and that which is selfish in nature is always dependent upon that for which one is selfish. The theme of desires in Daoism is often misunderstood. This is evident in passages, such as, "The nature of water is clear, yet soil sullies it. The nature of humans is tranquil, yet desires disorder it."[90(p101)] The common interpretation of this philosophy is that to align with the Dao, one must operate without any desires. However, this interpretation is not entirely true.[4] Perhaps it may be easier to classify desires into three categories: *self-sustaining, aspirational, and selfish* (SAS). Self-sustaining desires are necessary to care for oneself, including basic survival needs, such as eating when hungry, sleeping when tired, or drinking when thirsty. Aspirations include desires to heighten wisdom, balance, well-being, self-respect, and meaning. In contrast, desires resulting in experiences, such as gluttony, exploitation, or inappropriate lust, would be selfish, not beneficial, or contributing to a path that leads to a still and peaceful mind.

Practice

1. Categorize your desires. Note which ones are self-sustaining, aspirational, and selfish.

2. Begin building your habits by first living a few hours without selfish desires and write about your experience. If successful, follow through with a day, a week, a month, a year, etc., without selfish desires. How does your life experience change?

3. Clarify your values and take the appropriate steps. Figure out what *moves* you and identify the steps needed to meet those values. As an example, if you are moved by the virtue displayed by somebody who is community oriented, benevolent, and cares for the environment, you may identify a few values that all fall under relationship. To be more conscious of what you purchase, for example, you can use the following website that rates the degree to which the company adheres to optimal conditions for animals, the planet, and work conditions: https://goodonyou.eco. As another option, you may want to play a more active role in creating a community that relates to your interests.

To live according to the Dao, one lives in a place that encompasses, unites, and transcends both good and evil. Indeed, "de" from the Daodejing is also translated as "virtue," and alignment with the Dao leads to what humans consider virtuous behavior.

For freedom to exist in the world, there must be a choice. From the Laozi, "All things arise, and he does not turn away from them, He produces them but does not take possession of them."[4(p101)] Classical Daoism does not directly address the question of free will. From my reading of it, I would speculate that it would fall into the category of what we call compatibilism. While there may be some degrees of freedom (e.g., we can choose to live with or against nature), these degrees are constrained by laws and mysterious cycles of nature. From a more technical perspective, one can accept determinism from a biological level, yet freedom may exist at the psychological level. From an evolutionary stance, determinism works when habits are successful, but habitual sequences of behavior are too rigid to account for chance and unpredictability. This is an evolutionary purpose of free will and one of the main reasons for neuroplasticity. We can change through time, and this change adapts to the conditions presented to the organism. Humans can also think about thinking (i.e., metacognition), and even act against some of their most primitive impulses to survive (e.g., fasting—hunger, suicide—living). Humans can readily sacrifice themselves for an ideology or endure extreme pain to preserve their integrity.

In Daoism, there is no good or bad; rather, there are different paths one can take that may be either aligned with nature or misaligned. As a musician, I am partial to musical terms to describe classical Daoist ethics. An acronym used to describe alignment is ARC, as it requires *attunement* (e.g., through stillness) to nature, followed by a unique *resonance*, which is the expression of "de." This leads to an overall *concordance*. The acronym for misalignment is MDD, as it begins with a *misattunement* to nature, which results in *dissonance*, and in more severe cases, complete *discordance*. The other benefit of using such terms is that it does not oversimplify the matter. There are times, for example, when dissonance may amplify an overall musical piece, and in fact are intentionally incorporated—perhaps similar to the asymmetry of an artwork that makes it stand out all the more. There is dissonance driven by beauty and wholeness, and dissonance driven by chaos and ignorance; these subtle differences are important to consider. In behavioral terms, dissonance might lead to a productive form of guilt whereby the person attributes an issue to their behavior and error-corrects, whereas discordance would be a deeper shame-based response, possibly tethered to a learned helplessness. Thus, while alignment and misalignment may appear as black or white, keep in mind this is just like everything else: a paradoxical pair.

One of the well-known ideas in the Daodejing (DDJ) is that because there is the concept of good, the concept of bad is also born. Once this relationship emerges, their dependence on one another becomes more complex, and this is further elaborated in Chapter 27 of DDJ. The "bad" person enables a "good" person to be a teacher of the bad. If you think about it further, "bad" people lead to the employment of thousands of individuals, further opening up the opportunity for the "good" to provide benevolent services that may help others change for the better. The chapter closes with a message that even if the "bad" do not respect or listen to the "good," the value of this process would still be the same. The bad person enables the good person to be good or even another bad person to become good. What can be implied from this chapter is further support because though nature has no preference, with fortune and misfortune occurring in many people, alignment with the Dao leads to actions congruent with many virtues.

Humans have both prosocial and antisocial tendencies that can be elicited in the right context. If you could save a stranger from certain death but would not reap any social or financial reward, would you still help? For most of us, this is a rhetorical question, the answer to which is yes. Misalignment typically arises when there is emotional agitation, excessive desires and/or maladaptive and biased thoughts. In stillness, there is peace, and with a peaceful mind, would there be violence? To follow nature's way means there is no need for a laundry list of do's and don'ts, or moral codes one has to enforce effortfully. There is no overseer waiting to punish you or bless you. There is simply a choice to make: you can approach your life in an adaptive and beneficial way, or one where maladaptive decisions lead to disorder and suffering. In this sense, Daoism is an immensely freeing philosophy.

> He who is identified with Dao—Dao is also happy to have him. He who is identified with virtue—virtue is also happy to have him. And he who is identified with the abandonment of Dao—the abandonment of Dao is also happy to abandon him. It is only when one does not have enough faith in others that others will have no faith in him.[4(p141)]

That being noted, even if we are completely in harmony with our inner patterns, we may still encounter challenges in our relationship with the world. To live in society also means to agree to an implicit social contract (e.g., general social etiquette) and explicit (e.g., laws). Misalignment to the natural unfolding of our fundamental nature may occur when we confront obstacles that may stagnate, disrupt, or lead to a turbulent expression of nature's principles.

The metaphor of a tree is commonly used when describing the healthy maturation of a human. For example, we begin in the mud, and just as trees grow upward toward the heavens, so should humans. Daoism would invert this. Perhaps we can use the Banyan tree as an example. Banyan trees have aerial seeds that are dispersed through birds. When the seeds land on branches, they grow downward and then spread laterally. Similarly, in Daoism, our original nature is already perfect, and it's harmoniously interconnected with nature at large. We only have to realize this by dissolving our thought patterns and aligning with nature's principles as they uniquely present to us.

Reflection

1. Try viewing challenges you encounter in your life through the lens of balance.
   a. What might be imbalanced in your life, or within you that has led to the problem?
   b. How do you equilibrate?
2. Reflect on guilt, shame, or another experience you feel unsettled by.
   a. What does it feel like to reframe this experience as a behavior or part of you that is misaligned instead of wrong, bad, or corrupt?
   b. Where does it lie on the spectrum of misattunement, dissonance, and discordance (MDD)?

M------------------------------------D------------------------------------D

   a. What steps do you need to take to recover alignment?
   b. Are there other experiences or behaviors that can be amplified within the spectrum of attunement, resonance, and concordance (ARC)?

A------------------------------------R------------------------------------C

Endnotes

* *Primordial equilibrium* is not a Daoist term. I am using it to distinguish between fundamental dynamics and the varieties of balances that exist in the phenomenal world.

XIV

STILLNESS

*"The sage is still not because he takes stillness to be good
and therefore is still. The ten thousand things are insufficient to
distract his mind—that is the reason he is still. Water that is still
gives back a clear image of beard and eyebrows; reposing in
the water level, it offers a measure to the great carpenter.
And if water in stillness possess such clarity, how much more must
pure spirit. The sage's mind in stillness is the mirror of
heaven and earth the glass of ten thousand things."*
—THE ZHUANGZI

*"He did not move. He was still as the rocks themselves.
Stillness spread out from him, like rings from a stone dropped
in water. His silence became not absence of speech, but a
thing in itself, like the silence of the desert."*
—URSULA LE GUIN

Image 13: A personal photograph of a banyan tree on Old Cutler Road in Miami, Florida

As the banyan tree matures, its roots spread deep into the earth. Daoism seeks to cultivate deep roots into nature. The condition that facilitates this rooting is stillness, which is both a state of mind and an action. "Men do not mirror themselves in running water—they mirror themselves in still water."[9(p35)] When our minds are lodged in duality and abstraction, our minds may become opaque; this opacity is clarified by stillness. Stillness does not mean stagnation, just as a plant may appear still, yet be growing, moving imperceptibly. When the mind is still, the world within grows and gathers, pure and connected. We re-cognize the present anew. The Latin root for recognize is *re* which means "again" and *cognoscere* which means "to know," directly meaning "to know again." We engage with what is known, but this time, outside of biases. Clarity gives way to the spontaneous expression of nature's process. Therefore, nothingness nourishes *Potency*. We tune our minds through stillness and harmoniously attune to the rhythms of nature. Stillness allows us to embody *Potency*, as actions become efficacious yet effortless.

Thus, we consider the mind a mirror. A clear mirror reflects all things in the world, whether they are judged as "unpleasant," or "beautiful." "Unpleasant" things do not damage mirrors. A mirror does not cling to the images it reflects. Once something is out of view, no trace of it is left behind. This is not the same as our narrative selves, which may become so easily unsettled by the most minute unpleasant experience. Stillness is a way to clean our mirrors so that not only do we reflect the world as it is, but we allow what is within ourselves to shine forth with clarity. This allows for a pure and seamless connection between the inner and outer world. According to the Neiye, "equanimity" is "the true condition of the mind."[7(p50)] and our "ruling principle is to be tranquil."[7(p58)] When the mind is quiescent, the Dao emerges.

The Liezi[3] emphasizes that in this state, the mind is in a state of spontaneous preparedness: a disposition marked by perspicacity and readiness for what might come. This is further described in verse fifteen of the Daodejing, "the ancients were subtle, mysterious, profound, responsive… Watchful, as though crossing a winter stream. Alert, like people aware of danger."[36(verse 15)] To be perspicacious is to have an immediate insight into things, like a seasoned chess player who already knows, several steps ahead, what may come to be. Belgian surrealist Rene Magritte depicted this perfectly in a painting called *Perspicacity* (*La Clairvoyance*, 1936). In it, the painter is looking at an egg but painting a bird in flight.

Stillness is the center from which a sage operates. It is the first state enveloped and produced by nothingness and the Dao. Only nothingness is irreducible. Within pure life are active principles (i.e., the Dao) that operate with transparency. Sekida[68] identified the aim of Zen to be a state of *samadhi*, which is a complete stillness of conscious activity. He further asserted that stillness of activity eliminates awareness of time, space, and causation. Samadhi dissolves the ego. Although activity is stilled, a wakeful state remains. To be free is to be free of one's own selfish desires and realize that our becoming is continuous with the transformations of the cosmos. This agrees with the work of Zhuangzi.

> I look for the roots of the past, but they extend back and back without end. I search for the termination of the future, but it never stops coming at me. Without end, without stopping, it is the absence of words, which shares the same principle with things themselves.[10(p293)]

In the absence of words is silence, and silence is still. Nature operates through cycles; the sun rises and sets, seasons change, there are good days and bad days, and misfortune may suddenly appear as fortune. The Dao unifies and transcends all opposites, and aligning with it requires the stilling of the mind. An empty mind transcends opposing forces besides the perpetual cycling through emotional seasons. You find your home in an inner sanctuary defined by constancy, detached from the drastic swings of each cycle. From The Huainanzi:

> Therefore those who break through to the way return to clarity and tranquility. Those who look deeply into things end up not acting on them. If you use calmness to nourish your nature, and use quietude to transfix your spirit, then you will enter the heavenly gateway.[13(p19)]

BODY LIKE WITHERED WOOD, MIND LIKE DEAD ASHES: DAOIST MOVING MEDITATION

"My body is in accord with my mind, my mind with my energies, my energies with my spirit, my spirit with nothing. Whenever the minutest existing thing or the faintest sound affects me, whether it is far away beyond the eight Borderlands, or close at hand between my eyebrows and eyelashes, I am bound to know it. However, I do not know whether I perceived it with the seven holes in my head and my four limbs, or knew it through my heart and belly and internal organs. It is simply self-knowledge."

—LIEZI

*"Only then, when I had come to the end of everything
inside me and outside me, my eyes became like my ears,
my ears like my nose, my nose like my mouth;
Everything was the same. My mind concentrated in
my body relaxed, bones and flesh fused completely,
I did not notice what my body leaned against and my feet trod,
I drifted with the wind east or West, like a leaf from a tree
or a dry husk, and never knew whether it was the
wind that rode me or I that rode the wind."*

—LIEZI

In Taiji, one practices "stillness in movement," which refers to complete mental serenity as the body moves fluidly. Maintaining and improving Qi has to do with movement meditations, such as Kung Fu, Qigong, or Taiji. Modern-day Daoist practice is popular for Qigong, Taiji, and Wudang style martial arts. Taking care of the body is critically important among Daoists because it improves the experience of vitality and connectedness. The Neiye specifies that *Potency* does not arise unless our body is aligned, *and* our minds tranquil. Daoism and Western science remind us that the mind isn't confined to the brain; it also encompasses the body and relationships. In this conceptualization, mental health can stem from physical health and vice versa. The body is a "lodging place," a vessel for Nature to express itself. *Body like withered wood, mind like dead ashes* is a Daoist saying from The Zhuangzi, which refers to the optimal condition of the body as supple, with the mind being nonattached to everything that hinders a complete engagement with the flow of nature. One could further elaborate on this, by suggesting the process of transformation through fire: more specifically, the burning away of maladaptive attachments.

Scientists have found that the following practices improve well-being.

Benefits of Qigong

▶ It reduces cravings and withdrawal symptoms in people struggling with substance abuse.[212]

▶ Improves mental and physical health in adults at risk for coronary heart disease.[213]

▶ Reduces stress and increases quality of life.[214]

▶ Improves the self-perception, physical strength, and depressive symptoms of depressed elderly people with chronic diseases.[215]

▶ Increases social support satisfaction and decreases loneliness in socially isolated older adults.[216]

▶ Decreased patients' chronic lower back pain after three months of therapy.[217]

▶ Increases sleep quality and decreases fatigue in patients undergoing chemotherapy for non-Hodgkin's lymphoma.[218]

▶ Some suggest in a study by Liu and colleagues[219] that studying the effects of Qigong practices on adolescents can be an effective therapy modality to enhance psychological well-being, reducing feelings of depression and anxiety.

▶ Improves balance, muscle strength, and flexibility.[220]

▶ In a systematic review, Aman and colleagues[221] investigated the effectiveness of proprioceptive training in improving motor functions. The study found evidence that proprioceptive training can yield meaningful improvements in somatosensory and sensorimotor function.

▶ It may improve focus. Henz and Schollhorn[222] looked at brain activity using EEG to investigate if Qigong had the same effects as mental and physical training. Focusing on the breath, mind, and body is necessary for Qigong. You can learn to better regulate your thoughts by practicing regularly.

▶ May improve well-being equals mood, anxiety, depression, stress management, and quality of life.[223]

Benefits of Taiji and Overall Health

▶ Lowers blood pressure, improves lipid metabolism, and protects the cardiovascular system.[224]

▶ Improves cellular immune functioning by enhancing the protection of lymphocytes and the immunoregulation of cells in older adults.[224]

▶ As an aerobic exercise, it improves cardiopulmonary function and improves symptoms in patients with chronic obstructive pulmonary disease.[224, 225]

▶ Helps reduce the frequency of falls in older adults by improving balance control through the enhancement of static balance, muscular strength, physical agility, and coordination skills.[224, 225]

▶ Promotes psychological well-being in individuals struggling with depression, anxiety, hostility, and delusions.[223, 224]

▶ Daily practice can improve the sleep quality of those with moderate-to-severe sleep disorders and shorten sleep onset latency.[223, 224, 225]

▶ Increases brain volume and improves memory and executive function in older adults.[224]

▶ Improves mood and self-esteem in patients with TBIs.[226]

▶ Decreases the risk of circulatory system diseases, such as hypertension, stroke, coronary heart disease, and chronic heart failure.[225]

▶ Effective in the treatment of musculoskeletal system or connective tissue diseases such as osteoarthritis, fibromyalgia, and chronic low back pain.[225]

▶ Increases balance and motor function in patients with Parkinson's disease.[224, 225]

Brain Region/Function	Impact	Citation
Prefrontal Cortex (PFC)	Improved activation, increased connectivity, enhanced mental control abilities, better cognitive performance	Xie and colleagues (2019)
Motor Cortex (MC)	Improved activation, increased connectivity, enhanced control over movement and coordination	
Occipital Cortex (OC)	Improved activation, increased connectivity, enhanced visual processing abilities	
Whole Brain Network	Enhanced local efficiency, improved information processing, improved cognitive function	Cui and colleagues (2021)
Olfactory Cortex	Enhanced information integration, improved sense of smell and taste	
Thalamus	Enhanced information relay, improved sensory perception and cognitive flexibility	
Precuneus	Improved self-awareness, enhanced memory retrieval and integration	
Cognitive Flexibility	Significantly improved ability to adapt, switch between tasks, and think creatively	
Grey Matter Volume (GMV)	Increased GMV in specific brain regions associated with better memory, emotional processing, and cognitive abilities	
Functional Connectivity (FC)	Increased connectivity between brain regions involved in memory, attention, and cognitive control	
Executive Control Network Connectivity	Improved emotion regulation, enhanced self-awareness, reduced sensitivity to outcomes	Liu and colleagues (2018)
DLPFC-MFG (Middle Frontal Gyrus) Functional Connectivity	Mediated the impact of self-awareness on sensitivity to outcomes	
Fractal Stride Time Dynamics	Associated with better adaptability, resilience, and reduced risk of falls	Gow and colleagues (2017)
Decreased FC between DLPFC and 1. Left superior frontal gyrus/ACC and 2. Left putamen/insula	Improved mental control function (subtest in the Wechsler Memory Scale, WMS)	Tao and colleagues (2017)
Left Thalamus GMV	Enhanced emotional stability, slowed gray matter atrophy, improved meditation level	Liu and colleagues (2019)
Left Hippocampus GMV	Improved emotional stability, reduced risk-taking tendency, slowed gray matter atrophy	

Table 9: Benefits of Taiji on Brain Structure and Function

PRINCIPLE VI

SPONTANEITY

Nature's expression is immediate and spontaneous. It does not mull over ideas before following through; otherwise, our experience of life would not be fluid, instead filled with gaps, moments of non-creation, followed by partial creations and full creations with no order. Its process is continuously in motion, with all of existence forming and becoming with constant rhythm. We exist within this dynamic process, part and parcel of this experiential flow. The fact that the collective intelligence of humanity could not understand the nature of reality implies that nature is far more complex than our intelligence can grasp. Allowing nature to guide us means trusting the spontaneous signals that our intuition provides us. Nature's language is spontaneous, immediate, experiential, and non-verbal. Intuitive insight and experiences come from a place beyond conscious awareness. Science can be helpful in steering us toward the right contexts for trusting its signals.

To be spontaneous does not mean to simply express any urge and indulge every desire. That would be impulsivity. Impulsivity neglects complexity and context, whereas spontaneity considers them. Spontaneity is wisdom, a direct expression of your innermost nature. It is favored in Daoism because it relates to activity naturally arising from the experience of the "great unity," not the self.

Spontaneity as a principle of being means to be engaged with the world playfully. In play, our most natural self comes out as we allow our most genuine responses to emerge unhindered. It is to aspire toward the synchronization of our intuition and our actions in the outside world. A misconception of Daoism is that Daoists shun effort. In fact, in many cases, effort is required, particularly toward practices that may facilitate an attunement to nature. This is because we have become misaligned with nature. To increase one's ability to be effortless and spontaneous is something to aim for, but active involvement is required to get there.

When spontaneity is a guiding principle, focus on the present moment and trust your salience network (your internal "director") in natural settings—to attend the world with lightness so that you can engage others as an outpouring of nature, which may lead to the generation of novelty.

Spontaneity as a principle of doing relates to the actual cultivation of practices to move and express oneself with complete freedom. In scientific terms, learning begins as effortful, but when something is learned, it becomes automated as information becomes merged into implicit systems. Thus, "The wise student hears of the [D]ao and practices it diligently"[36 (verse 41)] or From The Huainanzi: "Those who penetrate through to the way...regulate the genuine response of their natures, cultivate the techniques of the mind, nourish these with harmony, take hold of these through suitability."[90 (p257–258)] Making sure the body remains healthy is significant. Enhancing our vitality, mobility, strength, and flexibility allows us to more fully express our potentials, and keep our minds from ruminating about physical discomfort, which may prevent us from being present.

Hunter-gatherers adapt flexibly to the presenting conditions of the environment and the pressures. In their free time, you might find them engaged in storytelling, dance, or music. Spontaneity also is born in the present, and so we would likely find a more spontaneous way of engaging in dialogue with others. As we'll discuss, they are also far more active in their physical lives than we are. Movement brings a host of benefits and continues on into their sixties and seventies. From an evolutionary perspective, what this means is that we evolved to be athletic and without surprise, when we are, our health and experience are enriched, and when we are not, the opposite is true.

Under the principle of spontaneity, we encounter play and movement, those vibrant expressions of life's unbidden joy. Play releases us from the constraints of rigid purpose, allowing creativity to flourish, while movement reflects the vitality of existence, a reminder that life is a dance best lived in the freedom of the present moment.

XV

PLAY

"My childhood play took me to extremes, and all of them,
I now understand, were a fun way to test the social realities
into which one is born. Surely this is a most important
evolutionary function of play—finding out what is
fun and fair or not fair on the field of life."
—JAAK PANKSEPP

"The creation of something new is not accomplished by the intellect
but by the play instinct acting from inner necessity."
—C.G. JUNG

A playful attitude lies at the heart of The Zhuangzi. This is clear in many of his humorous stories and responses. He was ahead of his time for integrating play into his teachings. The following is a great example.

Once, when Zhuangzi was fishing in the Pu river, the king of Chu sent two officials to go and announce to him: "I would like to trouble you with the administration of my realm." Zhuangzi held on to the fishing pole and, without turning his head, said, "I have heard that there is a sacred tortoise in Chu that has been dead for three thousand years. The king keeps it wrapped in cloth and boxed, and stores it in the ancestral temple. Now would this tortoise rather be dead and have its bones left behind and honored? Or would it rather be alive and dragging its tail in the mud?" "It would rather be alive and dragging its tail in the mud," said the two officials. Zhuangzi said "Go away! I'll drag my tail in the mud!"[10(p137)]

In this passage, Zhuangzi playfully dismantles desires that others would typically find quite appealing, knowing well that his freedom to live would be at risk in such a scenario. The idea of the tortoise being wrapped may also allude to living in a restrained way. In play, humans transcend ordinary concerns, birthing a more authentic mode of existence. Play reflects states of *wuwei*, as the individual becomes more spontaneous, creative, and relaxed. Inauthentic states of being often emerge when we feel threatened or feel the need for social comparison.

One major finding in science is that mild-to-moderate levels of stress or eustress are conducive to growth and learning. What people tend to forget is that stress is essentially neutral. Stress is active in threat and excitement. Eustress refers to the activation of the sympathetic system toward goals that are not considered overwhelming, whereby the individual believes himself/herself to have sufficient resources to handle them.[233] Eustress, however, can be present in learning under traditional environments and ones that are playful.

Another major finding indicates that our primary emotional systems are dedicated play.[94] One purpose of play is to practice real-world applications in a safe space. In groups, we may develop a variety of skills (e.g., social, technical) besides the generation and awareness of one's role in social hierarchies. During play, cultural norms and knowledge from friends or playmates are shared. Play may also promote bonds and reveal mate compatibility. From an evolutionary perspective, play can help us learn and grow. During play, individuals experience flow and intrinsic motivation, and both experience positive and negative effects. Negative emotions like frustration can occur when the player makes an error; however, this can be seen as a sign that they are sufficiently invested in the learning process and are building a healthy balance between enjoyment and challenge. Research has revealed an intimate relationship between emotion and cognition, with emotions substantially influencing perception, attention, learning, memory, reasoning, and problem solving. A fMRI comparison between a game- and non-game-based numerical learning task yielded some differentiable neural activation patterns.[*]

Children develop important communication skills through play; as adolescents and beyond, they will continue to work on communication through academic writing and acquiring second languages. One popular implementation of play in academic writing is genre manipulation and experimentation. For example, a high school student can become familiar with Shakespeare by creating their own modern script. A university student learning citation systems can experiment with forming their own citation rules and comparing them to MLA. By allowing students to bend formal conventions in a safe environment, they can express and explore their unique strengths and identities. Although play is a specific activity, playfulness is an attitude that appears to involve several categories: humor and laughter, cultivating relationships, creativity, and mastery orientation. Playfulness helps to reframe situations to be more entertaining, interesting, and/or stimulating, such as by focusing on motivation and enjoyment. This is especially important for academic writers and second language learners who can encounter tediousness, overwhelming difficulty, and/or boredom.[235, 236]

As adults, some forms of play remain the same, whereas others evolve. Sports and games endure as important routes for bonding. The ideal ratio of dominance to submissive dynamics in humans is 60/40 in play.[94] Exceed this ratio and the losing players will be less likely to engage in continual play. For learning and growth, play remains to be an important avenue. This may include reading a new book, learning a new skill, or picking up a new hobby. It is quite obvious that when somebody is interested and intrinsically motivated to learn something new in a safe setting, they will probably excel more rapidly than if they were remanded to. Moreover, qualitatively, it is quite common to find increased engagement in classrooms when a professor is humorous. Humor enhances memory recall and reduces the chronic release of cortisol, which can harm learning and memory processes.[237] While purposeful practice and the eustress involved with hard work and dedication is beneficial, it is also completely supported by science to include "purposeless" play as a way to enhance learning.

THEORY, SCIENCE, AND PRACTICE

Wandering in Nature

"And into the forest I go, to lose my mind and find my soul."
—JOHN MUIR

Image 14: Photograph of a trek I undertook with a friend in Bhutan.

Daoism emphasizes the blurring of lines between inner and outer worlds; therefore, one's environment significantly impacts their internal state. Hinton[15] emphasized that Daoist artist-intellectuals would wander nature's rivers and mountains with the belief that these landscapes were the greatest embodiment of the Dao. Indeed, imposing human technology onto that which is natural is construed as being relatively distant from the Way.

> What we call "heaven" is pure and untainted. Unadorned and plain, it has never begun to be tainted with impurities. What we call "human" is biased… Thus, that the ox treads on cloven hooves and grows horns and that the horse has a mane and square hooves, this is heavenly [i.e., natural]. Yet to put a bit in a horse's mouth and to put a ring through an ox nose, this is human. Those who comply with Heaven roam with The Way. Those who follow the human interact with the mundane.[10(p19)]

Here I consider the research regarding benefits of hiking and being immersed in nature for the practice now known as "Shinrin Yoku" or *"forest bathing"* in Japan. Any hiking enthusiast would agree that one feels refreshed or even reborn after hiking a beautiful trail. There is something about being immersed in all that is natural without interference from human effort that renews one's experience of the world. This is also not "woo woo"; there is objective evidence. Walking in nature has been found to be correlated with a variety of benefits (see Table 10).

Suggested Benefits	Associated Measures	Sources
Reduced feelings of fatigue	+ Subjective values and decreased oxygenated hemoglobin (oxy-Hb)	Imamura and colleagues (2022)
Therapeutic effect on chronic heart failure (CHF) patients	+ Decrease of oxidative stress levels + Decreased inflammatory activation (oxidative stress hypothesis)	Mao and colleagues (2012)
Therapeutic effect on hypertension	+ Blood pressure indicators + Cardiovascular disease-related pathological factors	Mao and colleagues (2012)
Improved parameters related to cardiovascular and metabolic disorders	+ Increased score for vigor + Decreased scores for depression, anxiety, fatigue, and confusion + Decreased urinary adrenaline + Greater adiponectin	Li and colleagues (2016)
Treating inflammatory diseases	+ Biogenic volatile organic compounds: 23 terpenes and terpenoids emitted in forested areas of the Northern Hemisphere display anti-inflammatory activities.	Kim and colleagues (2020)
Enhancing heart rate and blood pressure functions	+ Pulse rate, systolic and diastolic blood pressure were significantly lower. + Negative mood subscale scores of "tension-anxiety", "anger-hostility", "fatigue-inertia", "depression-dejection", and "confusion-bewilderment" were significantly lower. + Positive mood subscale score of "vigor-activity" was higher.	C. P. Yu and colleagues (2017)
Improvement for individuals experiencing depressive tendencies	+ Decrease in systolic blood pressure and diastolic blood pressure + Decrease in negative profile of mood state (poms) items	Furuyashiki and colleagues (2019)
Boost immunity and health protection	+ B-costol and sesquirosefuran, organic compounds emitted by the common lily peace plant, Spathiphyllum, related to potential antiviral and anti-COVID properties	Roviello and colleagues (2021) Peterfalvi and colleagues (2021)
Increased sleep efficiency for postmeno-pausal women experiencing insomnia	+ Significant reduction of cortisol + Polysomnography findings related to sleep efficiency (e.g., latency to sleep onset)	H. Kim and colleagues (2020)

Table 10: Benefits of Forest Bathing

Another interesting phenomenon is the overview effect, which was first noted when astronauts attained their first glimpse of Earth in space. Many have reported intense experiences of awe that led to feelings of deep connectedness to the environment and humanity. Importantly, this attitudinal shift has also led many to become proactive in caring for our precious world.

Image 15: A view of Earth from space

Art

Expressing creativity is another way of cultivating Shen. Hinton[15] also stressed that Daoist intellectuals would also engage in poetry and painting in the hopes of realizing the Dao more rapidly. The idea that art expresses emotions and experiences that cannot be expressed in words is well-known to most people. Whether the work of art is through poetry, prose, painting, music, or dance, it can contain a greater expression of the ineffable than words. Art therapy, which is often neglected or seen as an auxiliary form of treatment, may be beneficial to individuals with mental illnesses (see Table 11).

Suggested Benefits	Associated Measures	Sources
Improved visuospatial skills, visual exploration strategies, and motor function in patients with mild-to-moderate Parkinson's disease	• Navon Test and Rey-Osterrieth Complex Figure Test: The Navon Test assesses resource allocation during processing of visual information with neural correlates that include extrastriate visual areas. • Extended recruitment of anatomic and functional networks that support contrast coding, depth perception, visual transience, organization of 3-D texture, spatial reasoning, and other functions.	Cucca and colleagues (2021)
Improved prereflective perceptual processes for participants diagnosed with schizophrenia	• Reports of a sense of relaxation and a sensorimotor engagement with the art materials • Excerpts from the participants' life stories became woven into the artwork images, directly in images, or by association at the interviews.	Mitchell and Meehan (2022)
Patients with Alzheimer's disease: increased quality of life, reduction of behavioral symptoms of dementia, and positive effects on cognitive functions	• Decreased disengagement • Executive functioning, language access, and comprehension • Social interest, engagement, and pleasure Measured by • Greater Cincinnati Chapter Well-Being Observation Tool	Savazzi and colleagues (2020)
For stroke patients, creative art therapy combined with conventional physical therapy can significantly decrease depression, improve physical functions, and increase quality of life compared with physical therapy alone.	• Improved assessment measures on cognition, physical functions, and quality of life and reduced anxiety and depression	Kongkasuwan and colleagues (2016)
Increased self-esteem and social functioning	• Behavioral activation • Self-efficacy • Social connectedness • Individual and group identity	Rastogi and Kempf (2022) Vaartio-Rajalin and colleagues (2021)
Reduction of anxiety and stress	• Statistically significant lowering of cortisol levels • Participants' written responses: art-making session was relaxing, enjoyable, helpful for learning about new aspects of self, initial struggle to later resolution, and about flow/losing themselves in the work. • Significant decreases in anxiety symptoms	Kaimal and colleagues (2016) Beerse and colleagues (2019)

Suggested Benefits	Associated Measures	Sources
Decrease psychosocial stress	• Increases in positive affect, creative agency, and self-efficacy • Decreases in negative affect, anxiety, perceived stress, and burnout Using assessment tools • Creative Self-Efficacy and Identity • General Self-Efficacy Scale • Positive and Negative Affect Schedule • Perceived Stress Scale	Kaimal and colleagues (2019)

Table 11: Benefits of Art Therapy

Image 16: One of my patient's drawings, partly a metaphor signifying the ongoing construction of his self and the efforts required in doing so.

Endnotes

* [1] Stronger activation of the anterior insula in the game version may reflect interactions with the amygdala by integrating the emotional experience with the learning process. More pronounced activation of the hippocampus also may reflect interactions with the amygdala through mediating encoding of salient stimuli. Interestingly, increased activation of the frontal medial cortex (fMC) was found in the non-game version despite the brain area's implicated role in emotional and stimulus-reward processing. This may be explained by a need for a stronger fMC response to compensate for the absence of intrinsic motivational states. Importantly, extrinsic motivation, such as the teacher's approval, may prioritize avoidance of failure over learning, whereas intrinsic motivational states associated with play, such as improving skills, may incorporate one's mistakes into improved learning.[234]

XVI

MOVEMENT

"In governing the self, it is best to nurture the spirit.
The next best is to nurture the body."
—THE HUAINANZI

Spontaneity is characterized by vitality and movement of body and mind. In Daoism, one of the major goals is to be full of life, to feel vitalized and vigorous. The etymology of vigor comes from the Latin *vigere*, meaning "to be lively." Ultimately, by aligning with nature, one experiences vigor, a form of *Potency*. This is clear in The Zhuangzi: "the highest happiness, keeping alive—only inaction gets you close to this!"[10(p140)] People find this in states of *wuwei* or in modern-day flow. In this context, you find meaning through what brings vitality to your everyday life. It is not so much something that can be imposed upon your existence. Rather, it is discovered, similar to the assertions of Viktor Frankl. As I argued in my previous book,[19] this may include the feeling of being *moved* through self-transcendent experiences (STEs), which include a psychophysiological response. STEs may include admiration, inspiration, awe, and moral elevation.

Inner movements and outer movements overlap, yet they are also different from one another. Physical exercise, for example, has varying degrees and types of benefits to our inner lives. Much of this depends on the type of exercise engaged in. Exercise, meditation, and sleep are still by far the best ways to enhance cognition and boost mood. Regarding exercise, many benefits have been identified.

Summary	Reference
Exercise is associated with: • Increased cerebral blood flow • Increased oxygen to cerebral tissue • Increased gray matter volume in hippocampal and frontal regions • Increased Brain Derived Neurotrophic Factor (BDNF) • Increased self-control, sexual satisfaction, emotional stability, assertiveness, and confidence • Improved learning, memory, attention, and executive processes • In children, higher academic achievement, verbal, perceptual, and arithmetic tests • In the elderly, reduced neurodegeneration and cognitive decline • Decreases in symptoms of anxiety, depression, hostility, tension, headaches • Preventative for addictive and unhealthy behaviors	Mandolesi et al. (2018)
Aerobic exercise • Improved executive functioning • Improved attention • Improved spatial and episodic memory • Improved processing speed (with high intensity) • Increased frontal + prefrontal cortex (PFC), anterior hippocampus, and hippocampal volume • Increased BDNF Weightlifting • Improved short-term and long-term memory • Improved executive functioning • Improved selective attention and conflict resolution • Increased IGF-1 > enhanced cognition • Together = global improvements in cognition Yoga • Improved working memory • Improved attention • Improved inhibitory control • Greater volume in left hippocampus and PFC • Increased efficiency in DLPFC	Mandolesi et al. (2018) Netz (2019) Dunsky et al. (2017) Brunner et al. (2017) Gothe et al. (2018)

Table 12: Benefits of Exercise

Findings such as these support the idea of embodied cognition, meaning cognition is not just in the brain but influenced by the body. A meta-analysis[260] encountered that cardiovascular exercise overall triggers mechanisms within our neurobiological system that boost memory processing. If you were to have two three-minute bouts of intense treadmill running prior to engaging in an associative vocabulary task, your concentration of neurochemicals involved in your consolidation of memory would increase. If you were to perform six minutes of moderate to intense cycling immediately after looking at twenty photographs, you could recall more information about those photos than without performing the exercise. This finding was also noted in individuals with mild cognitive impairment.

Over a twelve-month period of continued cardiovascular exercise, your brain will increase in volume in the hippocampal area, an area associated with improvement in visuo-spatial memory. What this means practically is if you are trying to learn information more effectively, engaging in cardio-based exercises right after studying. It takes time for information learned to be processed in your brain. Exercise provides this break, while increasing blood flow and releasing many neurochemicals helpful to this process, besides improving your sleep (which is crucial for memory consolidation).

Of particular interest to us are the benefits that can be derived from exercises that mimic the rhythm of hunter-gatherers. For instance, high-intensity interval training (HIIT), which requires individuals to alternate between low-intensity and high-intensity movement (e.g., twenty-second sprint, sixty-second walk, repeat 8x), has been shown to improve executive functioning (e.g., cognitive control and working memory) in children[261] and improve cognitive flexibility in older adults.[262] These are interesting findings because children may have more difficulties with inhibition and working memory because of a frontal lobe that is not yet developed. These abilities are quite important for optimizing their functioning in this age range. As for older adults, these functions have matured, and the challenge is the automaticity of thought patterns, which may prevent them from experiencing the world differently. While it may be helpful in predictable circumstances (e.g., when a heuristic is beneficial), cognitive flexibility may allow for novelty in unpredictable circumstances, enabling greater problem solving, well-being, and adaptation. The cross-talk between exercise and cognition continues to be examined with great excitement. There are studies[263] suggesting how strength training leads to the highest probability of reducing the rate of cognitive decline in individuals who have dementia.

Cognitive functioning is only one branch of psychological life. Another frontier is mood. Cardiovascular exercise is more beneficial for reducing depression and anxiety when compared to strength training, and even more so when there is a lack of involvement in either cardio or strength. Importantly, the highest outcomes were found when cardio and strength training were both involved.[264] If you had to choose just one, and you are experiencing symptoms of depression, it may be more beneficial for you to engage in cardio-based exercises over strength training. It is interesting how and why distinct exercises may affect specific functions and experiences.

Yoga, as another example, with its flow of postures and sustained positions, may lead to increases regulatory ability of practitioners over the sympathetic system (e.g., fight/flight), and HPA axis (e.g., endocrine system). Besides cognition, it can decrease symptoms of depression and anxiety.[265] Thus, preliminary evidence suggests that, in time, findings in science may suggest specific exercises for specific cognitive deficits, or conditions, but for now, more research is needed. We know that movement improves human functioning on multiple dimensions of existence. Movement is evolutionarily beneficial, and as a result, reinforced in the aforementioned improvements.

It is unnatural for humans to remain sedentary for long periods of time. People who sit for long periods of time have a significantly higher mortality rate. Even minor adjustments in posture may yield some fascinating results. In one study, researchers found that standing subjects improved their speed of processing and cognitive control compared to sitting subjects.[266] Standing up generates a sense of alertness and arousal in comparison to seated positions. Another study[267] found that upright positions led to higher self-esteem, positive mood, and less fear. There is also a correlation between increased processing speed and attention with positive moods.[268] The ideal sit-to-stand ratio ranges between 1-1 to 3-1, suggesting per hour of sitting, you should stand one to three hours. On a related note, different postures may also yield different creative abilities. One study found that open upright postures may lead to significant improvements in creative thinking compared to closed postures.[269] Certainly, all these studies teach us that the body impacts the brain, but the alteration of body posture and movement may only make certain thoughts and experiences possible. It is for this reason that science is advancing toward the idea of embodied cognition.

When examining the Hadza hunter-gatherer community, one study[270] found that movement (tracked through a number of steps) followed an inverted U pattern depending on age and sex. Importantly, in this H-G community, the primary work for males is hunting and harvesting wild honey, while females gather foods, such as plants. In this context, between the ages of thirty to forty-five, males walked on average fourteen km, and females walked eight km a day. Males peaked at thirty-two years old, averaging fifteen km a day, and females between seventeen and twenty years old peaked at nine km a day. The average steps ranging from the ages of eighteen to seventy-five, Hadza males walked on average 18,434 steps (approximately 14 km/8.7 miles), and females 10,291 steps (approximately 7 km, 4.2 miles) per day. Importantly, many Hadza males and females between sixty and seventy years old continue to exercise and move at such distances. In our WEIRD society, the average for males is

5,332 and females 4,064 steps. The contrast is stark, and our society has no shortage of health difficulties. One must wonder how rates might decrease if we matched our activity level to that which we evolved for.

Practice

Recast in scientific terms, to say we strayed from nature is to say we have strayed from a species' typical environment and development. The following table provides guidance as to general changes in life that can help shift you toward species-typical conditions without abandoning civilization. For a more personalized approach, explore the lifestyles of hunter-gatherer groups that lived in regions near your ancestral origins.

	Species Atypical	Species Typical
Parenting	Two working parents without help, sleep-training (e.g., "cry it out," Ferber Method), pure formula feeding early on (unless absolutely necessary), reduced responsiveness to foster "independence," rigid routines (disrespecting child's biological rhythms and training them to fit parents' needs), "helicopter parenting."	Alloparenting, safe co-sleeping, breastfeeding, lots of warm physical contact, flexible routines (based on their biological rhythms), "free-range parenting." (For more specifics, vist evolvednest.org, and the work of Mckenna, J. Safe Infant Sleep)
Movement per day	• 5,332 steps per male • 4,064 steps per female	Avg. 18–75 y/o • 18,434 steps (Hadza estimatesfor male) • 10,291 steps (Hadza estimates for female) • Other estimates: 8–12 km (4.9–7.45 miles) a day
Exercise	Sendentary - Low	Exercise: interval training, lots of walking, climb, crawl, carry, HIIT
Culture	• Individualistic • Isolation, self-absorbed • Competition over coopera-tion	• Collectivistic, emphasis on community, focused on others, respecting oneself. • Cooperation over competition
Diet	• Ultra-processed foods, added sugar, nonorganic, GMO, factory-farmed, grain-fed meat with antibiotics	• Whole natural foods, naturally occurring sugar (e.g., fruits and honey), organic, non-GMO, free range, grass fed, fermented foods. • Can incorporate intermittent fasting
Consumption	Mindset: Excess • Eco/human/animal-un-friendly products	Mindset: Sufficiency • Eco, human/animal-friendly products Check goodonyou.eco
Environmental Relationship	• Isolated in concrete jungle, fearful of nature • Out of sync with natural cycles	• Frequently visiting the natural world • Attuned to natural light cycles, wake up with sun, get sunlight exposure first thing in the morning (10 min.)
Technology and real-world balance	• Technological reliance, prioritize self-image/virtual image over face-face interactions	• Less technological reliance, prioritize face-face interactions and real-world skills
Sleep	• Sleeping less than six hours a day	• Six to eight hours of sleep (three hours after sunset, wake up just before sunrise or during). • Possibly segmented sleep, if that suits you (with brief naps midday).

	Daoism considers the body part of the mind, and, although it wasn't discussed, it also emphasizes the importance of diet. To be a force of nature is to be a force *for* nature. One of the best things we can do for ourselves, as expressions of nature, is to fully nuture our potential. There are many creative ways we can enhance our health. More suggestions: • Allocate time for social engagement, introspection, and play • Engage in novel activities to enrich and improve brain functioning • Make sure you are on a healthy diet Daoist-influenced suggestions: • Meditation • Taiji • Qi-Gong • Participate in the Arts • Nature walks, hikes, forest bathing

Table 13: Modern lifestyle vs. Hunter-Gatherer Adapted Lifestyle

TRANSFORMATION

Movement implies change, and change leads to transformation. Transformation is the realization of a creative aim. Change involves tempo; changes that are too rapid may become chaotic, and changes that are too slow may become rigid. Once a creative idea matures fully, it endures in a more stabilized rhythmic becoming: transformation. This process of transformation informs nature's equilibrium that changes may or may not be necessary. Transformation occurs at many levels; we all experience a transformation of consciousness every time we are dreaming. Sometimes, we undergo a complete transformation, such as in death.

The inner principle of transformation is about embracing and being proactive about ongoing changes. It means to be very clear about recognizing what is out of our control, and in our control, and fully embracing it. If you must let go of something you cherish, you grieve it, yet you may also look forward to what letting go of it might bring you. You consent to, accept, and even facilitate these changes.

Transformation of attention is about incorporating new ways of attending to oneself, others, and the world. To accept incoming changes that we may experience as undesirable, we need to discover new ways of attending the experience. William James introduced the idea that governing the foundations of our experience is what we pay attention to and how we pay attention to it. Mcgilchrist[45] builds on this by asserting we can consider attention a moral act. The way we focus our attention shapes our reality and affects how we interact with others and the world around us. Since we can only focus on so much at once, we should be careful and deliberate about where we direct our attention.

Transformation on the outside is simply to commit to the changes and embody the actions necessary for the transformation to occur. It may involve strategy or planning, so long as they are not working against the principles of nature. There is a reason the Daodejing contains chapters on governing strategies and even war.

Hunter-gatherers do not remain stagnant. They transform with the selective pressures of their environment and neighboring cultures.[271] As an example, Central African hunter-gatherers, having had direct contact with Bantu farmers, developed an inter-relationship whereby musical instruments, tools, and vocabulary co-evolved. To survive, transforming practices are necessary, and as generations pass generations, so does culture evolve in tandem.

At last, we arrive at the principle of transformation, which is found in cultivation and what I call Neurodaonamics. Cultivation speaks to the deliberate tending of our inner potential, a practice that requires patience and care. This chapter reveals the phases of growth we might encounter in one traditional path of cultivation—meditation, as you embark on this journey.

Neurodaonamics, a term of my own creation, captures the ceaseless interplay of alignment and misalignment with the seven principles that shape our lives. This concept serves as a lens where we can explore how these principles manifest, how we might embody them, and the pitfalls to be mindful of along the way. Whether used in the therapeutic space or for personal growth, this chapter sheds light on the continuous rhythm of transformation—not as a singular event, but as an unfolding process, drawing us ever closer to the great mystery of life.

XVII

CULTIVATION

"Genuine, like a piece of uncarved wood,
Open and broad, like a valley, Merged and undifferentiated,
like muddy water. Who can make muddy water gradually
clear through tranquility? Who can make the still
gradually come to life through activity?"
—LAOZI

"People say to me so often, 'Jane, how can you be so peaceful...'
I always answer that it is the peace of
the forest that I carry inside."
—JANE GOODALL

Nature is a process; there is no terminal point to the unfolding of its creative advance. As Zhuangzi's philosophy emphasizes, one of life's constants is "the transformation of things" (物化, wuhua). Similarly, in our lives, we are constantly pending in the illusion of fulfillment. In meditation, it is best not to have any goals. To harbor expectations may derail the process. While scientific investigations and Daoist writings have detailed many benefits, the actual practice is central, with these other details being peripheral. If you are sitting, can you just sit? If you are walking, can you just walk?

In this context, there are those who have provided us with maps, yet even these maps are just that—maps. They are re-presentations of individual journeys within their mind. Maps may change just as everything in the world does. So, I urge you to focus on the process, not the results. We know the results exist, but it is the actual process that matters.

The earliest documentation of meditation stages in Daoism comes from a twelve-sided jade knob dated circa 380 BCE, and a jade sword hilt dated circa 400 BCE. The inscription notes:

> To circulate the vital breath: breathe deeply, then it will collect. When it is collected, it will expand. When it expands, it will descend. When it descends, it will become stable. When it is stable, it will be regular. When it is regular, it will sprout. When it sprouts, it will grow. When it grows, it will recede. When it recedes, it will become heavenly. The dynamism of heaven is revealed in the ascending; The dynamism of earth is revealed in the descending. Follow this and you will live; oppose it and you will die.[2(p29)]

As seen from the passage above, the inscription tracks the development of breath meditation that begins as an effortful activity to one that becomes effortless and natural. The balance of heaven or nature, and earth or humanity are captured in the inhalation and exhalation. Overall, Roth described three core stages that appear in early Daoist texts related to meditation. In the first stage, which he termed a preamble preparatory stage, he described *apophatic practices* including the dissipation of "perception, thought, desires and feelings."[*2(p297)] The second is labeled as Sorites: consecutive stages of meditation, involves a series of stages describing what is experienced with advancement. Finally, the third stage, called Denouement, describes the practical and mental benefits of attaining these stages.

A table examining several texts can be found i1 Roth.[2(p313)] The passage of interest resides in Chapter 23 of The Zhuangzi entitled

Gengsang Chu. Here I will describe these stages from Brook Ziporyn's translation.[9(p191–192)]

We begin with the preamble, which includes practices that completely disempower four categories that are further elaborated into twenty-four descriptors:

1. "Retract the wills raging arousal," which includes rank, wealth, prominence, prestige, fame, and advantage;
2. "Untie the mind's entanglements," which includes "appearances, actions, sexual beauty, conceptual coherence, emotional energies, and intentions";
3. "Undo the constraints on the intrinsic powers," which includes "dislikes, desires, joy, anger, sorrow and happiness";
4. "Pierce through the blockages of *the course*," which includes "avoidance, approaching, taking, giving, understanding and ability."

As one continues to practice, they move through four stages becoming: (a) aligned, (b) still, (c) clear, and (d) empty. The benefit of this is that the individual "is able to 'do nothing, and yet leaving nothing undone.'"[9(p192)] What this final phrase refers to is the idea that once one has reached emptiness, they will spontaneously engage in the appropriate action at the appropriate time and place. There is no need for effortful action guided by the self. Since the self has become empty; it is as if there is no one there acting.

A more comprehensive trajectory of transformation is noted in the Daoist horse taming pictures, which, admittedly, was created after the four core classical texts being used in this book; however, it still emphasized quietist-based practices, which correspond well with classical Daoism. These pictures are equivalent to the Ch'an Buddhist's ox-herding pictures. The Daoist horse-taming pictures contain thirteen illustrations, with the first ten centered on horse-taming and the final three not being equine-centered. Each of these illustrations is accompanied by poetic verses by Gao Daokuan (1195–1277). Roughly speaking, the wild horse can be understood as NETS (i.e., narratives, emotions, thoughts, and sensations) within the self. The following are the ten images equine-centered images. A detailed analysis and the complete set of thirteen can be found in Louis Komjathy's[14] *Taming the Wild Horse*. I provide my own summaries described in the list below.

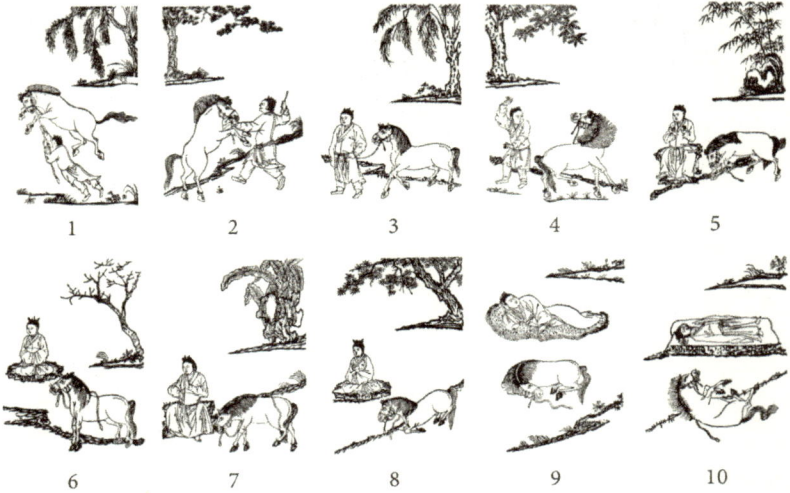

Image 17: Taming the Wild Horse series: From *Shàngshèng xiūzhēn sānyào* 上乘修眞三要 (Three Essentials for Cultivating Perfection According to the Highest Vehicle; DZ 267; ZH 1037). Courtesy of Dr. Louis Komjathy (Center for Daoist Studies)

1. *Untrained:* The horse is wild and chaotic. It drags you with its movements. Discipline is required.
2. *Training begins:* The horse revolts in resistance when its freedom to be reckless is challenged. You are holding the lead

closer to its face. Mild discipline is insufficient, and one must continue training one's mind with double the effort to reduce excessive thinking and conditioned behaviors. With time, the mind becomes more settled.

3. *Restrained:* Although you still hold the lead, it is loosened. The horse now gains more trust because it may sense you have good intentions. Meditation practice no longer requires as much effort as it did in the first two phases. The horse cannot be trusted without the lead, but it tends to follow your lead, meaning thoughts are still chaotic and potentially unstable, but with continued dedication and practice, the mind can settle more quickly.

4. *Training continues:* You are no longer holding on to the lead although it is still there, hanging. You are dancing and the horse follows you. You are adept at catching primal chaotic expressions and calming yourself. There is a joy in the deepening of this relationship, and as clarity and stillness increase, problematic conditioned behaviors are released.

5. *Trained:* You are seated with your hands up in a gesture of noninterference. At this point, there is observation with no clinging to appearances. Having internalized practices, you are free of conditioned responses and reactivity and do not need to continue observing in an effortful way. Fully trained, the horse rests and is "on call." You have dominion over your cognitive faculties, and you can use them when you please, as well as tune out when unnecessary. You are more attuned to your true nature and joyful.

6. *Unhindered:* You are seated in meditation as the horse stands. You are sincerely committed to the practice, and your experience is being carefree.

7. *At leisure (I):* You are playing the lute seated as the horse stands beside you with a lowered head. You now rest in the state of freedom and independence. You are completely joyful in solitude, and engaged in activities that are in harmony with

your being. You may forget about mundane concerns and even your existence. Time becomes of no importance as you abide in emptiness. Thoughts that are chaotic, disruptive, unpredictable, erratic, conditioned, and undisciplined are all silenced and settled in stillness. There is no effort in observation and no discipline necessary for practice. There is an expansion and a connection to the deep patterns of nature (Li). Cultivation becomes self-directed.

8. *At leisure (II):* You are seated as the horse rests. You are completely carefree and open to the process of becoming. There is a deep enjoyment of nature and the living world, with a sense of increased harmony. You also have the experiential awareness that there are, without a doubt, others who share your aspirations and path. This may reflect a resonance with the writings of others who previously only led to intellectual understanding, with some possible skepticism, but now have an emotional and experiential quality.

9. *Resting together:* You and the horse are lying down, resting together. Clear of thoughts, and agitation completely stilled, the mind is in a deep state of serenity. The horse is asleep, having complete trust in you, as if you were another horse. There is a mutual realization of true nature. There is but meditative absorption. The body is so still that it is like withered wood, as if nobody were home. No longer clinging, thoughts take on the quality of dead ashes. There is the dissolving of any boundaries and a spontaneous joy in this silence and connection to the world.

10. *United in forgetfulness:* You and the horse are lying on your backs, asleep, appearing dead. Language itself has disappeared as you unite with pure life. You have become boundless, experiencing all of existence within. There is pure consciousness, stillness, and peace. The Dao is realized within oneself and others, and all distinctions disappear. You are

preparing to become an "immortal being" (my interpretation: you lose the idea of death as you identify with the grander process of nature itself).

11. *Abiding in suchness:* There is a Daoist priest in this illustration. Thus, both the horse and the person are absent, in oblivion. Identity is fully released and the habitual mind completely still. There is a complete harmonization of the inner and outer world: a complete deconditioning. You exist in a nondual and nonconceptual space.

12. *Dharma body of clarity and purity:* This illustration depicts a child in meditation pose with a third eye on his forehead, conveying complete illumination and realization. The child is a symbol for a complete return to purity and simplicity: a return to the Dao.

13. A poem does not accompany the thirteenth illustration and only illustrates a Daoist elder in flowing robes. One has all the attributes of illustration twelve, in addition to living in formlessness, and there is not even a hint of a personal identity lingering. This reflects the complete emergence of original nature beyond space and time. One lives in oneness, the Dao. The individual becomes immortal (i.e., complete identification with nature itself, so there is no death, only transformation).

Thus, a chaotic, conditioned, agitated mind transitions through several phases as it is continually stilled. Eventually, it reaches complete equilibrium and identification with natural being. Meditation is one way of developing a deeper relationship with nature.

Reflection & Practice

These stages of meditation express that gaining inner freedom is a process.

Can you trust the science and the descriptions of others who have achieved a greater capacity for inner peace through these practices?

Can you relate to any of these phases?

What phase might you locate yourself in?

Remember, everyone starts with the first illustration. Can you be patient with yourself?

Can you enjoy where you are in the process?

Endnotes

* In the context of meditation, *apophatic practices* refer to a continual negation of imposed mental activity.

XVIII

THE NEURODAONAMIC APPROACH

"In fact the art of life is first to be alive,
secondly to be alive in a satisfactory way, and
thirdly to acquire an increase in satisfaction."
—ALFRED N. WHITEHEAD

The word *neurodaonamic* is a play on the words neuro, Dao, and dynamic. Given the substantial neuropsychological evidence supporting these principles, I have incorporated "neuro" into the concept. It is a neuropsychologically informed approach. Dao is, of course, "the Way," and in this book, a reference to the seven principles that emerged through dialogue between science and classical Daoism. Dynamic refers to movement and change, as well as the mechanics concerned with the interaction of different forces. The forces we are interested in are the forces of nature as they present within us and around us. There are two simple questions the neurodaonamic approach is interested in: (1) How are you misaligned with nature? And (2) How do you recover *Potency* (de,德)?* This term delineates an approach to transforming your life so that it is in alignment with the seven principles of nature.

While this may interest those interested in peak performance or self-actualization, it will also impact those with more challenging psychological difficulties. Instead of viewing oneself through a pathological lens with diagnoses and disorders, I offer you an alternative viewpoint (i.e., you are simply misaligned with nature).

How can we apply principles in a more pragmatic way? In this chapter, I *first* provide an abridged definition of each principle; *second*, I follow with typical ways people may become misaligned as captured by a *deficiency* on one end, *excess* on the other, with nature's principle centered in between; and third, I provide a "clinical" bin, where I note what diagnoses or symptoms might apply in the clinical world. A deeper clinical exposition of this method will have to be conducted independently of this work. At the end, I provide a single conceptualization from the perspective of trauma.

The number of situations where these principles may be applied are *ad infinitum*, and just like a fractal pattern, they apply to bio-psycho-socio-spiritual domains interdependently. If you are a therapist, this approach is not meant to replace any formal approach but may serve as an adjunctive model to conceptualize and assist others with self-actualizing. If you are not in the profession, this section is helpful in condensing some of these chapters and what they mean.

CREATIVITY

"There is a pleasure in the thought that the particular
tone of my mind at this moment may be new in the Universe;
that the emotions of this hour may be peculiar & unexampled
in the whole eternity of moral being. I lead a new life.
I occupy new ground...untenanted before."
—RALPH WALDO EMERSON

Creativity in nature appears through the very act of creation. It is the generator of diversity. The principle of creativity connects all things; it is not confined to the arts. Every moment humans live can be considered a creative act. As we are continually becoming someone new, every decision becomes the precursor to being an increasingly defined person.

In humans, creativity is a multifaceted and layered process, whereby novel and valuable ideas, solutions, or creations arise. In this work, we explore creativity of being, attending, and doing. We begin by incorporating practices in our everyday life that facilitate a connection with no-thingness (i.e., the fertile expanse, or playground of potential and possibility). A mind that is clear and still becomes serene. This is when we inhabit the *uncarved wood*. With this disposition, we harbor an intentional attitude of uncertainty, as we accept change as a necessity for balance and being open to the guidance of nature. This is the creativity of being. Attentional creativity is the flexibility each of us has in our ability to attend to the world and ourselves. To this effect, attention has been discussed as a moral action[45] as how we attend to things changes our natures and the nature of what we attend to. Our modern world is filled with distractions and deceptions. What do you choose to attend to? Finally, creativity of doing is the expression of nature's creative impulse and its interaction with the world.

Deficiency—Stagnation

Stagnation results from *clinging* and being *closed* with rigid *certainty* (three c's). What are we clinging to: our past, future, belongings, sensations, images, feelings, or thoughts? What are we closed to? Potential and possibilities? What are we certain of? Our narrative selves may prevent us from change.

Psychologically, we can be seduced by safety and familiarity, but it is ultimately a failure to adapt, grow, and consider the insight that can be drawn from each unfolding moment. Let's imagine an individual who loses their physical ability to engage in what they previously took great pleasure in. Resistance to change, clinging to the old self, closing off to possibilities, and rigid narratives oftentimes lead to increased depression, loss of sense of self-worth, disbelief, anger, and frustration. And while all this is typical of a grieving process, our progress does not depend on friction.

A person's value is depreciated only when they identify with their old self and are unwilling to let go of that image. Another perspective is that a new path is set with select boundaries for which the individual must now work with. It may highlight strengths that were unknown to the individual. There are countless cases in rehabilitation, where new strengths are given the opportunity to come to the forefront and new meaning is forged in the moment.

Another case to highlight this principle is the example of an individual with an addiction. Addictive cycles take effort, time, and money to maintain. It is logical that when an interfering addiction is subverted, energy, time, and financial expenditure are reclaimed. Hands, exhausted by clinging onto a frail line, are now available for use. New creative endeavors to replace them are to be expected if the habit is successfully transcended and energy is successfully diverted. A person may develop an increase in complexity, as pleasure and goals are no longer restricted to a single substance. Therefore, at its root, misaligning with creativity occurs through *clinging*, whether to a past identity, desires, objects, or habits. The narcissists cling to self-image to protect themselves from an inner fragility. The psychopath may cling to power. Someone with borderline pathology clings to fears of abandonment, and the list goes on. Clinging holds us back from movement, while simultaneously sapping a person's energy. It results in a mismatch between the mind of the individual and the ever-flowing current of the creative advance. Treatment would be geared toward "dislodging" the individual from their stagnation.

Related symptoms/diagnoses: Grandiosity, Narcissism, Borderline Pathology, ASPD, OCD, Paranoia, Addictions.

Excess—Instability

We are aware of many cases where disruptions in the mind can lead to instability. Nature's creative advance becomes creative instability. Such examples include those who become overwhelmed or inundated by nature's activities. This may come in the form of artists who are inundated by ideas accompanied by the necessity to produce them but cannot realistically do so. When a gift is simultaneously a curse, instability will invariably ensue.

From a clinical perspective, we may identify psychotic symptoms, drastic changes in emotion, rapid mood swings, and other erratic behaviors relating to uncontrollable compulsions as resting on this spectrum. "Neurodivergence" has always and will always be a part of nature's expression.

Related symptoms/diagnoses: Schizophrenia, Schizoaffective, Bipolar, Borderline, OCD, Autism Spectrum, DID.

PROCESS

"The process of creation is the form
of unity of the universe."
—ALFRED N. WHITEHEAD

"There are no fixtures in nature.
The universe is fluid and volatile."
—RALPH W. EMERSON

The process of nature is dynamic, present, ever flowing, and continuously integrating. To be aligned is to be attuned to its movements through intuition, open to its presence within us, and to flow with it like a coordinated dance.

Deficiency—Hyperopia

Here we find somebody with hyperopia or farsightedness. The individual can see in the distance, but things become blurry up close. This is, of course, a psychological metaphor for individuals who cannot be in the present and attuned to the process of nature as it unfolds. This is someone who may be overly *rational, narrative focused, and distracted (RND)*. To begin with, I follow Mcgilchrist's[45] idea of rational, which differs from reasonable. To be rational is abstract, decontextualized, and mechanistic thinking, whereas to be reasonable is thinking rooted in relationship, context, and intuition. To be rational does not consider the whole, whereas to be reasonable does. To be narrative focused is to believe only in the stories one tells oneself without openness to other opinions and thoughts. Third, to be distracted is to be unintentionally mind-wandering, obstructing the potential for flow. These disrupt the process because there is an inability to align itself with the fluid, unfolding, and interconnected character of reality. It is simply an echo chamber for the ego.

This individual, separated from the process in their abstract center, focuses on the world as if it is fixed to their beliefs. If someone views the world as transactional, relationships become transactional, and the potential that exists within their relationships is denied. Being is *dimmed*, in Heidegger's words.[272] This individual cannot enjoy the present phase in which they find themselves, as they distribute value unequally to their conception of different phases in life. The process is neglected for the goal (i.e., dopamine orientation), which leads to an everlasting dissatisfaction with minimal periods of joy. Existential guilt may be a prevalent experience for these individuals, as they never seem to meet their potential.

We emphasize the objectification of all life, discriminating, and categorizing all that we see. By doing so, we overshadow the fullness of experience with an observation that only captures a small slice of what is happening. Many of my clients arrive so focused on achieving the next goal that they essentially lose all the time dedicated to the process, and do not appreciate their achievement. The obsession with a particular goal creates "tunnel vision," which limits creativity and sacrifices other possible outcomes.

Our most precious asset is time, and if our minds are busy mulling over repeated goals and wandering aimlessly in possibilities, our experience of time actually contracts[273] and we feel life is passing us by. However, the more our mind wanders, the more likely it is that it will wander to unhappy spaces.[21] How do you recover your experience of time? By being present and engaged with all that experience has to offer. There is a time and a place to be oriented toward meeting a goal and time and place for being oriented toward process. The highest form is their integration, which is found in states of flow. Flow, however, is not always accessible, and outside those moments it's important to know the preferred mode. Let's look at how these two profiles differ.

Process Orientation	Goal Orientation
Exploration	Analysis
Discovery-driven	Solution-driven
Viewing the whole	Parts
Context	Content
Pure reception of experience	Proactive categorization of experience
Becoming	Being
Change	Stasis
Experience	Abstraction
Spontaneous	Effortful
Nature, interconnection	Self, isolation
People as subjects	People as objects
Present-oriented	Past- or future-oriented

Table 14: Process Versus Goal Orientation

To engage life as a process means not to value one point over another, but to treat them equally. Equality for all experiences! This also implies the necessity to be present with all experiences, whether they are "mundane," tragic and/or exciting. For those who have gained mastery over their NETS (i.e., narratives, emotions, thoughts, sensations), mundane activities may be perceived quite differently. If you use your breath as a tether to the present. and reach a state of consciousness that is clear of thoughts, you can lose yourself in the process of washing dishes. This meditative absorption can be quite pleasant and lead to therapeutic effects.

Related symptoms/diagnoses: Grandiosity, Narcissism, Borderline Pathology, ASPD, OCD, Paranoia, PTSD.

Excess—Myopia

Myopia is nearsightedness. Here we have individuals who can see things up close in the present, but cannot see far. They become overly concrete, which is also an issue because it neglects an entire dimension of nature—psychological experience, and the world of ideas. They may use the justification of "going with the flow," when in place there is really a lack of foresight. Seeing further into our perceptual horizon is reflected in the necessity to psychologically peer into probable futures to plan ahead. Planning is not against Daoist thinking, so long as it is resonant with our intuitive expressions. The idea is to sense what feels right and live well, in contrast to pursuing something that is simply pleasurable in the short term but violates what we deeply sense to be aligned with our values.

Related symptoms/diagnoses: ADHD, Impulsivity, Addictions, Anger management, PTSD.

RELATIONSHIP

"The great harmony is the harmony of enduring individualities,
connected in the unity of a background."
—ALFRED N. WHITEHEAD

"We live in succession, in division, in parts, in particles.
Meantime, within man is the soul of the whole;
the wise silence; the universal beauty, to which every part
and particle is equally related; the eternal one."
—RALPH W. EMERSON

The natural world is a vast network of interconnection, a truth that resonates within the deepest intuitions of humankind. The principle of a relationship can be defined as an experiential connectedness to others and the world. It is a switch of dominance from what Martin Buber famously called the I-It relationship to an I-Thou relationship. People are beings where an authentic encounter may blossom (I-Thou), in contrast to an object to be manipulated and exploited for utility or personal gain (I-It). To approach the world through the I-It lens is to diminish the true potential that resides in interaction. Existence is not fixed and mechanical, but alive and pulsing with meaning and possibility. A relationship is about the harmonious integration of similarities and differences. This manifests in the way we are being, attending, and engaging with the world. It is a recognition that the world, in its diversity, does not demand domination or control but instead calls for reverence and respect. When we meet the world in this way, our actions flow not from external rules but from an inner orientation—an alignment with the lived truth that every being, every encounter, has its own intrinsic value.

Deficiency—Isolation

What was meant to be the tool shed (our intellect) became our place of residence. Our NETS lead us to the experience that we are isolated beings imprisoned in our bodies: that we live solely for ourselves. Imagine how silly it would sound if an orange tree selfishly believed it existed for its own survival and flourishing. It is true that we have NETS not directly accessible to others, yet at the same time those NETS have all formed in relationship to our biology and experiences. They may be revealed indirectly through our behaviors. Our narrative self develops NETS, and once the barriers become weakened, a lifestyle closer to the facts becomes more accessible: a lifestyle closer to nature.

Misalignment from the principle of *relationship* is the loss of an *experiential connectedness* to one's *home* (i.e., family, natural world) and *others* (ECHO). This leads to the experience of *isolation*. One precondition of a successful relationship is reciprocity. Without the experience of connectedness, there is only a lack of empathy and an extremely competitive drive for personal success, many times at the expense of others. The constant denial of connection becomes justified in the belief that the world is cruel and everyone is here to fend for themselves. This misalignment may further yield an individual that adapts their beliefs to whatever suits them at the moment. This inconsistency further develops into a life that is conflicted, shallow, and out of touch with reality.

From another perspective, misalignment may occur in depressive conditions. In a depressive episode, the individual's ability to function and relate to the world becomes exceedingly restricted. The disproportionate number of negative cognitions distorts their connection with this principle, and what follows may be acute feelings of isolation. Trapped in desperation and despair, this condition may still lead to an unintentional self-absorbed state, given that depressive narratives continuously interfere with the energy and ability to be truly empathic. A similar story exists with anxiety, whereby circuits related to fight or flight inhibit other networks that allow them to think and feel otherwise. Most conditions can be conceptualized through challenges with relationships, whether with oneself or others (e.g., anxiety, schizophrenia, autism, bipolar, borderline, etc.).

One benefit of recovering the relational orientation is experiences of "oneness." Oneness is a true ground of relational experience that may lead to spontaneous compassion, in contrast to willful compassion for the sake of being a good person. Part of the problem is that although we may strive for the value of compassion, without the ground of experience to support it, we lose the *Potency* of true resolve. Importantly, "oneness" is an experience that presents a background to the perception of multiplicity. It is not that one suddenly perceives the world as an amorphous mess of activity. Paradoxically, oneness teaches us to better respect differences. The following is another rendition of a story from Zhuangzi.

> There was a king who was in awe of a magnificent seabird. He decided to honor it by bringing it to his palace, where the best musicians would play music for it. He put together a regal feast with rare dishes and expensive wine. The seabird responded with confusion, fearful of the music and saddened by being captured. The food and the wine were not delectable to it. It died in three days.[9]

The king followed the rule: treat others as you would treat yourself. Although his intentions were good, his ego impeded his consideration of what the bird might want. He did not respect differences. The rule might be better explained as treat others as they would like to be treated. If the king had been more empathic and experienced a deeper level of connection, he would have respected that each has their own nature, and the best way to honor the other is to honor their nature. Interconnection and separateness are both part of our experience, but interconnection precedes separateness at every level, except our experience of it. To move with nature is to exist in harmony with it, and by extension with other people.

Related symptoms/diagnoses: Depressive symptoms, Feelings of isolation, ADHD, Schizophrenia, Schizotypal, Anxiety, Autism Spectrum, Bipolar disorder, PTSD, etc.

Excess—Loss of Individuality

On the other extreme, there are groups of individuals who seem to solely exist to appease others. While this isn't a traumatic defense, such individuals may treat others as they would like to be treated, but they do not treat others as they would treat themselves. In fact, they fail to treat themselves, and simply conform to the expectations of others. Continual demands upon them lead to exploitation and the loss of a stable identity. In Daoist thought, one honors both individuality and connection to create an ideal balance. While the latter supersedes the former, it does not mean anyone has the right to claim your identity and freedom.

Related symptoms/diagnoses: Burnout, People pleasers, Exploitation, Victims of trauma, Manipulation.

WHOLENESS

"Life, death, preservation, loss, failure, success, poverty, riches,
worthiness, unworthiness, slander, fame, hunger, thirst, cold, heat—
these are alternations of the world…if you can harmonize
and delight in them, master them and never be at a
loss for joy…spring with everything, mingling with all
and creating the moment within your mind—
this is what I call being whole in power."
—THE ZHUANGZI

"Each thing is a half, And suggest another thing
to make it whole…odd, even; in, out; upper, under;
motion, rest; yea, nay. All are needed by each one.
Nothing is fair or good alone;
to empty here, you must condense there."
—RALPH WALDO EMERSON

Wholeness in the universe is not mere unity, but a dynamic interplay of diversity—a deep-seated tendency for disparate elements to weave themselves into a larger, coherent reality. Wholeness embraces opposites and contradictions, drawing them into an expansive totality where each part finds its role, its meaning, in relation to the whole.

Our mind, like the universe, is not just a collection of disconnected parts but a living system in which every aspect (e.g., fears, impulses, aspirations, etc.) finds its place. Mental health is not about the suppression of conflict or the elimination of unpleasant thoughts. It is about integration—about bringing the fragments of our inner life into a cohesive and meaningful whole. The wholeness of the mind mirrors the wholeness of the universe. Just as the cosmos integrates opposites, such as light and darkness, order and chaos, so too does the healthy mind. Wholeness does not eliminate tension but transforms it into a creative force, a source of growth and vitality. A person who embraces wholeness in their inner life becomes, in a sense, a microcosm of the larger universe: dynamic, integrated, and alive with possibility.

Allow your being to embrace the whole, attend to the widest possible range, and express this wholeness in a way that is suitable to the context.

Deficiency—Fragmented

Misalignment from the principle of *wholeness* is to fall prey to narrow and fragmented viewpoints. It is to *fragment* the whole, *exclude* facts, to be *narrow*-minded, to believe in firm *categories*, and to disregard *experience (FENCE)*. Singular perspectives become the perceived truth, preventing the integration of good and bad, and leading to a distorted individual view. This relates to the left-hemisphere interpreter, which is the tendency for the left hemisphere to make up responses with confidence, despite its accuracy. False certainty stagnates learning.

On the level of being, one may reject aspects of oneself and, in Jungian terms, form a shadow that may be internalized as hypercriticality or unjustly projected onto the world and others. Without the experience of wholeness, there lies the feeling of something being left out, incomplete, and disempowered. Unaware, a voice beckons from the bellows, and may even deploy regrettable behaviors of which an individual is not conscious until it is too late.

Many psychological conditions, such as borderline thinking characterized by vacillation between extremes of love and hate, or manic episodes marked by grandiose thoughts, show a lack of wholeness. Notably, many psychotherapeutic interventions involve learning how to regulate emotions to facilitate the ability to adopt different perspectives and integrate them into a greater pattern within the whole.

Related symptoms/diagnoses: Borderline pathology, Spectrum Symptoms, Depression, Anxiety.

Excess—Overgeneralization

Overgeneralization refers to those individuals who see the whole but do not see the parts. The problem with this is that there is an oversimplification of complexities. Overgeneralized statements neglect details that result in false statements. This is a major issue in modern society, especially in the world of politics. How many times have you seen a sweeping statement in the news that, while true, forgoes important details, rendering an incomplete picture? From another perspective, it is interesting to point out that when documentaries are released showcasing the details of particular cases (e.g., serial killers), they often elicit sympathetic responses to acts of extreme violence. These details play major roles in legal cases and sentencing.

From the perspective of psychological health, overgeneralization may cause misdiagnoses, which leads to improper treatment. A child may exhibit many signs of ADHD, but when considering the specific details, we find that the child simply had learning disabilities, and would thus exhibit such signs only in related classes. One cannot make a proper judgment when neglecting the details; wholeness requires both the forest and the trees that make it. Many distortions can arise from doing so: the magnification of one experience while discounting other experiences, thinking in extremes, or judgment of other people based on a single encounter.

Related symptoms/diagnoses: Cognitive Distortions, Heuristics, Defenses, Trauma, etc.

EQUILIBRIUM

"The lover of nature is he whose inward and
outward senses are still truly adjusted to each other;
who has retained the spirit of infancy
even into the era of manhood."
—RALPH WALDO EMERSON

"His single mind reposed, the ten thousand things submit...
emptiness and stillness reach throughout (Nature) and penetrate
the ten thousand things. This is...the mind of the
sage by which he shepherds the world."
—THE ZHUANGZI

Balance is about establishing a dynamic equilibrium. It is tension in a guitar's strings that enables them to resound harmoniously within its wooden frame out into its environment. An ideal zone of asymmetry in balance allows movement to progress in a beneficial way. Become aware of these zones in different domains of your life, attend to the areas that require nurturing, and engage in the appropriate acts that enhance balance.

Deficiency—Turbulence

Misalignment from the principle of equilibrium is reflected in turbulence, which is marked by imbalance and loss of stillness. People forget that for there to be a balance, there is a tension involved, yet this tension brings about stillness, though never the complete absence of movement. There is a dynamic equilibrium. Imbalance occurs when there is an excess or deficiency within distinct domains of existence. Equilibrium is a balance of asymmetry and symmetry in nature, with asymmetry being slightly dominant. Movement and progression require an asymmetrical balance. This asymmetry may manifest as the necessity for potential to be greater than what is realized, or for humans to feel at peace, yet spurred by curiosity to discover the world in all its wonder. A slight tilt in proportion stimulates exploration and growth.

Turbulence refers to individuals who disproportionately invest their time in particular sensations, images, feelings, thoughts, areas of life, or behaviors while disregarding or minimally considering the importance of other domains. Enough so that it offsets the ideal zone of dynamic equilibrium; in diagnostic terms, we might say clinical symptoms that significantly affect one's functioning in work, relationships, play, etc. This disproportion may manifest as unhealthy hedonism (sensations), fantasies (images), acting out rage (feelings), or obsessive thoughts or compulsive behaviors. One of the core illusions one confronts in these scenarios is that of comfort.

As an example, the hedonist (not from an epicurean sense) may defend their excessive pleasurable pursuits, despite their disruptions in other domains of life, because of a pessimistic and nihilistic view of the world. "The world is corrupt," "you only live once," "we are just animals," or "there is no greater meaning to life," may be common arguments. However, this implies a narrative that neglects other viewpoints. Each retort simply highlights the world's preponderance of non-criminals.

If one believes humans generate meaning, and they simultaneously believe humans are part of nature, then nature is generating meaning. Meaning thus becomes part of the underlying fabric of nature (in one view, through humans). From a larger scope, selfish pursuits of desire usually end up impacting others negatively (e.g., deceit, betrayal, exploitation, etc.) if not themselves (e.g., diseases, addiction, obesity, debt, etc.), which typically ends in the hedonist's downfall. The illusion of comfort pervades this type of being in the world. Trapped by their impulses and self-referring thinking, they do not wish to take on the necessary responsibilities required for growth. They *believe* they feel comfortable living out this hollowed existence, and resist evidence to the contrary until their life is in shambles. The fleeting feeling of balance is achieved only once a pleasurable aim has been met. As a result, the outcome of such a life is typically typified as chaotic, imbalanced, and possibly tragic.

From another perspective, loss of balance and stillness may appear as the ease with which feelings are triggered in ways that are inaccurate and maladaptive. When one recoils with anxiety that is not commensurate with a particular situation, one has become undermined by preconceived notions, faulty cognitive appraisals, and one's own imagination. When one makes assumptions that presuppose that one knows the future, one automatically finds oneself in error. Although some level of anxiety may be useful, because it creates homeostatic asymmetry that can promote progression, overwhelming amounts of anxiety that destabilize a system toward regression are not. When abstractions do not conform to the facts, we become imbalanced.

Related symptoms/diagnoses: Emotion or Behavior Dysregulation, Rumination, Mood swings.

Excess—Stasis

In this context, individuals misaligned with equilibrium are challenged by *stasis*. This is characterized by someone who may believe that there is a point in life where all things fall perfectly into order, and that this state can last forever if they only could find and maintain the right conditions. This individual may be excessively risk aversive, and comfortable with the monotony of their lives. By evading opportunities that require some level of risk, this person may then strive to continue maintaining a static and sterile life. They may feel a loss of meaning and feelings of emptiness, albeit with security.

From a macroscopic perspective, we can imagine a "workaholic" who has "no life" outside of their work and feels empty. Yet during their work, they realize they are just distracting themselves from a sense of emptiness. Their inner well-being becomes entirely contingent upon how their work life is progressing. On the other end of the continuum is *Puer aeternus*, or eternal child: in modern-day colloquialism known as a "failure to launch" individual. Such individuals cannot contribute to society in any meaningful way, and although they wish to be treated as grown-ups, they are frequently not, because they may feel threatened by the responsibilities that come with adulthood. These ideas of perfection end up becoming unhealthy and lead to burnout or severe regrets.

Clinically: "Failure to launch," existential dread (loss of meaning, emptiness).

SPONTANEITY

"It is a secret which every intellectual man quickly learns,
that, beyond…intellect, he is capable of a new energy, by
abandonment to the nature of things; that, beside his privacy of
power as an individual man, there is a great public power,
on which he can draw…he is caught up into the life of the universe,
his speech is thunder, his thought is law, and his words are
universally intelligible as the plants and animals."
—RALPH W. EMERSON

"What leaps into conscious attention is a mass of presuppositions
about Reality rather than the intuitions of Reality itself.
It is here that the liability of error arises."
—ALFRED N. WHITEHEAD

Spontaneity is not impulsivity; rather, it is the unpredictable unfolding of possibility with the consideration of context and the bounds of order. It is the dynamic pulse of the universe, forever generating the new while holding together the patterns of the old. Spontaneity reveals our universe as a living process—a field of surprise, emergence, and improvisation.

To be spontaneous is to be playful, lively, and in motion. Spontaneity allows the individual to tap into deeper reserves of potential, bypassing the over-regulated mechanisms of habit and routine to give birth to something new. It is a co-created act in the moment, a signal from nature interacting with a unique mind. Spontaneity is lost when we attend to any other temporal zone other than the present, and to be spontaneous is to have the courage to play out what is birthed in the moment.

Deficiency—Inhibited

Misalignment from the principle of spontaneity is one of the major hurdles for those who are intellectual or anxiety prone. There is an absence of playfulness, vitality, and physical movement (PVP). The prototypical individual operating under this illusion questions almost every decision that is to be made: from simple ones, such as deciding on what shirt to wear, to more complex and demanding tasks, such as what career to pursue. This serious-minded person may be focused on their conscious decision-making, untrusting of their intuitive mind. This tendency results in inefficiency, delayed processing times, and heightened errors in complex situations requiring an immediate response. There is too much energy expenditure on thinking, and thus they may constantly feel tired and might be restricted in physical movement. Such individuals rarely engage in playful behavior, which is a major problem, because play is a necessity for well-being. Wracked by insecurity about what might happen should they be spontaneous, they may keep everybody at arm's length, and as a result have only a few friends. This creates further restrictions in the ability for psychic gratification, generating a level of continuous psychological turmoil.

Related symptoms/diagnoses: Grandiosity, Narcissism, Depression, Borderline Pathology, ASPD, OCD, Paranoia, Anxiety.

Excess—Impulsivity

As mentioned earlier, spontaneity considers the context of particular situations. Impulsivity does not. It is simply acting out whatever ideas are evoked in the moment. The classic picture of someone who is impulsive is somebody who is continually interrupting others, or broadly acting in ways that continually violate social harmony (without reason).

This may be more biologically mediated, such as in individuals who have had a traumatic brain injury or genuine ADHD, but sometimes it can be more psychological, such as with individuals who have anti-social behaviors. In the latter case, they may justify their behaviors by concluding that their actions are simply a reflection of their deepest being, when really it is just a failure to self-regulate in moments of challenge. They may simply not have the insight, skills, or knowledge necessary to hold themselves back from acting out.

Related symptoms/diagnoses: ADHD, TBI, Antisocial, Oppositional-Defiant.

TRANSFORMATION

"With each new mind, a new secret of nature transpires."
—RALPH W. EMERSON

Change is the process that leads to transformation. When you have accepted change, the next step is to fully actualize the potential that lies within it. To do so, we have to first develop insight into the direction in which change is taking us. One way of doing this is to identify the signals. The most natural thing to do is to identify what I call vital signals.[17] Vital signals are physiological signals paired with psychological signals that arise within us when we feel moved. Feeling moved can arise from many sources, such as awe, moral elevation, admiration, and inspiration. Once you are aware of these in your being, you attend to them and cultivate their expression in your life.

Deficiency—Neglect

Misalignment from the principle of transformation refers to the decision not to neglect the person one is becoming. It may be easy to confuse creativity with transformation. However, I view them as sequential. To align with creativity is to open and receive the changes with consent, whereas transformation is to proactively accept and cultivate the new potential available in this transformation. It is reflected in the idea of *amor fati* from Nietzsche and the Stoics: to embrace and love your fate. To clarify a possible misconception, it is important to note that in Daoism much effort precedes effortless action. Wu Wei and/or flow is an aspiration.

Thus, one does not cling; however, one remains passive to the succeeding changes. Here, the individual refuses to seek the lessons and knowledge that can be learned from whatever change they are undergoing. Instead, they nod their heads with passive resignation. The neglecting change may occur as a result of a variety of responses, such as *acquiescing*, or even *regressing* to earlier phases (e.g., two steps forward, one step back) as a result of *evading* responsibilities (ARE).

Excess—Noise

Noise builds on instability. It is the next step, which can lead people who continually "put the cart before the horse." So eager to change, they not only cannot integrate wisdom from their previous experiences but also attempt to embody, put into action upcoming changes unrealistically. What separates instability and chaos is behavioral. While instability is primarily psychological, chaos is the expression of such actions. Somebody practicing mindfulness may suddenly act as if they are a "guru," or expert on the topic, without actually having any experiences that come along with such titles. In a more innocent fashion, someone becomes quickly frustrated by a lack of progression, believing they should be able to master some technique. There is a typical lack of patience, which may impact the determination and persistence required to master a designated skill. A full transformation is not met, as "prerequisites" have yet to be completed. This may lead to dysregulated emotional expressions, passive-aggressive tendencies, anxiety, or general neuroticism. Their actions then simply become noise, as opposed to a harmonious interaction with the parts that form who they are.

Reflection & Practice

These seven principles may serve as an adjunctive approach to psychotherapy. This *neurodaonamic* paradigm is non-pathologizing, because its premise is that some psychological difficulties arise when humans have become misaligned with nature. There is no good or bad, right or wrong, just alignment or misalignment. It may reduce shame and guilt that might be preventing healing. Instead of thinking "I am a bad person," which implies they may feel like they deserve to be punished, the inner dialogue would be, "I have become misaligned. How do I realign?"

The following two tables summarize each principle with its corresponding illusions and excesses.

7 Principles of Nature	Deficiency and some characterizations Mnemonic: SHIFTIN'
Creativity	Stagnation: Closed to possibility, certain of your decisions, and actively cling. Acronym: CCC
Process	Hyperopia: Overly rational, narrative focused, and distracted. Acronym: RND
Relationship	Isolation: Loss of experiential connectedness to one's home (e.g., family, the natural world) and others. Acronym: ECHO
Wholeness	Fragmentation: of the whole, excluding facts, narrow-mindedness, excessive categorization, and general incongruence with experience. Acronym: FENCE
Equilibrium	Turbulence: Resistance toward the responsibilities necessary to achieve higher-order dynamic equilibrium. Results in chaos, unsustainability, resistance, and dysregulation. Acronym: CURD
Spontaneity	Inhibited: Lack of playfulness, vitality, and physical movement. Acronym: PVP
Transformation	Neglect: Acquiesce, regress, or evade life's demands. Acronym: ARE

7 Principles of Nature	Excess and some characterizations Acronym: IM LOSIN'
Creativity	Instability: Overwhelmed by continuous ideas, identification with present ideas, lack of temporal integration
Process	Myopia: Pleasure oriented, disregard for intuitive aspirations, using "go with the flow" as justification for lack of planning and foresight
Relationship	Loss of individuality: "People pleasers," neglecting the self, loss of identity, identity tied to opinions of others.
Wholeness	Overgeneralization: See the whole but not the parts, oversimplification
Equilibrium	Stasis: Risk averse, belief in comfort over growth
Spontaneity	Impulsivity: Decontextualized impulsive actions
Transformation	Noise: Behavioral manifestation of instability: impatience, identification with roles not yet mastered

If you are a mental health practitioner, see how your patients' presenting problems might fit into this approach. If you are not, you may use some of these questions and identified goals to assist with your progress. When you know where the misalignment is, you can determine how alignment might be achieved. Beyond all the recommendations and reflections provided throughout this book, here are some practical ideas when adopting a neurodaonamic approach to life. Keep in mind, these are only a few examples you'll find in this book.

7 Principles of Nature	Questions	Goals
Creativity	• What potentials within you are seeking to express themselves, and why have they been held back? *Or* • How has the creative impulse of nature gone too far? What can be done?	• Identify potentials and the resistance to their expression. • Engage in activities and experiments to help reconnect with the creative advance. • Engage in daily meditation to return to nature. • What can you do to reduce instability? • Adopt a stance of uncertainty. • View change as balance. • View change as opportunity. • Embrace what is to come. • Explore how nothingness may be useful to integrate into your life. • Explore how emptiness has played a negative role in your life.
Process	• What is preventing you from engaging in the present (hyperopia)? • It's pleasurable, but is it costing your potential (myopia)? • Check in with yourself. Is the present the right time for a process orientation or goal orientation? To what end does either serve? • Can you tell the difference between your impulses and intuition? • How about when to best follow intuition over reason? • What activities trigger flow for you? If none, find something!	• Explore what NETS lead to loss of present orientation. • Explore what NETS are preventing the development of potential. • Help determine when process or goal orientation is maximally beneficial. • Distinguish between intuition vs. impulse. • Explore how intuition (MAST) manifests and has been helpful. • Find activities of interest that may lead to flow. • Learn moving meditations. • Adopt Wuwei as a way of life.
Relationship	• Do you have a healthy relationship with yourself? Others? The world? • How would your actions be different if you lived according to the idea "treat others as they would like to be treated"?	• Reestablish or improve connection to yourself, others, and the world. • Heighten empathy and compassion. • Learn how to make space for and respect differences.
Wholeness	• Ask people to reflect on their experience of a particular challenge. Where does it lead to in the present? • Are you accepting of the good and the bad?	• Learn RH and LH modes of experiencing the world. • Learn acceptance-based methods. • Challenge perspectives with alternate and opposing views.

7 Principles of Nature	Questions	Goals
Wholeness cont.	• Are you accepting of paradox? • Can you accept your perspective is limited (fragmentation and overgeneralization)? • Can you adopt a curious attitude vs. one of certainty?	• Distinguish between psychological facts vs. truths. • Integrate the "good" and the "bad."
Equilibrium	• Can you tell the difference between eustress and major stress? • How would you describe your ideal asymmetrical balance? • What changes in you when you adopt the idea that agitation comes from alignment or misalignment from nature? • Is there evidence of stasis or turbulence in your life?	• Help distinguish states of eustress from problematic stress. • Identify perceived imbalances that are due to excess or deficiency. • Reframe good and bad as aligned or misaligned, explore ensuing experiences.
Spontaneity	• Are you playing enough in life? • Are you taking things too seriously? Why? • Are you obsessed with control and too scared to be spontaneous? • Are you impulsive or inhibited? • How much movement is incorporated in your life?	• Figure out how more play may be of benefit. • Identify what prevents playfulness. • Incorporate more movement. • Distinguish between spontaneity and impulsivity.
Transformation	• How can you be proactive about embodying potentials that express themselves through you? Do you neglect them? Or do your behaviors come out like noise?	• Explore concrete methods that can facilitate the expression and embodiment of change.

As a final tool, it may be beneficial to rate yourself on where you currently believe you are by dotting yourself on the spectrum. If you are not in the center, ask yourself what life changes might be necessary to move you closer to one of the principles. I recommend you begin by moving one space or intersection at a time with very specific and concrete goals. If you are a mental health professional, you may use this to help track your patients' progress. Notably, anyone familiar with my previous book, *Reassembling Models of Reality*, may notice this table is quite similar to one I presented there. They both were inspired by the idea of the *golden mean* by Aristotle. The difference is that here I have provided actual principles, whereas the other is about finding what uniquely *moves* you, and that book may be used in tandem with this one. We are connected through these principles, but we also hold individualistic tendencies that bring us to life.

Deficiency	7 Principles of Nature	Excess
Stagnation	Creativity	Instability
Hyperopia	Process	Myopia
Isolation	Relationship	Loss of individuality
Fragmented	Wholeness	Over-generalization
Turbulence	Equilibrium	Stasis
Inhibited	Spontaneity	Impulsive
Neglected	Transformation	Noise

Brief Trauma Conceptualization

Trauma can lead to the misalignment of all principles and affect their functioning on both ends of the spectrum. To begin with, trauma arrests the natural flux of the self's creative unfolding, ushering in a state of *stagnation*. Stagnation may appear as repetitive, dysfunctional relational patterns and an inability to live beyond the defining experience. In captivity, instability may ensue as the mind becomes flooded with intrusive narratives, emotions, thoughts, and sensations (NETS). There is an inability to adapt to changes post-trauma, as the potential for positive outcomes is met with disbelief.

The natural process of becoming and being gets disrupted. The great stream in which personality is ever-forming loses its forward motion. Traumatized individuals vacillate between extremes, teetering into hyperopia in one instant and myopia in the next. Their intuition becomes clouded, a lost medium for truth, as they become seized by repeating narratives continually seeking ways to prevent the trauma from ever happening again. Feelings of being misunderstood and helplessness toward the tides of their inner lives, they may further experience alterations in their capacity for intuitive moral considerations. To recalibrate, some may adopt the mantle of hyperrationality, yet find no solace, only an increasingly divided self with moments of chaotic cognitive and emotional surges.[55] There is no potential for flow, as they are imprisoned in the past, eluded by the present, and fearful of an ominous future. As the horizon narrows, so does the atmosphere thicken with danger.

Traumatized individuals may experience alterations in social cognition.[38] These faculties are warped, as misinterpretations of social interactions accrue. They may also become more *isolated* as they continue to avoid all situations with any semblance of a past wound. Some may have the defense of becoming a "people pleaser," as a hedge against further harm, a method that prevents abusive situations from occurring again. Yet in the act of compliance, there is a loss of individuality, a power ceded to the abuser themselves.

All three neural networks become incoherent, resulting in *fragmentation*.[55] The traumatized person can no longer operate as a *whole*, rather torn between contradictory forces. As a result, their views become biased, careening toward pessimism and protection. They struggle to attune to experience, as their unsettled inner world continues to consume their being. *Overgeneralizations* take root, and details are overlooked, as any behavior that reminds them of the trauma leads to suspicion and the grip of paranoia.

Naturally, all this amounts to *turbulence* as they continue to strive for *equilibrium*. Emotions are rampant, and thoughts are racing, encouraging chaos. In time, their potential becomes limited to very specific behaviors, relationships, and places. Life is lived with an aversion to risk, as risk may potentially lead to another traumatic experience. This leads to *stasis*.

A precondition for *stasis* is being overly *inhibited*. Unable to be *spontaneous,* due to fears of the outcome. On the other hand, because of continual concerns about the future, their hyperarousal may lead to impulsive actions. Such actions may have protected them from trauma, but do not serve them in the present.

Finally, because of an inability to adapt to changing conditions, their potential transformation is neglected. They *acquiesce* to changes, *regress* to earlier stages of development, or *evade* them altogether. Subsequent behaviors simply become *noise*, misattuned to themselves, others, and the principles of nature. Different phases involved with transformation are interrupted, as impatience and fear dictate their reality. Their original nature becomes more deeply hidden, as greater discord ensues.

Endnotes

* Recover comes from the Latin word *recuperare*, meaning to "get again." Given that original nature is always with us, *Potency* awaits for our original nature to be discovered in awareness anew.

CONCLUSION

"If you will stay close to nature, to its simplicity,
to the small things hardly noticeable, those things can
unexpectedly become great and immeasurable."
—RAINER MARIA RILKE

"I would like to beg you dear Sir, as well as I can,
to have patience with everything unresolved in your heart
and to try to love the questions themselves as if they were locked
rooms or books written in a very foreign language.
Don't search for the answers, which could not be given to you now,
because you would not be able to live them. And the point is
to live everything. Live the questions now. Perhaps then,
someday far in the future, you will gradually, without
even noticing it, live your way into the answer."
—RAINER MARIA RILKE

Through these principles, we trace the vast arc of existence: creativity, the engine of novelty, calls forth form, and the principle of process reminds us that life is no fixed state but a perpetual becoming. Relationships root us in the web of connections that make meaning possible, while wholeness gathers and unites the fragments of our experience. Equilibrium steadies the ever-shifting flow, while spontaneity breathes vitality into our days, and transformation, the final rhythm, expresses our deeper attunement with the unfolding mystery of life itself. Aligned with these principles, we embody the *Utmost Potency*. According to The Huainanzi:[13(p274)]

Therefore, the rule of the Perfected Person is like this:

His mind is coextensive with his spirit;

His physical form is in tune with his nature.

When he is still, he embodies *Potency*;

When he acts, he patterns himself on penetration.

He follows his spontaneous nature and aligns himself with inevitable transformations.

In Daoism, pure life unifies, whereas thinking divides. The individual moves through life cycling between filling oneself with knowledge and releasing one's attachment to it. This notion is found in The Huainanzi: "When they are empty, they go; When they are full, they return."[13(p91)] Attunement to the way of Nature requires the mind to be stilled, enabling the individual to join the process of becoming rather than working against it. Consequently, life becomes directed by intuition, not contrivance; expressions become spontaneous, not forceful; the mind becomes flexible, not rigid; and behaviors become effortless, not labored. The approach of Daoism is not to resist human nature, but to accept it and model its evolution toward the grander process from which it comes: nature. The way of nature is not the same as the way of egocentricity. Though our thinking minds are a product of nature, we have evolved to the point of being able to operate against it. To experience the Way, one must become like still water, a metaphor for emptying the mind of internal activity for organicity to emerge. This yields a more objective worldview and freedom from unnecessary distractions.

Refining the mind so it aligns with nature takes time, but there are activities that may be of benefit. The following is a final list of recommendations one might engage in to help facilitate the process. Sarris, Manincore, Hargraves, and Tsonis[274] had the clever idea of reviewing the literature as it relates to the four elements (fire, water, earth, air). Many of their findings will be summarized here, alongside support from other research articles.

Nature-Attuned Activities in Modern Day

▶ Exposure to nature (earth) may enhance overall health because studies have indicated that increased urbanization and industrialization negatively affect health.[274]

▶ Engaging in horticulture (earth) has been shown to enhance mental health and well-being. It has been specifically shown to reduce cortisol levels and depressed mood and improve quality of life.[274]

▶ Sauna use (fire), or "sauna bathing," involves short-term exposure to high temperatures from 113° to 212° F. There is a strong correlation between sauna use and reduced mortality and morbidity. Sauna use has also been found to have cardiovascular, neurological, and metabolic benefits.[274, 275, 276]

▶ Exercising outdoors (earth, air) is associated with increased energy and flow experience, as well as decreased "tension, confusion, anger, and depression."[274(p3)] For example, activities such as hiking and running may be beneficial.

▶ Forest bathing (earth, air) involves spending time in forests and has been shown to enhance "mental health while altering physiological stress and immune biomarkers."[274 (p3)]

▶ Light exposure (fire) influences our health, well-being, and performance. Light therapy helps treat circadian rhythm sleep disorders and depression.[277, 274]

- ▶ Direct bright light or sun exposure (fire) in the morning affects our circadian rhythm, which has been shown to improve sleep quality and promote more advanced sleep onset.[277, 278]
- ▶ Avoiding light exposure at night helps prevent shifts in our circadian rhythm. Light exposure at night results in the delay of melatonin onset, which is associated with increased mortality rates, mood disturbances, health issues, and poor performance.[277, 278]
- ▶ Improving sleep hygiene is beneficial in alleviating symptoms of mental health disorders, regardless of their severity, and even in the presence of comorbid health conditions.[279]
- ▶ Breathing-focused biofeedback techniques (air) have been shown to reduce anxiety and perceived stress through the modulation of the amygdala and hippocampus, the areas of the brain affecting stress and memory.[274]
- ▶ Reducing one's screen time and increasing regular exercise has been found to lower the risk of "depression, anxiety, low self-esteem, and life dissatisfaction."[280(p2)]
- ▶ Daily meditation decreases negative mood and anxiety and increases attention, working memory, and recognition memory. Short daily meditation practices can provide similar health benefits as long-duration and higher-intensity practices.[281]
- ▶ Exercise has been shown to improve neuroplasticity by triggering the processes in which neurotrophins affect energy metabolism. Brain-derived neurotrophic factor (BDNF) is the most susceptible neurotrophin to be regulated by exercise.[282, 283]

To be attuned to the Dao is to be lodged in its home, nothingness. Within nothingness is *primordial chaos.* An unstructured, undifferentiated formless state of possibilities before creation. From the Dao, an all-encompassing principle that organizes and directs the development of life, there arose the state of the uncarved wood, an individual's raw potential, or original nature. To be in Dao is to exist in the fertile expanse where time stands still. Time loses meaning because primary identity shifts into alignment with the timeless principle. Distance in space loses its felt degrees of separation because of deep interconnectivity in its undifferentiated formless state. Death loses significance because it is perceived and experienced as another transformation of the Dao. Anxiety from change dissipates, as it is simply seen as part of Dao's process of equilibrium. The intolerance of uncertainty fades, as it gives way to the adventure of potential and possibility. It is, in essence, alongside chance, the requirement for freedom. The Dao is self-generating, meaning it is root and branch. It is complete fulfillment, so temptations surrender their grasp to Dao's quiescence. In a sense, to be with Dao is to favor loss over gain.

Patterns from the whole are recognized in patterns within yourself. If you are struggling to tune your mind and attune to the flow of nature, learn from observations in nature. Novel ways of being begin with effort, and know that science supports the fact that effortful activity eventually becomes effortless. Cultivate your mind and body so that it becomes the ideal "conduit." To embody the formless principles of nature, you must pierce through the shallow activity of the mind and open to the intuitive signals and movements arising from pure life.

To flow with the dynamic patterns of nature, bow to the creative dynamics of nature, engage directly with its process, attune to the underlying relationships, accept the wholeness of its presentation, equilibrate to its movements, express its signals with spontaneity, and help cultivate its transformations. Allow your mind to become a presence that nurtures nature's potential, rather than a tool to carve out artificialities.

Clinging will surrender to the present, and you will seamlessly integrate with the whole. The world of experience is continually co-created and gathered within us. Dynamic and connected, we become part and parcel of the process. Following nature's way, we cultivate *Potency,* and the self becomes whole, balanced, and harmonious. We become adaptive, yet genuine; spontaneous, yet attuned; integrated, yet distinct; simple, yet complex; balanced, yet dynamic; playful yet wise; and savage, yet virtuous.

I'll end with a poem I wrote.

CALL TO NON-ACTION

My original nature houses inexhaustible potential,
yet my heart-mind pulsates with a signature rhythm.
Dissolve their borders,
and revel in Potency!

Nothingness is timeless, being endures, having distracts.
Nothingness is boundless, being integrates, having weakens.
Find your abode in nothingness, nurture your being, and have with sense!
Find serenity through stillness and clarity.

Direct encounters with reality are what I seek
so that I may truly live.
Financial security, safety, and good health
are the limits of having.
Loving relationships, joy in play, and meaning in activities
are the prizes of being.
Flourishing
is the nature of nothingness.

Possessing, demanding, expecting,
compulsions, jealousy, and entitlement—
all specters of having.
Clinging, the root of stagnation.

To integrate rage, fear, lust, and panic
is to move with shadows, empowered and energized with direction.
To act from rage, fear, lust, and panic
is to identify with shadows, disempowered, restless and fragmented with angst.

Slice through the mirage of rage and find the ruby within!
Pierce through the façade of fear and find the topaz within!
Slash through the deception of lust and find the emerald within!
Parry the blow of panic and find the sapphire within!
Seek sanctuary in the uncarved wood.
Discover vitality and adventure in uncertainty
and merge with the unending process of creativity and transformation!

ACKNOWLEDGMENTS

In preparation for this book, I read several versions of the Daodejing and Zhuangzi, each of which I found to be valuable in its own way. For the Daodejing, my preferred scholarly translations were by Wing-Tsit Chan and D.C. Lau, and the layman's translation by Gia-Fu Feng and Jane English. For The Zhuangzi, I prefer Burton Watson, A.C. Graham, and Brook Ziporyn's versions. I also found great inspiration from books by other authors, such as Deng Ming-Dao, Ray Grigg, Harold Roth, Livia Kohn, Eva Wong, David Chai, and David Hinton.

I have also consulted with Deng Ming-Dao,* Larson Di Fiori, Ph.D.,† Ray Grigg,‡ and Livia Kohn, Ph.D.,§ all of whom I would like to thank for furthering my knowledge of Daoism to ensure accurate interpretation and understanding from a variety of angles: traditional, scholarly, and independent.

In addition, I joined Livia Kohn's Dao Explorer lecture series, and kindly accepted an invitation from Larson to join Brown University's Virtual Contemplative Mentors in Residence program (both of which I highly recommend!). I have been practicing meditation for more than a decade with special interests in Daoism and Zen, and I host meditation groups in my practice. In addition, I have publications related to mindfulness, and worked closely with Dr. Dan Siegel, internationally acclaimed author, educator, and founding co-director of the Mindful Awareness Research Center (MARC) at UCLA. Finally, I practice Qi Gong and Taijiquan under the direction of Sam Wuest, a certified teacher of Daoist Gate Internal Arts who has studied Longmen Daoism formally under Zhou Xuan Yun and Lindsey Wei. He is a licensed acupuncturist and a teacher of Taiji, Qigong, and Traditional Chinese Medicine. I would like to extend my gratitude to him as he was also gracious enough to review this work to provide additional support and certify accuracy.

I am moved to extend my heartfelt gratitude to my students—Jason Ouyang, Kristina Nguyen, Ryan Karasik, and Aaliyah Jones—at the Center for Neuropsychology and Consciousness, whose diligent efforts with feedback, tables, and the pursuit of relevant literature have been of inestimable value. My esteemed colleagues, Terry Marks-Tarlow and Darcia Narvaez, have my sincerest thanks for their remarkable insights, and my dear friend, Josh Bermudez, for his discerning contributions to the refinement of the first five chapters. Finally, to my beloved wife, Jessica Shraybman, I owe a profound debt for her editorial care and the wisdom of her counsel throughout the writing of this book.

Endnotes

* Deng Ming-Dao is a well-known Daoist author and practitioner. He was a student of Kwan Saihung, a Daoist monk who was raised and educated on Huashan and an initiate of the Zhengyi Sect.

† Larson Di Fiori, Ph.D., is a visiting Assistant Professor at Brown University. He is the associate DUS of Contemplative Studies. He holds a master's in Chinese Studies from the University of Oxford and a Doctorate in Religious Studies from Brown University, with his primary concentration in Daoism and Classical Chinese Religion/Philosophy.

‡ Ray Grigg is a popular Daoist and Zen author; he is an independent practitioner.

§ Livia Kohn, Ph.D., is an Emeritus Professor of Religion and East Asian Studies at Boston University. She is a prolific Daoist Scholar, author, and practitioner.

REFERENCES

1. Diamond, J. (2012). The world until yesterday, what we can learn from traditional societies. Penguin Books.

2. Roth, H. D. (2021). *The contemplative foundations of classical Daoism.* State University of New York Press.

3. Lieh-Tzu. (1995). *Lieh-Tzu: A Taoist guide to practical living.* (E. Wong, Trans.). Shambhala. (Original work published ca. 400 BCE).

4. Lao Tzu. (1963). *The way of Lao Tzu (Tao-Te Ching).* (W.T. Chan, Trans.). Bobbs-Merrill Comp. (Original work published ca. 400 BCE).

5. Lao Tzu. (1963). *Tao Te Ching* (D.C. Lau, Trans.). Penguin Classics. (Original work published ca. 400 BCE).

6. *Sima, Qian, approximately 145 B.C., approximately 86 B.C. (1993). Records of the grand historian. Qin dynasty. Research Centre for Translation, Chinese University of Hong Kong. Renditions-Columbia University Press.*

7. Neiye. (1999). *Original Tao, Inward training (Nei-yeh) and the foundations of Taoist mysticism.* (H. D., Roth Trans.) Columbia University Press. (Original work published ca. 350 BCE).

8. Kohn, L. (2014). *Zhuangzi: Text and context.* Three Pines Press.

9. Zhuangzi. (2020). *Zhuangzi: The complete writings* (English ed., B. Ziporyn, Trans.). Columbia University Press. (Original work published ca. 369-286 BCE).

10. Zhuangzi. (2013). *The complete works of Zhuangzi* (B. Watson, Trans.). Columbia University Press. (Original work published ca. 369-286 BCE).

11. Zhuangzi. (2001). *Chuang-Tzu: The inner chapters* (A. C. Graham, Trans.). Hackett Publishing Company. (Original work published ca. 369-286 BCE).

12. Wong, E. (2011). *Taoism: An Essential Guide.* Shambhala.

13. Liu, A. (2010). *The Huainanzi (Translations from the Asian Classics)* (J. S. Major, S. Queen, A. Meyer, H. D. Roth, Eds. & Trans.). Columbia University Press. (Original work published ca. 200 B.C.E.).

14. Komjathy, L. (2017). *Taming the wild horse: An annotated translation and study of the Daoist horse taming pictures.* Columbia University Press.

15. Hinton, D. (2020). *China Root: Taoism, Ch'an, and Original Zen.* Shambhala.

16. Grigg, R. (1994). *The Tao of Zen.* Tuttle Publishing.

17. Grigg, R. (2021). *The Zen Tzu.* Xlibris US.

18. Marks, T. (2008). Psyche's veil: Psychotherapy, fractals and complexity. Routledge.

19. Chan, A. (2021). *Reassembling models of reality: Theory and clinical practice.* W. W. Norton & Company.

20. Hu, S. (2015). Hu Shi: Biological evolutionism and Zhuangzi (J. Liu. Trans.). In J. Liu (Ed.), *Zhuangzi and Modern Chinese Literature* (pp. 46–58). Oxford University Press. (Original work published ca. 1944–1945) https://doi.org/10.1093/acprof:oso/9780190238155.003.0003.

21. Filotas, E., Parrott, L., Burton, P. J., Chazdon, R. L., Coates, K. D., Coll, L., Haeussler, S., Martin, K., Nocentini, S., Puettmann, K. J., Putz, F. E., Simard, S. W., & Messier, C. (2014). Viewing forests through the lens of Complex Systems Science. *Ecosphere, 5*(1). https://doi.org/10.1890/es13-00182.1

22. Siegel, D. J. (2020). *The developing mind: How relationships and the brain interact to shape who we are.* Guilford Press.

23. Morais, L. H., Schreiber, H. L., & Mazmanian, S. K. (2021). The gut microbiota-brain axis in behaviour and brain disorders. *Nature Reviews Microbiology, 19*(4), 241–255. https://doi.org/10.1038/s41579-020-00460-0.

24. Shaik, L., Kashyap, R., Thotamgari, S. R., Singh, R., & Khanna, S. (2020). Gut-brain axis and its neuro-psychiatric effects: A narrative review. *Cureus, 12*(10), e11131. https://doi.org/10.7759/cureus.11131.

25. Palmer, C. (2022). *Brain energy: A revolutionary breakthrough in understanding mental health and improving treatment for anxiety, depression, OCD, PTSD and more.* BenBella Books, Inc.

26. Doan, T., Ha, V., Strazdins, L., Le, Q., Nguyen, T., Nguyen, Q., Nguyen, K., Broom, D., Stocks, N., Glover, J., Tran, B., & Nguyen, H. (2022). Healthy minds live in healthy bodies—effect of physical health on mental health: Evidence from Australian longitudinal data. *Current Psychology, 42*, (18702–18713). https://doi.org/10.1007/s12144-022-03053-7.

27. Cozolino, L. (2014). *The neuroscience of human relationships: Attachment and the developing social brain* (2nd ed.). W. W. Norton & Co.

28. Kim-Spoon, J., Herd, T., Brieant, A., Peviani, K., Deater-Deckard, K., Lauharatanahirun, N., Lee, J., & King-Casas, B. (2021). Maltreatment and brain development: The effects of abuse and neglect on longitudinal trajectories of neural activation during risk processing and cognitive control. *Developmental Cognitive Neuroscience, 56*. https://doi.org/10.1016/j.dcn.2021.100939.

29. Smail, M. A., Smith, B. L., Nawreen, N., & Herman, J. P. (2020). Differential impact of stress and environmental enrichment on corticolimbic circuits. *Pharmacology, Biochemistry, and Behavior, 197*, 172993. https://doi.org/10.1016/j.pbb.2020.172993.

30. Walker, W. H., Walton, J. C., DeVries, A. C., & Nelson, R. J. (2020). Circadian rhythm disruption and mental health. *Translational Psychiatry, 10*(1), 28. https://doi.org/10.1038/s41398-020-0694-0.

31. Goldberger, A. L. (2006). Giles F. Filley lecture. Complex systems. *Proceedings of the American Thoracic Society, 3*(6), 467–471. https://doi.org/10.1513/pats.200603-028ms.

32. Marks-Tarlow, T., Shapiro, Y., Wolf, K. P., & Friedman, H. (2020). *A fractal epistemology for a scientific psychology: Bridging the personal with the transpersonal.* Cambridge Scholars.

33. The Science of Psychotherapy. (2022, January 5). *Terry Marks-Tarlow, fractals and psychotherapy.* [Video]. YouTube. https://youtu.be/i54JJR2t1Lo.

34. Carney, J. (2020). Thinking avant la lettre: A review of 4E cognition. *Evolutionary Studies in Imaginative Culture, 4*(1), 77–90. https://doi.org/10.26613/esic/4.1.172.

35. Kohn, L. (1989). *Taoist meditation and longevity techniques. center for Chinese studies.* The University of Michigan.

36. Lao Tzu. (1971). *Tao Te Ching (English and Chinese edition)* (G.-F. Feng & J. English, Trans.). Vintage Books. (Original work published ca. 400 BCE).

37. Swann, N. C., Tandon, N., Pieters, T. A., & Aron, A. R. (2013). Intracranial electroencephalography reveals different temporal profiles for dorsal-and ventro-lateral prefrontal cortex in preparing to stop action. *Cerebral Cortex, 23*(10), 2479–2488. https://doi.org/10.1093/cercor/bhs245.

38. Chan, A. et. al. (2024). Trauma and the default mode network: Review and exploratory study. *Frontiers in Behavioural Neuroscience, 18.* https://doi.org/10.3389/fnbeh.2024.1499408.

39. Killingsworth, M. A., & Gilbert, D. T. (2010). A wandering mind is an unhappy mind. *Science, 330*(6006), 932-932. https://doi.org/10.1126/science.1192439.

40. Chan, A., & Siegel, D. J. (2018). Play and the default mode network: Interpersonal neurobiology, self, and creativity. In T. Marks-Tarlow, M. Solomon, & D. J. Siegel (Eds.), *Play and Creativity in Psychotherapy* (pp. 39–63). W. W. Norton & Company.

41. Girardeau, J. C., Sperduti, M., Blondé, P., & Piolino, P. (2022). Where Is My Mind…? The Link between Mind Wandering and Prospective Memory. *Brain Sciences, 12*(9), 1139. https://doi.org/10.3390/brainsci12091139.

42. Schimmelpfennig, J., Topczewski, J., Zajkowski, W., & Jankowiak-Siuda, K. (2023). The role of the salience network in cognitive and affective deficits. *Frontiers in Human Neuroscience, 17*, 1133367. https://doi.org/10.3389/fnhum.2023.1133367.

43. Northoff, G. (2022). Spatiotemporal Psychopathology—a novel approach to brain and symptoms. *Archives of Neuropsychiatry*, 59, S3–S9.

44. Chan, A., Northoff, G., Karasik, R., Ouyang, J., & Williams, K. (2022). Flights and perchings of the BrainMind: A temporospatial approach to psychotherapy. In P. B. Stapleton, O. Baumann, & D. Church (Eds.), *The future of psychology: Approaches to enhance therapeutic outcomes*. Frontiers Media S.A. https://doi.org/doi: 10.3389/978-2-83251-265-4.

45. McGilchrist, I. (2009). *The master and his emissary: The divided brain and the making of the Western world*. Yale University Press.

46. Burger, J. R., & Fristoe, T. S. (2018). Hunter-gatherer populations inform modern ecology. *Proceedings of the National Academy of Sciences*, *115*(6), 1137–1139. https://doi.org/10.1073/pnas.1721726115.

47. Beerman, M., & Sieben, A. (2023). The connection between stress, density and speed in crowds, *Nature Scientific Reports, 13,* 13626.

48. Kim, E., & Kim, J. (2023). Neurocognitive effects of stress: a metaparadigm perspective. *Nature Molecular Psychiatry, 28,* 2750-2763.

49. Diamond, J. (1987). The worst mistake in the history of the human race. *Discover Magazine,* 64–66.

50. Chaudhary, N., & Salali, G. D. (2022). Hunter-Gatherers, Mismatch and Mental Disorder. In *Evolutionary Psychiatry* (pp. 64–83). Cambridge University Press.

51. Narvaez, D. (2013). The 99 percent—Development and socialization within an evolutionary context: Growing up to become "a good and useful human being" In D. P. Fry (Ed.), *War, peace, and human nature: The convergence of evolutionary and cultural views* (pp. 341–357). Oxford University Press. https://doi.org/10.1093/acprof :oso/9780199858996.003.0017.

52. Jaspers, K. (1953/2021). *The origin and goal of history*. Routledge.

53. The CNC Dialogues. (2024, May 15). *Iain Mcgilchrist and Aldrich Chan: The Divided Brain, Truth, Beauty, Consciousness*. [Video]. YouTube. https://youtu.be/ TRfqvMBS3V0?si=2hXkwEz3fpqv8N1w.

54. Cazalis, V., Loreau, M., Barragan-Jason, G. (2022). A global synthesis of trends in human experience of nature. *Frontiers in Ecology and the Environment*, 21(2):85–93. https://doi.org/10.1002/fee.2540.

55. Chan, A. (2016). *The fragmentation of self and others: The role of the default mode network in PTSD* [Doctoral dissertation, Pepperdine University] (UMI No. 10102804). ProQuest Dissertations & Theses.

56. Narvaez, D. (2024). Returning to evolved nestedness, wellbeing, and mature human nature, an ecological imperative. *Review of General Psychology, 28*(2), 83–105. https://doi.org/10.1177/10892680231224035.

57. Chai, D. (2019). *Zhuangzi and the becoming of Nothingness.* State University of New York Press.

58. Hinton, D. (2016). *Existence: A story.* Shambhala.

59. Whitehead, A. N. (1933). *Adventures of ideas.* Macmillan.

60. Mcgilchrist, I. (2021). *The matter with things: Our brains, our delusions, and the unmaking of the world.* Perspectiva Press.

61. Kastrup, B. (2019). *The idea of the world: A multi-disciplinary argument for the mental nature of reality.* John Hunt Publishing.

62. Hoffman, D. (2019). *The case against reality: Why evolution hid the truth from our eyes.* W. W. Norton & Company.

63. Hoffman, D., & Prakash, C. (2014). Objects of consciousness. *Frontiers in Psychology, 5*(577), 1–22.

64. Nishida, K. (1990). *An inquiry into the good* (M. Abe & C. Ives, Trans.). Yale University Press. (Original work published ca. 1921).

65. James, W. (1948). *Some problems with philosophy.* Dover.

66. Kohn, L. (2010). *Sitting in oblivion: The heart of Daoist meditation.* Three Pines Press.

67. Roth, H. D. (2018). Cognitive attunement in the Zhuangzi. C. Defoort & R. Ames (Eds.), *Having a word with Angus Graham: At Twenty-five years into his immortality* (pp. 47–78). University of Hawaii Press.

68. Sekida, K. (1975). *Zen training: Methods and philosophy.* John Weatherhill.

69. Vandekerckhove, M., & Panksepp, J. (2009). The flow of anoetic to noetic and autonoetic consciousness: A vision of unknowing (anoetic) and knowing (noetic) consciousness in the remembrance of things past and imagined futures. *Consciousness and Cognition, 18*(4), 1018–1028. https://doi.org/10.1016/j.concog.2009.08.002.

70. Damasio, A. (2010). *Self comes to mind: Constructing the conscious brain.* Pantheon/Random House.

71. Austin, J. H. (1998). *Zen and the brain: Toward an understanding of meditation and consciousness* (Reprint edition). MIT Press.

72. Austin, J. H. (2013). *Meditating selflessly: Practical neural Zen.* MIT Press Ltd.

73. Austin, J. H. (2013). Zen and the brain: Mutually illuminating topics. *Frontiers in Psychology, 4.* https://doi.org/10.3389/fpsyg.2013.00784.

74. Tang, Y.-Y., Hölzel, B. K., & Posner, M. I. (2015). The neuroscience of mindfulness meditation. *Nature Reviews Neuroscience, 16*(4), 213–225. https://doi.org/10.1038/nrn3916.

75. Chan, A., & Siegel, D. (2017). Play and the default mode network: Interpersonal neurobiology. In T. Marks-Tarlow, D. J. Siegel, & M. Solomon (Eds.), *Play & creativity in psychotherapy* (pp. 39–50). W. W. Norton.

76. Corbetta, M., & Shulman, G. L. (2002). Control of goal-directed and stimulus-driven attention in the brain. Nature *Reviews Neuroscience, 3*(3), 201–215. https://doi.org/10.1038/nrn755.

77. Fujino, M., Ueda, Y., Mizuhara, H., Saiki, J., & Nomura, M. (2018). Open monitoring meditation reduces the involvement of brain regions related to memory function. *Scientific Reports, 8*(1). https://doi.org/10.1038/s41598-018-28274-4.

78. Wu, R., Liu, L.-L., Zhu, H., Su, W.-J., Cao, Z.-Y., Zhong, S.-Y., Liu, X.-H., & Jiang, C.-L. (2019). Brief mindfulness meditation improves emotion processing. *Frontiers in Neuroscience, 13.* https://doi.org/10.3389/fnins.2019.01074.

79. Norris, C. J., Creem, D., Hendler, R., & Kober, H. (2018). Brief mindfulness meditation improves attention in novices: Evidence from ERPs and moderation by neuroticism. *Frontiers in Human Neuroscience, 12.* https://doi.org/10.3389/fnhum.2018.00315.

80. Moore, A., Gruber, T., Derose, J., & Malinowski, P. (2012). Regular, brief mindfulness meditation practice improves electrophysiological markers of attentional control. *Frontiers in Human Neuroscience, 6*, Article 18. https://doi.org/10.3389/fnhum.2012.00018.

81. Jha, A. (2022, January 26). *A mindfulness of breathing exercise with neuroscientist Amishi Jha.* Mindful. https://www.mindful.org/the-mindfulness-of-breathing-exercise-with -neuroscientist-amishi-jha/.

82. Fox, K. C. R., Nijeboer, S., Dixon, M. L., Floman, J. L., Ellamil, M., Rumak, S. P., Sedlmeier, P., & Christoff, K. (2014). Is meditation associated with altered brain structure? A systematic review and meta-analysis of morphometric neuroimaging in meditation practitioners. *Neuroscience & Biobehavioral Reviews, 43*, 48–73. https://doi.org/10.1016/j.neubiorev.2014.03.016.

83. Tanaka, M., Nakashima, R., Hiromitsu, K., & Imamizu, H. (2021). Individual differences in the change of attentional functions with brief one-time focused attention and open monitoring meditations. *Frontiers in Psychology, 12.* https://doi.org/10.3389/fpsyg .2021.716138.

84. Eskildsen, S. (2015). *Daoism, meditation, and the wonders of serenity: From the latter Han Dynasty (25–220) to the Tang Dynasty (618-907).* State University of New York Press.

85. Komjathy, L., & Townsend, K. (2022). *Entering stillness: A guide to Daoist practice.* Square Inch Press.

86. Roth, H. D. (2020). *Daoist apophatic meditation: Selections from the classical Daoist textual corpus.* https://archive.org/details/daoist-apophatic-meditation-harold-d.-roth/page/n1 /mode/2up.

87. Wong, E. (2015). *Being Taoist: Wisdom for living a balanced life.* Shambhala.

88. Peirce, C. (1935). *Pragmatism and pragmaticism and scientific metaphysics* (Vols. V and VI, Collected Papers of Charles Sanders Peirce) (Edited by C. Hartshorne & P. Weiss). Belknap Press.

89. Prochaska, J.O. & DiClemente, C.C. (1982). Transtheoretical therapy: toward a more integrative model of change. *American Journal of Health Promotion, 12*(1), 11–12.

90. Liu, A. (2012). *The essential Huainanzi.* (J. S. Major, S. Queen, A. Meyer, H. D. Roth, Eds. & Trans.). Columbia University Press. (Original work published ca. 200 BCE.)

91. Robichaud, M., & Dugas, M. J. (2006). A cognitive-behavioral treatment targeting intolerance of uncertainty. In G.C.L. Davey & A. Wells (Eds.), *Worry and Its Psychological Disorders* (pp. 289–304). Wiley. https://doi.org/10.1002/9780470713143.ch17.

92. Bartal, I. B.-A., Decety, J., & Mason, P. (2011). Empathy and pro-social behavior in rats. *Science, 334*(6061), 1427–1430. https://doi.org/10.1126/science.1210789.

93. Panksepp, J. (1981). The ontogeny of play in rats. *Developmental Psychobiology, 14*(4), 327–332. https://doi.org/10.1002/dev.420140405.

94. Panksepp, J. (1998). *Affective neuroscience: The foundations of human and animal emotions.* New Oxford University Press.

95. Schaik, C. P., Bshary, R., Wagner, G., & Cunha, F. (2021). Male anti-predation services in primates as costly signalling? A comparative analysis and review. *Ethology, 128*(1), 1–14. https://doi.org/10.1111/eth.13233.

96. Masserman, J. H., Wechkin, S., & Terris, W. (1964). "Altruistic" behavior in rhesus monkeys. *The American Journal of Psychiatry, 121*(6), 584–585. https://doi.org/10.1176/ajp.121.6.584.

97. de Waal, F. B., Leimgruber, K., & Greenberg, A. R. (2008). Giving is self-rewarding for monkeys. *Proceedings of the National Academy of Sciences, 105*(36), 13685–13689. https://doi.org/10.1073/pnas.0807060105.

98. Warneken, F., Hare, B., Melis, A. P., Hanus, D., & Tomasello, M. (2007). Spontaneous altruism by chimpanzees and young children. *PLOS Biology, 5*(7). https://doi.org/10.1371/journal.pbio.0050184.

99. Schmidt, M. F., & Sommerville, J. A. (2011). Fairness expectations and altruistic sharing in 15-month-old human infants. *PLOS ONE, 6*(10). https://doi.org/10.1371/journal.pone.0023223.

100. Hamlin, J. K., & Wynn, K. (2011). Young infants prefer prosocial to antisocial others. *Cognitive Development, 26*(1), 30–39. https://doi.org/10.1016/j.cogdev.2010.09.001.

101. Jin, K. S., Houston, J. L., Baillargeon, R., Groh, A. M., & Roisman, G. I. (2018). Young infants expect an unfamiliar adult to comfort a crying baby: Evidence from a standard violation-of-expectation task and a novel infant-triggered-video task. *Cognitive Psychology, 102*, 1–20. https://doi.org/10.1016/j.cogpsych.2017.12.004.

102. Narvaez, D. (2014). *Neurobiology and the development of human morality*. W. W. Norton.

103. Narvaez, D. (2013). Wisdom as mature moral functioning: Insights from developmental psychology and neurobiology. In M. Jones, P. Lewis, & K. Reffitt (Eds.), *Character, Practical Wisdom and Professional Formation across the Disciplines* (pp. 24–40). Mercer University Press.

104. Hoffmann, J. A., von Helversen, B., & Rieskamp, J. (2013). Deliberation's blindsight: How cognitive load can improve judgments. *Psychological science, 24*(6), 869–879. https://doi.org/10.1177/0956797612463581.

105. Hogarth, R. M. (2010). Intuition: A challenge for psychological research on decision making. *Psychological Inquiry, 21*(4), 338–353. https://doi.org/10.1080/1047840x .2010.520260.

106. Julmi, C. (2023). Analysis and intuition effectiveness in moral problems. *Journal of Business Ethics*. https://doi.org/10.1007/s10551-023-05407-y.

107. Bechara, A., Damasio, H., Tranel, D., & Damasio, A. R. (1997). Deciding advantageously before knowing the advantageous strategy. *Science, 275*(5304), 1293–1295. https://doi.org/10.1126/science.275.5304.1293.

108. Bechara, A., Damasio, H., & Damasio, A. R. (2000). Emotion, decision making and the orbitofrontal cortex. *Cerebral Cortex, 10*(3), 295–307. https://doi.org/10.1093/cercor /10.3.295.

109. Kahneman, D. (2011). *Thinking, fast and slow*. Farrar, Straus and Giroux.

110. Clark, A. (2015). *Surfing uncertainty: Prediction, action, and the embodied mind*. Oxford University Press.

111. Belloc, M., Bilancini, E., Boncinelli, L., & D'Alessandro, S. (2019). Intuition and deliberation in the stag hunt game. *Scientific Reports, 9*(1), 1–7. https://doi.org /10.1038/s41598-019-50556-8.

112. Nalliah, R. P. (2016). Clinical decision making—choosing between intuition, experience and scientific evidence. *British Dental Journal, 221*(12), 752–754. https://doi. org/10.1038/sj.bdj.2016.942.

113. Pétervári, J., Osman, M., & Bhattacharya, J. (2016). The role of intuition in the generation and evaluation stages of creativity. *Frontiers in Psychology, 7*. https://doi.org/10.3389 /fpsyg.2016.01420.

114. Brown, H., Proulx, M. J., & Stanton Fraser, D. (2020). Hunger bias or gut instinct? responses to judgments of harm depending on visceral state versus intuitive decision-making. *Frontiers in Psychology, 11*, Article 2261. https://doi.org/10.3389/fpsyg .2020.02261.

115. Dunn, B. D., Galton, H. C., Morgan, R., Evans, D., Oliver, C., & Meyer, M., & Dalgleish, T. (2010). Listening to your heart: How interoception shapes emotion

experience and intuitive decision making. *Psychological Science, 21*(12), 1835–1844. https://doi.org/10.1177/0956797610389191.

116. Balas, R., Sweklej, J., Pochwatko, G., & Godlewska, M. (2012). On the influence of affective states on intuitive coherence judgments. *Cognition & Emotion, 26*(2), 312–320. https://doi.org/10.1080/02699931.2011.568050.

117. Kump, B. (2022). No need to hide: Acknowledging the researcher's intuition in empirical organizational research. *Human Relations, 75*(4), 635–654. https://doi.org/10.1177/00 18726720984837.

118. Pretz, J. E. (2008). Intuition versus analysis: Strategy and experience in complex everyday problem solving. *Memory & Cognition, 36*(3), 554–566. https://doi.org/10.3758/mc .36.3.554.

119. Wang, Y. (2002). Philosophy of change and the deconstruction of self in the Zhuangzi. *Journal of Chinese Philosophy, 27*(3), 345–360. https://doi.org/10.1163/15406253 -02703006.

120. Edelman, G. M. (2003). Naturalizing consciousness: a theoretical framework. *Proceedings of the National Academy of Sciences of the United States of America, 100*(9), 5520–5524. https://doi.org/10.1073/pnas.0931349100.

121. Northoff, G., & Panksepp, J. (2008). The trans-species concept of self and the subcortical–cortical midline system. *Trends in cognitive sciences, 12*(7), 259–264. https://doi.org/10 .1016/j.tics.2008.04.007.

122. James, W. (1950). *The principles of psychology.* Dover. (Original work published 1890).

123. Lieberman, D. Z., & Long, M. E. (2019). *The molecule of more: How a single chemical in your brain drives love, sex, and creativity-and will determine the fate of the human race.* BenBella Books.

124. Reber, A. S. (1967). Implicit learning of artificial grammars. *Journal of Verbal Learning and Verbal Behavior, 6*(6), 855-863. https://doi.org/10.1016/s0022-5371(67)80149-x.

125. Ahissar, M., & Hochstein, S. (2004). The reverse hierarchy theory of visual perceptual learning. *Trends in Cognitive Sciences, 8*(10), 457–464. https://doi.org/10.1016/j.tics .2004.08.011.

126. Seitze, A. R., & Watanabe, T. (2009). The phenomenon of task-irrelevant perceptual learning. *Vision Research, 49*(21), 2604–2610. https://doi.org/10.1016/j.visres .2009.08.003.

127. Bargh, J. A., & Chartrand, T. L. (2014). The mind in the middle: A practical guide to priming and automaticity research. In H. T. Reis & C. M. Judd (Eds.), *Handbook of research methods in social and personality psychology* (pp. 311–344). Cambridge University Press. https://doi.org/10.1017/cbo9780511996481.017.

128. Bandura, A. (1971). *Social learning theory.* Morristown, NJ: General Learning Press.

129. Csikszentmihalyi, M. (1990). *Flow: The psychology of optimal experience.* Harper & Row.

130. Tse, D. C., Nakamura, J., & Csikszentmihalyi, M. (2020). Living well by "flowing" well: The indirect effect of Autotelic personality on well-being through flow experience. *The Journal of Positive Psychology, 16*(3), 310–321. https://doi.org/10.1080/17439760 .2020.1716055.

131. Slingerland, E. (2014). *Trying not to try.* Random House, LLC.

132. Limb, C. J., & Braun, A. R. (2008). Neural substrates of spontaneous musical performance: An fMRI study of Jazz improvisation. *PLOS ONE, 3*(2). https://doi.org/10.1371/journal .pone.0001679.

133. Liu, S., Chow, H. M., Xu, Y., Erkkinen, M. G., Swett, K. E., Eagle, M. W., Rizik-Baer, D. A., & Braun, A. R. (2012). Neural correlates of lyrical improvisation: An fMRI study of freestyle rap. Scientific Reports, 2(1), 834. https://doi.org/10.1038/srep00834.

134. Ulrich, M., Keller, J., Hoenig, K., Waller, C., & Grön, G. (2014). Neural correlates of experimentally induced flow experiences. *Neuroimage, 86,* 194–202. https://doi.org/10 .1016/j.neuroimage.2013.08.019.

135. Ulrich, M., Keller, J., & Grön, G. (2016). Neural signatures of experimentally induced flow experiences identified in a typical fMRI block design with BOLD imaging. *Social Cognitive and Affective Neuroscience, 11*(3), 496–507. https://doi.org/10.1093/scan/nsv133.

136. Espana, R., Schmeichel, B., & Berridge, C. (2016). Norepinephrine at the nexus of arousal, motivation and relapse. *Brain Research, 1641,* 207–216. https://doi.org/10.1016/j.brainres .2016.01.002.

137. Linden, D., Tops, M., & Bakker, A. B. (2021). The neuroscience of the flow state: Involvement of the locus coeruleus norepinephrine system. *Frontiers in Psychology, 12.* https://doi.org/10.3389/fpsyg.2021.645498.

138. Zhang, Y., Feng, Y., & Song, L. (2021). Research in the flow experience of Tai Chi Chuan. *Research Square,* 1-21.

139. Csikszentmihalyi, M. (2014). Flow and the foundations of positive psychology: *The collected works of Mihaly Csikszentmihalyi.* Springer Netherlands.

140. Kotler, S., Mannino, M., Kelso, S., & Huskey, R. (2022). First few seconds for flow: A comprehensive proposal of the neurobiology and neurodynamics of state onset. *Neuroscience and Biobehavioral Reviews, 143.* https://doi.org/10.1016/j.neubiorev.2022 .104956.

141. Ivey, P. (2000). Cooperative reproduction in Ituri forest hunter-gatherers: who cares for Efe infants? *Current Anthropology, 41,* 856–866.

142. Ingold, T. (2000). *The perception of the environment: Essays on livelihood, dwelling and skill* (1st ed.). Routledge. https://doi.org/10.4324/9780203466025.

143. Amsterdam, B. K. (1968). *Mirror behavior in children under two years of age* [Doctoral dissertation, University of North Carolina]. University Microfilms (Order No. 6901569), Ann Arbor, MI, 48106.

144. Amsterdam, B. K. (1972). Mirror self-image reactions before age two. *Developmental Psychobiology, 5*(4), 297–305. https://doi.org/10.1002/dev.420050403.

145. Bard, K. A., Todd, B. K., Bernier, C., Love, J., & Leavens, D. A. (2006). Self-awareness in human and chimpanzee infants: What is measured and what is meant by the mark and mirror test? *Infancy, 9*(2), 191–219. https://doi.org/10.1207/s15327078in0902_6.

146. Rochat, P., & Zahavi, D. (2011). The uncanny mirror: A re-framing of mirror self-experience. *Consciousness and Cognition: An International Journal, 20*(2), 204–213. https://doi.org/10.1016/j.concog.2010.06.007.

147. Siegler, R. S. (1998). *Children's thinking* (3rd ed.). Prentice Hall.

148. Saxe, R. (2006). Why and how to study theory of mind with fMRI. *Brain Research, 1079*(1), 57–65. https://doi.org/10.1016/j.brainres.2006.01.001.

149. Uddin, L. Q., Kaplan, J. T., Molnar-Szakacs, I., Zaidel, E., & Iacoboni, M. (2005). Self-face recognition activates a frontoparietal "mirror" network in the right hemisphere: an event-related fMRI study. *NeuroImage, 25*(3), 926–935. https://doi.org/10.1016/j.neuroimage.2004.12.018.

150. Maister, L., Hodossy, L., & Tsakiris, M. (2017). You fill my heart: Looking at one's partner increases interoceptive accuracy. *Psychology of Consciousness: Theory, Research, and Practice, 4*(2), 248–257. https://doi.org/10.1037/cns0000110.

151. Knickmeyer, R. C., Gouttard, S., Kang, C., Evans, D., Wilber, K., Smith, J. K., Hamer, R. M., Lin, W., Gerig, G., & Gilmore, J. H. (2008). A structural MRI study of human brain development from birth to 2 years. *The Journal of Neuroscience: The Official Journal of the Society for Neuroscience, 28*(47), 12176–12182. https://doi.org/10.1523/JNEUROSCI.3479-08.2008.

152. Cavalli, G., Heard, E. (2019). Advances in epigenetics link genetics to the environment and disease. *Nature, 571,* 489–499. https://doi.org/10.1038/s41586-019-1411-0.

153. Cozolino, L. (2010). *The neuroscience of psychotherapy: Healing the social brain (The Norton Series on Interpersonal Neurobiology)*. W. W. Norton & Company.

154. Shah, P. E., Fonagy, P., & Strathearn, L. (2010). Is attachment transmitted across generations? The plot thickens. *Clinical Child Psychology and Psychiatry, 15*(3), 329–345. https://doi.org/10.1177/1359104510365449.

155. Ramachandran, V. S., & Rogers-Ramachandran, D. (2008). Sensations referred to a patient's phantom arm from another subject's intact arm: Perceptual correlates of mirror neurons. *Medical Hypotheses, 70*(6), 1233–1234. https://doi.org/10.1016/j.mehy.2008.01.008.

156. Wilson, D. S. (2019). *This view of life: Completing the Darwinian Revolution*. Pantheon.

157. Markus A and Shamay-Tsoory SG (2024). Hyperscanning: from inter-brain coupling to causality. *Frontiers in Human Neuroscience, 18*, 1497034. https://doi.org/10.3389/fnhum.2024.1497034.

158. Pérez, A., Carreiras, M., & Duñabeitia, J. A. (2017). Brain-to-brain entrainment: EEG interbrain synchronization while speaking and listening. *Scientific Reports, 7*(1). https://doi.org/10.1038/s41598-017-04464-4.

159. Northoff, G. (2018). *The spontaneous brain: From the mind-body to the world-brain problem*. MIT Press.

160. de Prado Bert, P., Mercader, E. M., Pujol, J., Sunyer, J., & Mortamais, M. (2018). The effects of air pollution on the brain: A review of studies interfacing environmental epidemiology and neuroimaging. *Current Environmental Health Reports, 5*(3), 351–364. https://doi.org/10.1007/s40572-018-0209-9.

161. Zare Sakhvidi, M. J., Yang, J., Lequy, E., Chen, J., de Hoogh, K., Letellier, N., Mortamais, M., Ozguler, A., Vienneau, D., Zins, M., Goldberg, M., Berr, C., & Jacquemin, B. (2022). Outdoor air pollution exposure and cognitive performance: Findings from the enrolment phase of the constances cohort. *The Lancet Planetary Health, 6*(3). https://doi.org/10.1016/s2542-5196(22)00001-8; Roth, H. D. (1997). Evidence for stages of meditation in early Taoism. *Bulletin of the School of Oriental and African Studies, 60*(2), 295–314. https://doi.org/10.1017/s0041977x00036405.

162. Bremer, B., Wu, Q., Mora Álvarez, M. G., Hölzel, B. K., Wilhelm, M., Hell, E., Tavacioglu, E. E., Torske, A., & Koch, K. (2022). Mindfulness meditation increases default mode, salience, and central executive network connectivity. *Scientific Reports, 12*(1). https://doi.org/10.1038/s41598-022-17325-6.

163. Gazzaniga, M. S., Bogen, J. E., & Sperry, R. W. (1962). Some functional effects of sectioning the cerebral commissures in man. *Proceedings of the National Academy of Sciences of the United States of America, 48*(10), 1765–1769. https://doi.org/10.1073/pnas.48.10.1765.

164. Gazzaniga, M. S., Bogen, J. E., & Sperry, R. W. (1965). Observations on visual perception after disconnexion of the cerebral hemispheres in man. *Brain: A Journal of Neurology, 88*(2), 221–236. https://doi.org/10.1093/brain/88.2.221.

165. Gazzaniga, M. S. (1995). Consciousness and the cerebral hemispheres. In M. S. Gazzaniga (Ed.), *The cognitive neurosciences* (pp. 1391–1400). The MIT Press.

166. Gazzaniga, M. S. (1995). Principles of human brain organization derived from split-brain studies. *Neuron, 14*(2), 217–228. https://doi.org/10.1016/0896-6273(95)90280-5.

167. Gazzaniga, M. S. (2005). Forty-five years of split-brain research and still going strong. *Nature Reviews Neuroscience, 6*(8), 653–659. https://doi.org/10.1038/nrn1723.

168. Schore, A. N. (2003). *Affect regulation and the repair of the self*. W.W. Norton & Company.

169. Schore, A. N. (2019). *Right brain psychotherapy*. W. W. Norton & Company.

170. Schore, A. N. (2003). *Affect dysregulation and disorders of the self.* W. W. Norton & Company.

171. J. B. (2006). *My stroke of insight: A brain scientist's personal journey.* Plume.

172. Zaidel, Dahlia & Marjan, Hessamian. (2010). Asymmetry and symmetry in the beauty of human faces. *Symmetry, 2*(1). http://doi.org/10.3390/sym2010136.

173. Wang, Y. (2003). *Linguistic strategies in Daoist Zhuangzi and Chan Buddhism: The other way of speaking.* Routledge.

174. Sainsbury, R. M. (2009). *Paradoxes* (3rd ed.). Cambridge University Press.

175. Hoffman, D.D., Singh, M. & Prakash, C. (2015). The interface theory of perception. *Psychonomic Bulletin & Review, 22*, 1480–1506. https://doi.org/10.3758/s13423-015-0890-8.

176. Louis, F. (2003). The genesis of an icon: The "taiji" Diagram's early history. *Harvard Journal of Asiatic Studies, 63*(1), 145. https://doi.org/10.2307/25066694.

177. Wilhelm, R. (1962). *The secret of the golden flower: A Chinese book of life.* Echo Point Books & Media.

178. Rosen, D. (1997). *The Tao of Jung: The way of integrity.* Penguin Group.

179. Neumann, E. (1969). *Depth psychology and a new ethic.* Shambala Publications.

180. Raichle M. E. (2010). Two views of brain function. *Trends in Cognitive Sciences, 14*(4), 180–190. https://doi.org/10.1016/j.tics.2010.01.008.

181. Kapur, N., Pascual-Leone, A., Sala, S. D., Manly, T., Mayes, A., Ramachandran, V. S., & Cole, J. (2011). *The paradoxical brain.* Cambridge University Press.

182. Moscovitch, M., Winocur, G., & Behrmann, M. (1997). What is special about face recognition? Nineteen experiments on a person with visual object agnosia and dyslexia but normal face recognition. *Journal of Cognitive Neuroscience, 9*(5), 555–604. https://doi.org/10.1162/jocn.1997.9.5.555.

183. Etcoff, N. L., Ekman, P., Magee, J. J., & Frank, M. G. (2000). Lie detection and language comprehension. *Nature, 405*(6783), 139–139. https://doi.org/10.1038/35012129.

184. Sacks, O. (1985). *The man who mistook his wife for a hat.* Harper & Row.

185. Warrington, E. K., & Davidoff, J. (2000). Failure at object identification improves mirror image matching. *Neuropsychologia, 38*, 1229-1234. https://doi.org/10.1016/s0028-3932(00)00040-3.

186. Beversdorf, D. Q., Smith, B. W., Crucian, G. P., Anderson, J.M., Keillor, J.M., Barrett, A.M., Hughes, J.D., Felopulos, G.J., Bauman, M.L., Nadeau, S.E., & Heilman, K.M. (2000). Increased discrimination of "false memories" in autism spectrum disorder. *Proceedings of the National Academy of Sciences, 97*(15), 8734–3737. https://doi.org/10.1073/pnas.97.15.8734.

187. Goodwin, F. K., & Jamison, K. R. (2007). *Manic-Depressive Illness: Bipolar Disorders and Recurrent Depression* (2nd ed.). Oxford University Press.

188. Pring, L., & Hermelin, B. (2002). Numbers and letters: Exploring an autistic savant's unpracticed ability. *Neurocase, 8*(4), 330–337. https://doi.org/10.1076/neur.8.3.330.16193.

189. Baron-Cohen, S. (2008). *Autism and Asperger syndrome*. Oxford University Press.

190. Göhlsdorf, N. (2020). "The magical device": Temple Grandin's hug machine. *Material Cultures of Psychiatry*, 228–255. https://doi.org/10.1515/9783839447888-016.

191. Pring, L., & Ockelford, A. (2005). Children with Septo-optic dysplasia—musical interests, abilities and provision: The results of a parental survey. *British Journal of Visual Impairment, 23*(2), 58–66. https://doi.org/10.1177/0264619605054777.

192. Helm-Estabrooks, N., & Ramsberger, G. (1986). Treatment of agrammatism in long-term Broca's aphasia. *British Journal of Disorders of Communication, 21*(1), 39–45. https://doi.org/10.3109/13682828609018542.

193. Cohen, J., Mccabe, E. M., Michelli, N. M., & Pickeral, T. (2009). School climate: Research, policy, practice, and teacher education. *Teachers College Record: The Voice of Scholarship in Education, 111*(1), 180–213. https://doi.org/10.1177/016146810911100108.

194. Farah, M. J., Wilson, K. D., Drain, H. M., & Tanaka, J. R. (1995). The inverted face inversion effect in prosopagnosia: evidence for mandatory, face-specific perceptual mechanisms. *Vision Research, 35*(14), 2089–2093. https://doi.org/10.1016/0042-6989(94)00273-o.

195. de Gelder, B., & Rouw, R. (2000). Paradoxical configuration effects for faces and objects in prosopagnosia. *Neuropsychologia, 38*(9), 1271–1279. https://doi.org/10.1016/S0028-3932(00)00039-7.

196. Rouw, R., & de Gelder, B. (2002). Impaired face recognition does not preclude intact whole face perception. *Visual Cognition, 9*, 689–718. https://doi.org/10.1080/13506280143000223.

197. Hawley, C. A., & Joseph, S. (2008). Predictors of positive growth after traumatic brain injury: A longitudinal study. *Brain Injury, 22*(5), 427–435. https://doi.org/10.1080/02699050802064607.

198. Strasser-Fuchs, S., Enzinger, C., Ropele, S., Wallner, M., & Fazekas, F. (2008). Clinically benign multiple sclerosis despite large T2 lesion load: Can we explain this paradox? *Multiple Sclerosis Journal, 14*(2), 205–211. https://doi.org/10.1177/1352458507082354.

199. Feuillet, L., Dufour, H., & Pelletier, J. (2007). Brain of a white-collar worker. *The Lancet, 370*(9583), 262. https://doi.org/10.1016/s0140-6736(07)61127-1.

200. Adler, A. (1943). Neuropsychiatric complications in victims in Boston's Cocoanut Grove disaster. *Journal of the American Medical Association, 123*, 1098–1101. https://doi.org/10.1001/jama.1943.02840520014004.

201. O'Brien (1993). Loss of memory is protective (letter). *British Medical Journal, 307*, 1283.

202. Gil, S., Caspi, Y., Ben-Ari, I. Z., Koren, D., & Klein, E. (2005). Does memory of a traumatic event increase the risk for posttraumatic stress disorder in patients with traumatic brain injury? A prospective study. *American Journal of Psychiatry, 162*, 963-9.

203. Bryant, R., Creamer, M., O'Donnel, M., Silove, D., Clark, C., & McFarlane, A. (2009). Post-traumatic amnesia and the nature of post-traumatic stress disorder after mild traumatic brain injury. *Journal of the International Neuropsychological Society, 15*(6), 862–867. https://doi:10.1017/S1355617709990671.

204. Xavier, A. C., Ge, Y., & Taub, J. W. (2009). Down syndrome and malignancies: A unique clinical relationship. *The Journal of Molecular Diagnostics, 11*(5), 371–380. https://doi.org/10.2353/jmoldx.2009.080132.

205. Wekerle, H., & Hohlfeld, R. (2010). Beneficial brain autoimmunity? *Brain, 133*(8), 2182–2184. https://doi.org/10.1093/brain/awq206.

206. Nesse, R. (2019). *Good reasons for bad feelings*. Penguin Random House.

207. Sherman J. A. (2012). Evolutionary origin of bipolar disorder-revised: EOBD-R. *Medical hypotheses, 78*(1), 113–122. https://doi.org/10.1016/j.mehy.2011.10.005.

208. Brüne, M. (2016). *Textbook of evolutionary psychiatry and psychosomatic medicine: The origins of psychopathology* (2nd ed.). Oxford University Press.

209. Andrews, P. W., & Thomson, J. A., Jr (2009). The bright side of being blue: Depression as an adaptation for analyzing complex problems. *Psychological review, 116*(3), 620–654. https://doi.org/10.1037/a0016242.

210. Whitehead, A. N. (1929). *Process and reality*. Macmillan.

211. Freud, S. (1930). *Civilization and its discontents*. Hogarth.

212. Abbott, R., & Lavretsky, H. (2013). Tai Chi and Qigong for the treatment and prevention of mental disorders. *The Psychiatric Clinics of North America, 36*(1), 109–119. https://doi.org/10.1016/j.psc.2013.01.011.

213. Hung, H.-M., Yeh, S.-H., & Chen, C.-H. (2015). Effects of qigong exercise on biomarkers and mental and physical health in adults with at least one risk factor for coronary artery disease. *Biological Research for Nursing, 18*(3), 264–273. https://doi.org/10.1177/1099800415617017.

214. Hwang, E.-Y., Chung, S.-Y., Cho, J.-H., Song, M.-Y., Kim, S., & Kim, J.-W. (2013). Effects of a brief qigong-based Stress Reduction Program (BQSRP) in a distressed Korean population: A randomized trial. *BMC Complementary and Alternative Medicine, 13*(1). https://doi.org/10.1186/1472-6882-13-113.

215. Tsang, H. W. H., Tsang, W. W. N., Jones, A. Y. M., Fung, K. M. T., Chan, A. H. L., Chan, E. P., & Au, D. W. H. (2013). Psycho-physical and neurophysiological effects of qigong on depressed elders with chronic illness. *Aging & Mental Health, 17*(3), 336–348. https://doi.org/10.1080/13607863.2012.732035.

216. Chan, A., Yu, D., & Choi, K. (2017). Effects of Tai Chi Qigong on psychosocial well-being among hidden elderly, using elderly neighborhood volunteer approach: A pilot randomized controlled trial. *Clinical Interventions in Aging, 12,* 85–96. https://doi.org/10.2147/cia.s124604.

217. Blödt, S., Pach, D., Kaster, T., Lüdtke, R., Icke, K., Reisshauer, A., & Witt, C. M. (2014). Qigong versus exercise therapy for chronic low back pain in adults—a randomized controlled non-inferiority trial. *European Journal of Pain, 19*(1), 123–131. https://doi.org/10.1002/ejp.529.

218. Chuang, T.-Y., Yeh, M.-L., & Chung, Y.-C. (2017). A nurse facilitated mind-body interactive exercise (Chan-Chuang Qigong) improves the health status of non-Hodgkin Lymphoma patients receiving chemotherapy: Randomised controlled trial. *International Journal of Nursing Studies, 69,* 25–33. https://doi.org/10.1016/j.ijnurstu.2017.01.004.

219. Liu, X., Li, R., Cui, J., Liu, F., Smith, L., Chen, X., & Zhang, D. (2021). The effects of Tai Chi and qigong exercise on psychological status in adolescents: A systematic review and meta-analysis. *Frontiers in Psychology, 12.* https://doi.org/10.3389/fpsyg.2021.746975.

220. Klein, P., Picard, G., Baumgardeb, J., & Schneider, R. (2017). Meditative movement, energetic, and physical analyses of three qigong exercises: Unification of eastern and western mechanistic exercise theory. *Medicines, 4*(69). https://doi.org10.3390medicines 4040069.

221. Aman, J. E., Elangovan, N., Yeh, I.-L., & Konczak, J. Á. (2015). The effectiveness of proprioceptive training for improving motor function: A systematic review. *Frontiers in Human Neuroscience, 8.* https://doi.org/10.3389/fnhum.2014.01075.

222. Henz, D., & Schöllhorn, W. I. (2017). EEG brain activity in Dynamic Health Qigong training: Same effects for mental practice and physical training? *Frontiers in Psychology, 8.* https://doi.org/10.3389/fpsyg.2017.00154.

223. Wang, F., Man, J. K., Lee, E.-K. O., Wu, T., Benson, H., Fricchione, G. L., Wang, W., & Yeung, A. (2013). The effects of qigong on anxiety, depression, and psychological well-being: A systematic review and meta-analysis. *Evidence-Based Complementary and Alternative Medicine, 2013,* 1–16. https://doi.org/10.1155/2013/152738.

224. Guo, Y., Qiu, P., & Liu, T. (2014). Tai Ji Quan: An overview of its history, health benefits, and cultural value. *Journal of Sport and Health Science, 3*(1), 3–8. https://doi.org /10.1016/j.jshs.2013.10.004.

225. Huang, J., Wang, D., & Wang, J. (2021). Clinical evidence of Tai Chi Exercise Prescriptions: A systematic review. *Evidence-Based Complementary and Alternative Medicine, 2021,* 1–14. https://doi.org/10.1155/2021/5558805.

226. Laskosky NA, Huston P, Lam WC, Anderson C, Zheng Y, Zhong LLD (2023). Are tai chi and qigong effective in the treatment of TBI? A systematic review protocol. *Frontiers in Aging Neuroscience, 15*, 1121064. https://doi.org/10.3389/fnagi.2023.1121064.

227. Xie, H., Zhang, M., Huo, C., Xu, G., Li, Z., & Fan, Y. (2019). Tai Chi Chuan exercise related change in brain function as assessed by functional near–infrared spectroscopy. *Scientific Reports, 9*(1). https://doi.org/10.1038/s41598-019-49401-9.

228. Cui, L., Tao, S., Yin, H., Shen, Q., Wang, Y., Zhu, L., & Li, X. (2021). Tai Chi Chuan alters brain functional network plasticity and promotes cognitive flexibility. *Frontiers in Psychology, 12*. https://doi.org/10.3389/fpsyg.2021.665419.

229. Liu, Z., Wu, Y., Li, L., & Guo, X. (2018). Functional connectivity within the executive control network mediates the effects of long-term tai chi exercise on elders' emotion regulation. *Frontiers in Aging Neuroscience, 10*. https://doi.org/10.3389/fnagi.2018.00315.

230. Gow, B. J., Hausdorff, J. M., Manor, B., Lipsitz, L. A., Macklin, E. A., Bonato, P., Novak, V., Peng, C.-K., Ahn, A. C., & Wayne, P. M. (2017). Can Tai Chi training impact fractal stride time dynamics, an index of Gait Health, in older adults? Cross-sectional and randomized trial studies. *PLOS ONE, 12*(10). https://doi.org/10.1371/journal.pone.0186212.

231. Tao, J., Chen, X., Egorova, N., Liu, J., Xue, X., Wang, Q., Zheng, G., Li, M., Hong, W., Sun, S., Chen, L., & Kong, J. (2017). Tai Chi Chuan and Baduanjin practice modulates functional connectivity of the cognitive control network in older adults. *Scientific Reports, 7*(1). https://doi.org/10.1038/srep41581.

232. Liu, S., Li, L., Liu, Z., & Guo, X. (2019). Long-term tai chi experience promotes emotional stability and slows gray matter atrophy for elders. *Frontiers in Psychology, 10*. https://doi.org/10.3389/fpsyg.2019.00091.

233. Aschbacher, K., O'Donovan, A., Wolkowitz, O. M., Dhabhar, F. S., Su, Y., & Epel, E. (2013). Good stress, bad stress and oxidative stress: Insights from anticipatory cortisol reactivity. *Psychoneuroendocrinology, 38*(9), 1698–1708. https://doi.org/10.1016/j.psyneuen.2013.02.004.

234. Greipl, S., Klein, E., Lindstedt, A., Kiili, K., Moeller, K., Karnath, H. -O., Bahnmueller, J., Bloechle, J., & Ninaus, M. (2021). When the brain comes into play: Neurofunctional correlates of emotions and reward in game-based learning. *Computers in Human Behavior, 125*, Article 106946. https://doi.org/10.1016/j.chb.2021.106946.

235. Barabadi, E., Elahi Shirvan, M., Shahnama, M., & Proyer, R. T. (2022). Perceived functions of playfulness in adult English as a foreign language learners: An exploratory study. *Frontiers in Psychology, 12*. https://doi.org/10.3389/fpsyg.2021.823123.

236. Tardy, C. M. (2021). The potential power of play in second language academic writing. *Journal of Second Language Writing, 53*, 100833. https://doi.org/10.1016/j.jslw.2021.100833.

237. Bains, G. S., Berk, L. S., Daher, N., Lohman, E., Schwab, E., Petrofsky, J., & Deshpande, P. (2014). The effect of humor on short-term memory in older adults: A new component for whole-person wellness. *Advances in Mind-Body Medicine, 28*(2), 16–24.

238. Imamura, C., Sakakibara, K., Arai, K., Ohira, H., Yamaguchi, Y., & Yamada, H. (2022). Effect of indoor forest bathing on reducing feelings of fatigue using cerebral activity as an indicator. *International Journal of Environmental Research and Public Health, 19*(11), 6672. https://doi.org/10.3390/ijerph19116672.

239. Mao, G.-X., Cao, Y.-B., Lan, X.-G., He, Z.-H., Chen, Z.-M., Wang, Y.-Z., Hu, X.-L., Lv, Y.-D., Wang, G.-F., & Yan, J. (2012). Therapeutic effect of forest bathing on human hypertension in the elderly. *Journal of Cardiology, 60*(6), 495–502. https://doi.org/10.1016/j.jjcc.2012.08.003.

240. Li, Q., Kobayashi, M., Kumeda, S., Ochiai, T., Miura, T., Kagawa, T., Imai, M., Wang, Z., Otsuka, T., & Kawada, T. (2016). Effects of forest bathing on cardiovascular and metabolic parameters in middle-aged males. *Evidence-Based Complementary and Alternative Medicine*, 2016, 1–7. https://doi.org/10.1155/2016/2587381.

241. Kim, T., Song, B., Cho, K. S., & Lee, I. S. (2020). Therapeutic potential of volatile terpenes and terpenoids from forests for inflammatory diseases. *International Journal of Molecular Sciences, 21*(6), 2187. https://doi.org/10.3390/ijms21062187.

242. Yu, C. P., Lin, C. M., Tsai, M. J., Tsai, Y. C., & Chen, C. Y. (2017). Effects of short forest bathing program on autonomic nervous system activity and mood states in middle-aged and elderly individuals. *International Journal of Environmental Research and Public Health, 14*(8), 897. https://doi.org/10.3390/ijerph14080897.

243. Furuyashiki, A., Tabuchi, K., Norikoshi, K., Kobayashi, T., & Oriyama, S. (2019). A comparative study of the physiological and psychological effects of forest bathing (Shinrin-yoku) on working age people with and without depressive tendencies. *Environmental Health and Preventive Medicine, 24*(1). https://doi.org/10.1186/s12199-019-0800-1.

244. Roviello, V., Scognamiglio, P. L., Caruso, U., Vicidomini, C., & Roviello, G. N. (2021). Evaluating in silico the potential health and environmental benefits of houseplant volatile organic compounds for an emerging "indoor forest bathing" approach. *International Journal of Environmental Research and Public Health, 19*(1), 273. https://doi.org/10.3390/ijerph19010273.

245. Peterfalvi, A., Meggyes, M., Makszin, L., Farkas, N., Miko, E., Miseta, A., & Szereday, L. (2021). Forest bathing always makes sense: Blood pressure-lowering and immune system-balancing effects in late spring and winter in Central Europe. *International Journal of Environmental Research and Public Health, 18*(4), 2067. https://doi.org/10.3390/ijerph18042067.

246. Kim, H., Kim, J., Ju, H. J., Jang, B. J., Wang, T. K., & Kim, Y. I. (2020). Effect of forest therapy for menopausal women with insomnia. *International Journal of Environmental Research and Public Health, 17*(18), 6548. https://doi.org/10.3390/ijerph17186548.

247. Cucca, A., Di Rocco, A., Acosta, I., Beheshti, M., Berberian, M., Bertisch, H. C., Droby, A., Ettinger, T., Hudson, T. E., Inglese, M., Jung, Y. J., Mania, D. F., Quartarone, A., Rizzo, J.-R., Sharma, K., Feigin, A., Biagioni, M. C., & Ghilardi, M. F. (2021). Art therapy for Parkinson's disease. *Parkinsonism & Related Disorders, 84*, 148–154. https://doi.org/10.1016/j.parkreldis.2021.01.013.

248. Mitchell, J., & Meehan, T. (2022). How art-as-therapy supports participants with a diagnosis of schizophrenia: A phenomenological lifeworld investigation. *The Arts in Psychotherapy, 80*, 101917. https://doi.org/10.1016/j.aip.2022.101917.

249. Savazzi, F., Isernia, S., Farina, E., Fioravanti, R., D'Amico, A., Saibene, F. L., Rabuffetti, M., Gilli, G., Alberoni, M., Nemni, R., & Baglio, F. (2020). "Art, colors, and emotions" treatment (ACE-T): A pilot study on the efficacy of an art-based intervention for people with Alzheimer's disease. *Frontiers in Psychology, 11*. https://doi.org/10.3389/fpsyg.2020.01467.

250. Kongkasuwan, R., Voraakhom, K., Pisolayabutra, P., Maneechai, P., Boonin, J., & Kuptniratsaikul, V. (2016). Creative art therapy to enhance rehabilitation for stroke patients: A randomized controlled trial. *Clinical Rehabilitation, 30*(10), 1016–1023. https://doi.org/10.1177/0269215515607072.

251. Rastogi, M., & Kempf, J. K. (2022). Art therapy for psychological disorders and mental health. *Foundations of Art Therapy*, 335–377. https://doi.org/10.1016/b978-0-12-824308-4.00008-9.

252. Vaartio-Rajalin, H., Santamäki-Fischer, R., Jokisalo, P., & Fagerström, L. (2021). Art making and expressive art therapy in adult health and nursing care: A scoping review. *International Journal of Nursing Sciences, 8*(1), 102–119. https://doi.org/10.1016/j.ijnss.2020.09.011.

253. Kaimal, G., Ray, K., & Muniz, J. (2016). Reduction of cortisol levels and participants' responses following art making. *Art Therapy, 33*(2), 74–80. https://doi.org/10.1080/07421656.2016.1166832.

254. Beerse, M. E., Van Lith, T., & Stanwood, G. D. (2019). Is there a biofeedback response to art therapy? A technology-assisted approach for reducing anxiety and stress in college students. *SAGE Open, 9*(2), 215824401985464. https://doi.org/10.1177/2158244019854646.

255. Mandolesi, L., Polverino, A., Montuori, S., Foti, F., Ferraioli, G., Sorrentino, P., & Sorrentino, G. (2018). Effects of physical exercise on cognitive functioning and wellbeing: Biological and psychological benefits. *Frontiers in Psychology, 9*. https://doi.org/10.3389/fpsyg.2018.00509.

256. Netz, Y. (2019). Is there a preferred mode of exercise for cognition enhancement in older age?—a narrative review. *Frontiers in Medicine, 6*. https://doi.org/10.3389/fmed.2019.00057.

257. Dunsky, A., Abu-Rukun, M., Tsuk, S., Dwolatzky, T., Carasso, R., & Netz, Y. (2017). The effects of a resistance vs. an aerobic single session on attention and executive functioning in adults. *PLOS ONE, 12*(4). https://doi.org/10.1371/journal.pone.0176092.

258. Brunner, D., Abramovitch, A., & Etherton, J. (2017). A yoga program for cognitive enhancement. *PLOS ONE, 12*(8). https://doi.org/10.1371/journal.pone.0182366.

259. Gothe, N. P., Hayes, J. M., Temali, C., & Damoiseaux, J. S. (2018). Differences in brain structure and function among yoga practitioners and controls. *Frontiers in Integrative Neuroscience, 12*. https://doi.org/10.3389/fnint.2018.00026.

260. Roig, M., Nordbrandt, S., Geertsen, S. S., & Nielsen, J. B. (2013). The effects of cardiovascular exercise on human memory: a review with meta-analysis. *Neuroscience and Biobehavioral Reviews, 37*(8), 1645–1666. https://doi.org/10.1016/j.neubiorev.2013.06.012.

261. Moreau, D., Kirk, I., J., & Waldie, K.E. (2017). High-intensity training enhances executive function in children in a randomized, placebo-controlled trial. *Elife, 6*. https://doi.org/10.7554/elife.25062.

262. Mekari, et. al. (2020). High-Intensity Interval Training Improves Cognitive Flexibility in Older Adults. *Brain Sciences, 10*, no. 11: 796. https://doi.org/10.3390/brainsci10110796.

263. Huang, X., Zhao, X., Li, B., Cai, Y., Zhang, S., Wan, Q., & Yu, F. (2022). Comparative efficacy of various exercise interventions on cognitive function in patients with mild cognitive impairment or dementia: A systematic review and network meta-analysis. *Journal of Sport and Health Science, 11*(2), 212–223. https://doi.org/10.1016/j.jshs.2021.05.003.

264. da Costa, T. S. et. al. (2022). Effects of aerobic and strength training on depression, anxiety, and health self-perception levels during the COVID-19 pandemic. *European Review for Medical and Pharmacological Sciences, 26*(15), 5601–5610. https://doi.org/10.26355/eurrev_202208_29433.

265. Pascoe, M, Bauer, I. (2015). A systematic review of randomized control trials on the effects of yoga on stress measures and mood. *Journal of Psychiatric Research, 68*. https://doi.org/10.1016/j.jpsychires.2015.07.013.

266. Rosenbaum, D., Mama, Y., & Algom, D. (2017). Stand by your Stroop: Standing up enhances selective attention and cognitive control. *Psychological Science, 28*(12), 1864–1867. https://doi.org/10.1177/0956797617721270.

267. Nair, S., Sagar, M., Sollers, J., Consedine, N., & Broadbent, E. (2015). Do slumped and upright postures affect stress responses? A randomized trial. *Health Psychology, 34*(6), 632–641. https://doi.org/10.1037/hea0000146.

268. Awad, S., Debatin, T., & Ziegler, A. (2021). Embodiment: I sat, I felt, I performed— posture effects on mood and cognitive performance. *Acta Psychologica, 218*, 103353. https://doi.org/10.1016/j.actpsy.2021.103353.

269. Andolfi, V.R., Nuzzo, C.D., & Antonietti, A. (2017). Opening the mind through the body: The effects of posture on creative processes. *Thinking Skills and Creativity, 24*, 20–28.

270. Wood, B.M., Harris, J.A., Raichlen, D.A. et al. (2021). Gendered movement ecology and landscape use in Hadza hunter-gatherers. *Nature Human Behaviour, 5*, 436–446. https://doi.org/10.1038/s41562-020-01002-7.

271. Padilla-Iglesias, C., Blanco-Portillo, J., Pricop, B. et al. (2024). Deep history of cultural and linguistic evolution among Central African hunter-gatherers. *Nature Human Behaviour, 8*, 1263–1275 https://doi.org/10.1038/s41562-024-01891-y.

272. Heidegger, M. (2008). *Being and time*. HarperCollins.

273. Terhune, D. B., Croucher, M., Marcusson-Clavertz, D., & Macdonald, J. S. (2017). Time contracts and temporal precision declines when the mind wanders. *Journal of Experimental Psychology: Human Perception and Performance, 43*(11), 1864–1871. https://doi.org/10.1037/xhp0000461.

274. Sarris, J., de Manincor, M., Hargraves, F., & Tsonis, J. (2019). Harnessing the four elements for mental health. *Frontiers in Psychiatry, 10*. https://doi.org/10.3389/fpsyt.2019.00256.

275. Laukkanen, T., Kunutsor, S. K., Khan, H., Willeit, P., Zaccardi, F., & Laukkanen, J. A. (2018). Sauna bathing is associated with reduced cardiovascular mortality and improves risk prediction in men and women: A prospective cohort study. *BMC Medicine, 16*(1). https://doi.org/10.1186/s12916-018-1198-0.

276. Patrick, R. P., & Johnson, T. L. (2021). Sauna use as a lifestyle practice to extend healthspan. *Experimental Gerontology, 154*, 111509. https://doi.org/10.1016/j.exger.2021.111509.

277. Brown, T. M., Brainard, G. C., Cajochen, C., Czeisler, C. A., Hanifin, J. P., Lockley, S. W., Lucas, R. J., Münch, M., O'Hagan, J. B., Peirson, S. N., Price, L. L., Roenneberg, T., Schlangen, L. J., Skene, D. J., Spitschan, M., Vetter, C., Zee, P. C., & Wright, K. P. (2022). Recommendations for daytime, evening, and nighttime indoor light exposure to best support physiology, sleep, and wakefulness in healthy adults. *PLOS Biology, 20*(3). https://doi.org/10.1371/journal.pbio.3001571.

278. Facer-Childs, E. R., Middleton, B., Skene, D. J., & Bagshaw, A. P. (2019). Resetting the late timing of "night owls" has a positive impact on mental health and performance. *Sleep Medicine, 60*, 236–247. https://doi.org/10.1016/j.sleep.2019.05.001.

279. Scott, A. J., Webb, T. L., James, M. M.-S., Rowse, G., & Weich, S. (2021). Improving sleep quality leads to better mental health: A meta-analysis of randomised controlled trials. *Sleep Medicine Reviews, 60*, 101556. https://doi.org/10.31234/osf.io/t2efb.

280. Hrafnkelsdottir, S. M., Brychta, R. J., Rognvaldsdottir, V., Gestsdottir, S., Chen, K. Y., Johannsson, E., Guðmundsdottir, S. L., & Arngrimsson, S. A. (2018). Less screen time and more frequent vigorous physical activity is associated with lower risk of reporting negative mental health symptoms among Icelandic adolescents. *PLOS ONE, 13*(4). https://doi.org/10.1371/journal.pone.0196286.

281. Basso, J. C., McHale, A., Ende, V., Oberlin, D. J., & Suzuki, W. A. (2019). Brief, daily meditation enhances attention, memory, mood, and emotional regulation in

non-experienced meditators. *Behavioural Brain Research, 356*, 208–220. https://doi.org/10.1016/j.bbr.2018.08.023.

282. Knaepen, K., Goekint, M., Heyman, E. M., & Meeusen, R. (2010). Neuroplasticity—exercise-induced response of peripheral brain-derived neurotrophic factor. *Sports Medicine, 40*(9), 765–801. https://doi.org/10.2165/11534530-000000000-00000.

283. Vorkapic, C., Leal, S., Alves, H., Douglas, M., Britto, A., & Dantas, E. (2021). Born to move: A review on the impact of physical exercise on brain health and the evidence from human controlled trials. *Arquivos de Neuro-Psiquiatria, 79*(6), 536–550. https://doi.org/10.1590/0004-282X-ANP-2020-0166.

284. Drchancnc, "Center for Neuropsychology and Consciousness," YouTube, https://www.youtube.com/@drchancnc.